RICHARD III

Warwick School Library

RICHARD III

Michael Hicks

TEMPUS

Revised illustrated edition published 2000
Paperback edition first published 2001

PUBLISHED IN THE UNITED KINGDOM BY:

Tempus Publishing Ltd
The Mill, Brimscombe Port
Stroud, Gloucestershire GL5 2QG
www.tempus-publishing.com

PUBLISHED IN THE UNITED STATES OF AMERICA BY:

Tempus Publishing Inc.
2 Cumberland Street
Charleston, SC 29401
www.arcadiapublishing.com

Tempus books are available in France and Germany from the following
addresses:

Tempus Publishing Group   Tempus Publishing Group
21 Avenue de la République   Gustav-Adolf-Straße 3
37300 Joué-lès-Tours   99084 Erfurt
FRANCE   GERMANY

British Library Cataloguing in Publication Data.
A catalogue record for this book is available from the British Library.

ISBN 0 7524 2302 9

Typesetting and origination by Tempus Publishing.
PRINTED AND BOUND IN GREAT BRITAIN.

Contents

List of illustrations

Colour section

Picture research by Tom Cairns.
Photographs, unless otherwise stated, copyright Geoffrey Wheeler
195 Gloucester Place, London NW1 6BU, UK

Genealogies

The House of York in the 1450s

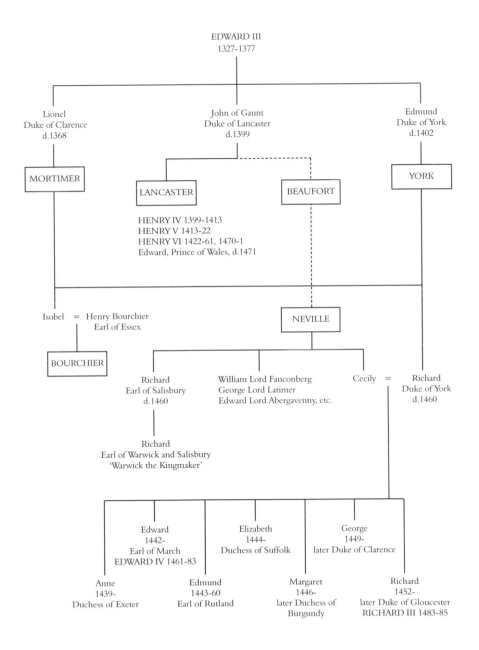

EDWARD III
1327-1377

Lionel
Duke of Clarence
d.1368

John of Gaunt
Duke of Lancaster
d.1399

Edmund
Duke of York
d.1402

MORTIMER

LANCASTER

BEAUFORT

YORK

HENRY IV 1399-1413
HENRY V 1413-22
HENRY VI 1422-61, 1470-1
Edward, Prince of Wales, d.1471

Isobel = Henry Bourchier
Earl of Essex

NEVILLE

BOURCHIER

Richard
Earl of Salisbury
d.1460

William Lord Fauconberg
George Lord Latimer
Edward Lord Abergavenny, etc.

Cecily = Richard
Duke of York
d.1460

Richard
Earl of Warwick and Salisbury
'Warwick the Kingmaker'

Edward
1442-
Earl of March
EDWARD IV 1461-83

Elizabeth
1444-
Duchess of Suffolk

George
1449-
later Duke of Clarence

Anne
1439-
Duchess of Exeter

Edmund
1443-60
Earl of Rutland

Margaret
1446-
later Duchess of
Burgundy

Richard
1452-
later Duke of Gloucester
RICHARD III 1483-85

The Warwick inheritance

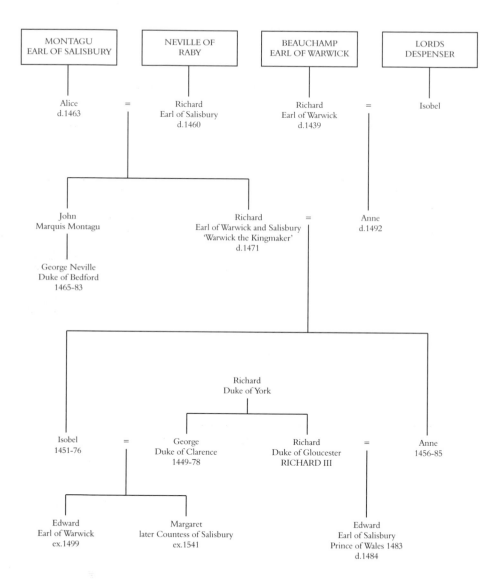

| MONTAGU EARL OF SALISBURY | | NEVILLE OF RABY | | BEAUCHAMP EARL OF WARWICK | | LORDS DESPENSER |

Alice
d.1463

=

Richard
Earl of Salisbury
d.1460

Richard
Earl of Warwick
d.1439

=

Isobel

John
Marquis Montagu

Richard
Earl of Warwick and Salisbury
'Warwick the Kingmaker'
d.1471

=

Anne
d.1492

George Neville
Duke of Bedford
1465-83

Richard
Duke of York

Isobel
1451-76

=

George
Duke of Clarence
1449-78

Richard
Duke of Gloucester
RICHARD III

=

Anne
1456-85

Edward
Earl of Warwick
ex.1499

Margaret
later Countess of Salisbury
ex.1541

Edward
Earl of Salisbury
Prince of Wales 1483
d.1484

The royal family on the death of Edward IV

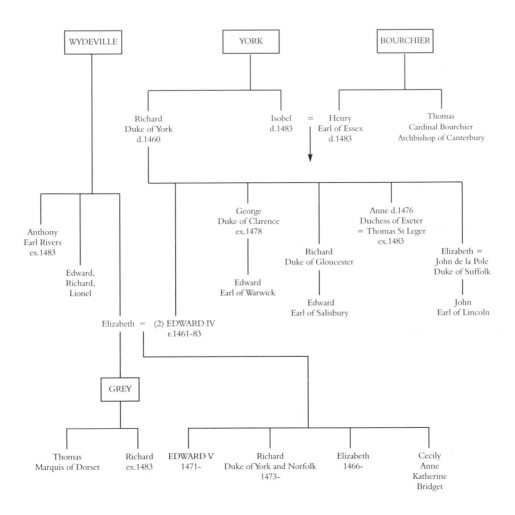

The title to the crown, 1483-5

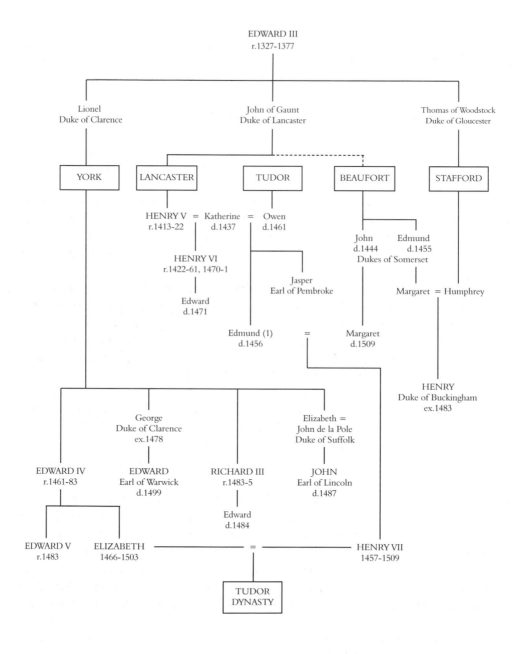

Introduction

Richard III and John are the two wicked kings in English history. Each had the ability and talents of a successful ruler, but each supposedly murdered his nephew and took his throne to the eternal destruction of his own reputation. Richard III was particularly unfortunate to enjoy the fruits of his supposed crime so briefly, to be followed by a Tudor dynasty so highly approved by historians (thus his defeat at Bosworth traditionally divides the Middle Ages from Modern History), and to have his story told by hostile historians of genius. It is Shakespeare's intense, compelling and utterly damning portrait of a usurper, tyrant and monster that has held the scene until today.

Real people are more complex than that. Nobody who ever lived could be as wicked as this or so lacking in redeeming features. So we argue from our twentieth-century vantage point. Richard's advocates, the Ricardians, have grown in the past century from an insignificant minority into an influential and ultimately dominant majority.

The credit belongs to the Richard III Society, founded in 1924 to clear his name, and to a host of novelists and historians. Richard III is now genuinely popular. In 1984 the Trial of Richard III was staged on television: in 1983 at Gloucester and in 1990 at Oxford this author engaged in debates on the resolution that 'Richard III was more sinned against than sinning'. Richard was acquitted at his television Trial and in both debates the resolution was carried overwhelmingly in his favour.

These results were certain before proceedings began. So thoroughly has public opinion been re-educated that a Ricardian orthodoxy has almost obliterated the Shakespearean tradition. It is the Tudor historians who now stand in the dock.

The Ricardians have rightly drawn attention to Richard's estimable career before his accession, his unjustified sufferings at the hands of Tudor propagandists, and the false charges that have been laid at his door. This book acknowledges such advances and seeks to build on them. Instead of the Tudor histories it relies overwhelmingly on contemporary sources. Instead of modern deductions about Richard's motives, it seeks to rescue his own pronouncements from the obscurity where they lie submerged and unrecognized in the hostile narratives of his contemporaries. It focuses on the issues and ideas expressed by Richard and his enemies, the very stuff of Ricardian politics and ideological warfare, and seeks to explain Richard's bewildering transformation in his own lifetime from the model of nobility via kingship to tyrant and monster.

My approach therefore is to give weight to what Richard and his contemporaries said as well as what they did. Their stated motives deserve as much attention as our cynical deductions from their actions. Of course there are dangers in this approach.

What people say may not always be true. There is always a gap between reality and our own perceptions. Room must be left for ignorance and error, propaganda and public relations. There are always those who wish to look better or different, and who want to impress others – mainly employers and potential employers – with qualities that they do not possess. Self-advertisement and propaganda are not the same as dishonesty or untruth. The most effective propaganda is the truth and propagandists can be convinced by their own messages. Even dishonest propaganda is of historical significance. It can assist our understanding of why and how things happened. What people believed about themselves, however mistaken, is often more important than the truth, especially if their belief actually determined their actions. This is particularly true of the career of Richard III. The real Richard was never as good or as bad as he was portrayed, but it was the successive images, not the reality, that influenced events. If we strip away the posturing, the denigration and the public profiles, we may approach closer to the real man. But which Richard was real?

This book is not therefore primarily a conventional life or history of the reign, for both of which Charles Ross's *Richard III* remains the standard work. It does not investigate Richard's patronage, which is exhaustively treated in Rosemary Horrox's *Richard III: A Study of Service*. It is not an account of Richard's posthumous vicissitudes, for which readers are referred to Jeremy Potter's *Good King Richard?* It focuses instead on Richard's reputation during his lifetime, its development or manufacture and repeated reshaping. Richard's successive reputations were a major influence – perhaps the most potent of all – both on his career and the politics of his time.

It is now over thirty years since I first encountered Richard III as a member of Charles Ross's Special Subject group at Bristol University. Charles encouraged me to undertake research, externally examined my thesis, advised and assisted me in many ways, and placed all Yorkist historians in his debt with his *Edward IV* and *Richard III*. I was equally fortunate to secure as my supervisor at Oxford John Armstrong, the editor of Dominic Mancini's *Usurpation of Richard III*. As the years have passed, my historical ideas have developed, not just on Richard, and this is a very different book from the one I would have written twenty or even ten years ago. It has evolved considerably since its own first edition in 1991. Nevertheless, as I have used their work, especially Armstrong's splendid edition of Mancini and Ross's paper on 'Rumour, Propaganda, and Public Opinion in the Wars of the Roses', I have been acutely conscious both of their influence and of the extent to which they have anticipated my own work. Thus this book is dedicated to their memory, the outstanding Ricardian scholars of the last two generations, now both, alas, no longer with us.

It is a pleasure to acknowledge the benefit this book has received from my contacts with many other medievalists. Most are acknowledged in the bibliography, but particular reference was made in the first edition to Professor Barrie Dobson, Professor Ralph Griffiths, Dr Gerald Harriss, Professor Tony Pollard, Dr Rosemary Horrox and Miss Margaret Condon. Generations of undergraduates have unwittingly assisted me in formulating my ideas. This substantially expanded edition draws on more recent publications, most notably by Professor Pollard again, by Dr Michael K. Jones, Livia Visser-Fuchs and Anne Sutton, which have enabled the arguments to be further developed and refined. A very special debt, as always, is due to my wife Cynthia, who has applauded every new discovery and charted every twist in interpretation in the last thirty years. For her and our three offspring, Richard – like his brother George before him and father-in-law Warwick since – has been a most demanding intruder into our domestic life.

All quotations from original sources, whether originally in Latin or Middle English, have been rendered in modern English.

1 The England of Richard III

The Ricardian achievement

Five centuries have passed since Richard III was king of England. He reigned for just two years. Then retribution swept away his throne, his life, his dynasty, above all his reputation. History records him as a monstrous irrelevance, an untoward interruption to stable government and the ruin of the House of York. It was over his dead body and over his shame that the Tudors inaugurated their golden age. His example was a dreadful warning to all usurpers and tyrants. For the Tudors, Richard was a usurper, a tyrant, a murderer and a monster: in sum, the enemy of God and Man, who received his just deserts as certainly in heaven as on earth. Nobody depicted this better than Shakespeare. Yet even the Tudor playwright found drama in Richard's fall and a tragic greatness in the man. Whatever else he was, Richard was undoubtedly a tragic figure: as complete a failure as the most inept of English kings. He left behind no legacy and no line and died for no cause. He fell because he took the crown: the fatal error from which there was no going back. He cannot have enjoyed those twenty-six months of anxiety which were all he was allowed.

Richard was ambitious. Who would not wish to be king? His opportunity came as Lord Protector of his teenage nephew and principal bulwark to his throne. The temptation proved too much. The system made him protector, but we cannot blame the system for what followed. Convention demanded that Richard should give his nephew loyal support. It was a convention that he both acknowledged and flouted. The law of inheritance declared that he could not succeed. That law Richard both recognized and perverted. Like his brother, Edward IV, he manipulated his own election. He achieved his accession by the proper procedures and through the correct channels but nevertheless it was might that was right. Richard reigned in spite of the system, in contempt of the publicly accepted norms of political conduct, and he paid the full price for it. The natural allies of the crown deserted him, even the lifelong adherents of his dynasty abandoned him, unnatural alliances were forged by his foes, and his triumph was brief indeed. As in our own world today, his *coup d'état* bestowed a momentary ascendancy that endured only until conventional values were reasserted. When the establishment revived, the system triumphed, and Richard was no more.

The Wars of the Roses

Richard III ruled from 26 June 1483 until 22 August 1485. His reign was the last, conclusive, phase of the Wars of the Roses. We all know the basic facts about these

Left: the Yorkist badge of the white rose and sun emblems combined in a 'rose au soleil'.
Right: The crowned Tudor red rose of Henry VII.

wars. The crown of England was the prize, the houses of Lancaster and York the contenders, and thirty years of bloody civil war were the means. From 1455 to 1485 a dynastic struggle raged. Bosworth was the decisive victory of the Lancastrian Henry VII over the Yorkist Richard III. The wounds were healed by the marriage of Henry Tudor to Elizabeth of York. The Tudor rose united the warring emblems – the red rose of Lancaster and white rose of York – and ushered in more than a century of domestic peace.

Yet almost all this is Tudor propaganda. The official Tudor view still holds sway more than five centuries after the accession of the house of Tudor and almost four centuries after its extinction. When Queen Elizabeth I died in 1603, such propaganda lost its political point, but it had outlasted all other viewpoints and no rival tradition remained to be revived. This Tudor propaganda was most memorably codified by Shakespeare and repeatedly revamped by Sir Walter Scott and many others. Yet it is almost entirely untrue. The Wars of the Roses did not so obviously begin in 1455 or end in 1485. Rather than a continuous conflict of unchanging contenders, the Wars of the Roses embrace several separate wars between different protagonists. The fighting was brief and the peace was long. For twelve years from 1471 to 1483 there were no battles. Twice there were decisive victories, in 1461 and 1471, but new issues and new personalities generated new frictions and hence new wars.

Dynasticism was *a* cause, not *the* cause, and not until 1483, if then, was the lure of a crown to prove irresistible. It is only in retrospect – and then only with a Tudor perspective – that the battle of Bosworth and the year 1485 are decisive. For Henry VII was not the natural heir of Lancaster, nor was he initially the bringer of concord.

Henry VI as he appears in stained glass at King's College Chapel, Cambridge.

To defend his usurpation, his predecessor had to be blackened. Surely nothing was worse than Richard III and nobody wished for a return to the horrors of his reign? King Henry was the saviour and hero and King Richard the tyrant and monster. So the propaganda ran, and so it has remained almost until now.

National humiliation, bankruptcy and domestic chaos preceded the civil war. In 1449-50, in just a few months, the English were bundled unceremoniously out of Normandy and Henry VI lost that second crown he had inherited in infancy. An outraged public bayed for reform at home, victory abroad and vengeance on those traitors who had succumbed to the resurgent French. No government could have satisfied such demands, certainly not that of Henry VI, nor did it. Henry exemplified the Christian virtues expected of kings but he did not have the capacity to make and implement policy. Generally uninterested in worldly affairs, without the will to impose his authority or the ability to decide for himself, he was content to be manipulated by those about him and was quite impervious to public opinion. At best impractical and inefficient, at worst other-worldly or mad, Henry VI was a vacuum at the heart of a government that cried out for crisis management.

Richard Duke of York (1411-60), the first cousin and subject of the king, father of the future Edward IV and Richard III, posed as saviour and strove to stop the slide. Repeatedly, by force and otherwise, the duke bypassed Henry to make government effective. Henry, however, remained king and always retained his right to rule. He repeatedly shrugged off his fetters and resumed his ineffective government. Once again the impossibility of restraining a king emerged as the inescapable flaw of the medieval English constitution. At length, frustrated and ambitious, Richard claimed the crown himself, asserting that his descent from Lionel Duke of Clarence, second son of Edward III (1327-77), took precedence over the Lancastrian line deriving from the third son, John of Gaunt. This was perhaps sound in theory, but kings did not reign by hereditary right alone, and York's claim appeared too harsh in practice to the incumbent king. York's own supporters recoiled and compromised. What York won was not the crown but the succession to it, coupled with the right to rule as protector during Henry's lifetime. It was too little for his own security, but too much for diehard Lancastrians. There followed not peace, but war, Richard's own death and the victory of his eldest son, who became Edward IV (1461-83). The knot was cut by a change of king and dynasty, and the future Richard III became a royal prince.

Peace did not return at once, but the victory of 1461 was nevertheless a decisive one that brought the deaths of many prominent Lancastrians and the submission of most of the rest. They included Edward IV's future queen Elizabeth and her Wydeville kinsfolk. Like it or not, the Yorkist was their king and they made the best of it. The king of a faction became the king of the whole nation with a mandate to restore good government and national pride. If he lacked Henry VI's Christian virtues, Edward was a bigger and more impressive man, more athletic and more soldierly, more resolute and more decisive, better able both to browbeat and to charm. Early in his reign, of course, he was scarcely a man at all. He was physically well-developed, but intellectually immature and untrained for government. His faults included sloth and lack of attention to business, greed and lust, self-glory and extravagance. Kingship was to be enjoyed, not worked at, and financial retrenchment, the methodical suppression of rebellion and painstaking diplomatic negotiations were best left to others.

Edward made many mistakes in these early years, none greater than his misjudged marriage, and the Lancastrian legacy was dispelled too slowly to arrest disillusionment. And when he did indeed assert himself, deciding his own policy and broadening his ministry, he shouldered aside those who had made him king and now were reluctant to relinquish power.

Those displaced were his Neville cousins: Richard Neville, Earl of Warwick and Salisbury, alias Warwick the Kingmaker, who died in 1471; Warwick's brothers and brothers-in-law; and his son-in-law George, Duke of Clarence (died 1478), middle brother of the Yorkist kings Edward IV and Richard III. First, in 1469, they tried to eliminate Edward's new favourites, killing several Wydevilles. They also attempted

Lionel, Duke of Clarence, second son of Edward III,
through whom Richard Duke of York claimed his
title to the throne. Drawn from the gilt bronze
'weeper' on the tomb of Edward III. (George and
Thomas Hollis, Monumental Effigies, *1839-42)*

to imprison the king and govern on his behalf. Then, in 1470, they tried to replace
him with Clarence. Only when all these manoeuvres failed and the Nevilles arrived
as refugees in France did they ally with erstwhile Lancastrians to restore Henry VI.
They succeeded: Henry VI reigned for a second time in 1470-1. Such a coalition of
incompatibles did not last. Warwick, Henry VI, and Prince Edward of Lancaster all
perished. Clarence made his peace, to be followed by other survivors, notably the
future Cardinal Morton and the foremost political thinker of the age, Chief Justice
Fortescue. Only the two Tudors, Jasper Earl of Pembroke and his nephew Henry,
stagnated in Brittany as irrelevant back numbers. If 1461 was decisive, 1471 was
doubly so. There was no basis for any future conflict: no rival claimants, no
significant exiles and no dangerous discontent.

New completely secure, Edward could safely invade France in 1475, albeit briefly,
recoup his finances, and stage Clarence's execution on trumped-up charges in the
packed parliament of 1478. These were the years when he reconstructed royal
finances from the virtual bankruptcy of Henry VI and justified his proud claim to

be 'guardian of the law'. Three sons were born to him and two survived to continue the dynasty. The Wars of the Roses were over. And yet, when Edward died in 1483, his youngest brother Richard ousted his sons, ruled for two stormy years and died disastrously. A new, Tudor, dynasty reigned and rode out crises as violent as those that swept Richard away. It too could have failed. Instead, Henry VII was victorious and it is his perspective that has shaped ours. Yet he would never have reigned had not the Yorkist consensus been broken and had not disaffected Yorkists in near desperation sought him out. In a very real sense, Henry VII was a Yorkist king. That, in turn, was the work of Richard III, who alienated those most loyal to his brother's son. It was Richard's *coup d'état* in 1483, culminating in his accession, that ended the Yorkist consensus, inaugurated a new era of civil war and let in the Tudors. The Wars of the Roses resumed. And it was Richard who was destroyed.

The political system

Such a catalogue of events cannot answer our questions. Why did the Wars of the Roses happen? Why was there civil war? What were the issues at stake? Why did Richard III reign and fall? How could such things happen, when they do not occur and could not recur in the England of today? Part of the answer why lies in a straightforward account of cause and effect, but such causes themselves arise from the political system of which they formed a part.

The England of Richard III was very different from England today. Late medieval England was overwhelmingly rural, a landscape of forest and marsh, thinly populated and with few substantial towns. Economy, society, government and technology alike were underdeveloped by the standards of our modern industrialized society. Yet when we turn to the people and their relationships, it all seems very familiar. We can recognize the ruthless and cynical pursuit of personal power and profit, identify with instinctive self-preservation in times of crisis, and recall modern instances of the 'ambition and lust for power' attributed to Richard III.

However, medieval men were not merely people of today clad in outlandish clothes and uttering dialect. Although they were biologically akin to us, their ways of thought were quite alien and their standards of political conduct were not ours. We cannot understand their civilization by reading back our motives into past situations, but must instead try to grasp the ideas of their age. That means not just the ideals and principles which they consciously expressed, but the assumptions, conventions, standards of conduct, and expectations that were often unconscious. Expressions of ideals and principles may be mere lip service, but assumptions about politics and society are implicit. The political theories of the time were formally codified by university academics in elaborate Latin treatises and expressed more informally by politicians and administrators in proclamations, sermons and manifestos, the propaganda of government and opposition.

Propaganda, by definition, aims to influence people and its medieval authors – Richard above all – believed that it did. But this could only happen if its ideology was shared by the target audience. And the target audience was not just the political elite, who could have read the propaganda when it was posted on market crosses and church doors, but the humble and illiterate majority who heard it proclaimed and whose specific interests and concerns were often directly invoked. Their actions could influence events, particularly when they acted en masse, and account therefore had to be taken of their views. They mattered politically. Hence the introduction of successive programmes of reform that appealed to their ideals and aspirations. Hence, too, the deliberate besmirching of opponents with shocking charges such as treason, devil worship, and the murder of a pregnant woman, with which Henry VI's government sought to dispel popular sympathy for the rebel leader, Jack Cade. In 1483 Richard III brought such techniques in the defamation of his opponents to a new level of sophistication and for his own advantage. Once king, however, he was judged, condemned, and vilified in the same way that he had previously reviled his enemies.

It was the greatest of medieval academics, such as St Thomas Aquinas and Giles of Rome, who developed the political ideas of the Wars of the Roses. Richard III possessed a copy of Giles's *Of the Rule of Princes* and presumably knew its contents. Among many anonymous figures who applied them in practice, three stand out. One wrote Richard III's proclamations and *Titulus Regius*, the official instrument of his election as king in 1483. Another was Bishop John Russell, Lord Chancellor and chief minister to Edward V and Richard III, when he composed the three sermons discussed here. As keynote addresses for three openings of parliament in 1483-4, these explored in theoretical terms the practical remedies for the pressing problems confronting a beleaguered regime. Equally practical in their propagandist purpose, if ostensibly theoretical, were the treatises of another of Richard's contemporaries, Sir John Fortescue, Chief Justice in the 1450s, written when he was chancellor-in-exile of Henry VI during the 1460s. These were no airy-fairy idealists formulating abstract theories, but men of affairs addressing contemporary politicians on matters that concerned them gravely and expecting what they said to have a decisive influence on events.

All wrote in an era of civil war of which they did not approve. Even at the height of the Wars of the Roses, such conflict was not the norm, but was seen as an aberration unnatural, undesirable, and in breach of God's divine plan. Peace and tranquillity were the ideal, their preservation was the chief function of government, and strife and division were to be eschewed.

War was to be entered into as a last resort: in 1471 Edward IV offered concessions to Warwick the Kingmaker in the vain hope of achieving 'peace and tranquillity' and 'to avoid the effusion of Christian blood'. War – especially civil war – was God's punishment for sin. Indeed the Tudors came to present all the troubles of the fifteenth century in this way. They saw the root cause as the usurpation of Henry IV in 1399, when Richard II – God's deputy – was deposed from his throne. Retribution was visited by God on Henry IV's grandson Henry VI. Yet Henry VI, too, had been an anointed king, who could not be unseated without sin, and even as God's instrument Edward IV earned the punishment that fell on his son, Edward V.

For Edward V's deposition, Richard III was punished when God pronounced his verdict at Bosworth. The Tudors connected the whole sequence of events by a divine cycle of crime and punishment that modern historians have called the Tudor Myth and which is alien to our modern ideas. But it was not alien at the time. The Tudor Myth imposed a particular pro-Tudor interpretation and purpose on the sequence, which identified the Tudors as God's intended objective, but the underlying concepts of sin, punishment, and divine intervention were widely shared, and had indeed been deployed by others for other purposes long before the Tudor victory had occurred or could even be anticipated. History, after all, was the story of God's judgements on mankind. There was a Lancastrian Myth long before there was a Tudor Myth. God took a close interest in the world and still intervened in human affairs.

To medieval Englishmen the creation story in Genesis was not a myth. It was the literal truth. It explained their world. They accepted that God had created everything in seven days according to a divine plan that was yet to be fulfilled. Since He was perfect, so too was everything He created, which was ideal both in itself and in relation to everything else. They thought of creation in terms of a great chain stretching from earth to heaven with inanimate things at the bottom, all the forms of life – vegetative, sensitive, and rational – above, and the angels and God at the top. Everything was encompassed in the chain, so that, Chief Justice Fortescue observed, 'there is no worm that crawls upon the ground, no bird that flies on high, no fish that swims in the depths, which the chain of this order does not bind in harmonious concord'. Harmony and concord were God's objective and to achieve it He had pre-programmed each creature with the relevant part of His divine plan. The instincts of each creature were part of the law of nature that God had created. God thought not of individual parts, but of wholes: not of individual bees or sheep, but of the hives and flocks to which they belonged; not of individual limbs, but of the human body of which they were part. These units were God's models for the society to which men belonged.

Human society was thus divine and was divided like the rest of creation into different ranks and occupations, all of which were interdependent and indeed necessary for the good of society as a whole. God wanted all creatures to work together with the harmony of a beehive or the human body. Unfortunately in the beginning Adam and Eve had used their capacity to think to disobey, had been expelled from the Garden of Eden, and had transmitted the capacity and desire to sin to all their successors. Mankind gave selfish desires priority over God's wishes or the good of society. God therefore intervened again to create a government to impose His will on mankind for its own good.

If society and government were both divine in origin and in purpose, it followed that they needed to be directed as God wanted. Some guidance was provided by the Bible, some by the Law of Nature, which could be deduced from other things that God had created. This was the idea behind the extended parallels drawn between human society and the models that God had provided, such as the human body. Comparison of human society with the human body dates back at least to the Greek philosopher Aristotle. St Paul discussed the members of the Church – or the mystical body of Christ – in terms of the limbs or members of the human body and was followed by such influential thinkers as St Augustine of Hippo, St Thomas Aquinas, Giles of Rome, and, in the fifteenth century, by Chief Justice Fortescue and Lord Chancellor Russell. It was such an influential concept that 'body politic' became an alternative term for 'society'. Sometimes the comparisons are detailed and literal. Thus Russell drew parallels with the head, shoulders, stomach, womb and intestines, feet, hands and eyes:

> The right eye is of understanding, the left is of affection [sensuality]. The due and beauteous proportion of man's two eyes is that the one be like the other both in colour and quantity. It is a monstrous sight that one man has two eyes of divers colours.

So a proper balance must be maintained. Similarly Fortescue identified the heart as the source of life, the blood as the will of the people, the head as the king, and law as the nervous system. Such deductions provided a basis for action.

To judge from the three sermons he drafted for the opening of parliament in 1483-4, the body politic dominated Russell's thinking. The many different ranks and occupations of people throughout the country comprised a single body. Pursuing the analogy, he concluded in the interests of 'due proportion and harmony' that everybody had his own function and place and must content himself with it. 'This is the means to keep the body in good health and estate. For that body is whole and strong, whose stomach and innards are served by the outward members, so that which suffices is well digested.' Admittedly it may seem to the feet and hands, 'which seem to do the most painful labour for man's living', that the 'middle members' such as the belly, stomach, and womb were contributing nothing to the whole, but actually their role was crucial. 'For when they be fed, they feed again, yielding unto every part of the body that without which no man may live, that is to wit, in all the vein's blood, digested out of the best of man's food and repast.' From this it followed that every limb and trade was needed for the good of society and that none could be spared. 'There is no member, however noble, that may say to the least and vilest of them all, "I have no need of thee", for each has been allocated his office and function.' As all were vital, all must do their duty and perform their office, not selfishly but for the general good of society as a whole:

> God wishes that our people of England, who all now separately pursue their own personal advantage and the accomplishing of their particular desires, would instead consider the common and public body of the realm, of which quite rightly a great person is often merely a small member.

Without working together to this common end, society could not function. To enforce His wishes, God had ordained in 'well governed cities' officials 'to oversee and

The painted effigy of Sir John Fortescue, Lancastrian Chief Justice, chancellor-in-exile of Henry VI and author of treatises on political theory, at Ebrington church, Gloucestershire.

not to permit any owner to abuse his own thing, lest that by the sloth and negligence of the landlords, cities and towns should fall to extreme decay and ruin'. So, too, with every kind of body: 'the body of man has his physician, the brutal beast his herdsman, the tree and herb his grafter or gardener, the stone his quarrier.' This body politic, too, 'may not be left without cure and good curators'. It was the role of government – God's government – to enforce God's wishes for the benefit of the human society He had created.

So government had been ordained by God, but God had left open the form of that government for the people themselves to decide. That was how people could reconcile the existence of different kinds of government – the republic of Venice, absolute and constitutional monarchies – with government's divine status. In England's case, so it was believed, the people had chosen limited monarchy. It was to protect their property and bodies, so Fortescue believed, that 'they submitted of their own will to the government of a king' and had elected the mythical Trojan Prince Brutus to rule over them. Because the people had limited the powers of the rulers they chose, so the king's power was limited or political rather than regal or absolute. He held power subject to the will of the people, and indeed shared power with them. They were essential to the body politic:

> And just as in the body natural [the actual physical body]… the heart is the source of life, having in itself the blood which it transmits to all the members thereof, whereby they are quickened and live, so in the body

politic the will of the people is the source of life, having in it the blood, namely, political forethought for the interest of the people, which it transmits to the head and all the members of the body, by which the body is maintained and quickened.

To Fortescue the lawyer, it was the law that was the nerves and transmitted throughout the whole the truth about the rights of every limb. 'And just as the head of the body natural is unable to change the laws of that body, or to deprive that same people of their substance against their wills', so too the king could not dispose arbitrarily of the lives and goods of the people but was bound instead to protect them. Thus government existed for the good of the people and not for the personal benefit of princes. 'The king is given for the sake of the kingdom and not the kingdom for the sake of the king,' wrote Aquinas. 'Hence all the power of the king ought to be applied to the good of his realm.' Henry VI's government observed that 'God made not the people for the princes, but he made the princes for the service and for the good and behoof of his people.' In 1469 Judge Yelverton stated that the judges exercised their discretion in the manner most beneficial to the common weal. And in 1484 Bishop Russell told Richard's parliament that 'all the terms and limitations of our thoughts we ought to refer to one singular point, that is to say, the advancing of the common weal'. By this he meant that the criterion to be applied to decide what was good and what bad was the common wealth or public good. Their touchstone, like ours, was the public interest.

And so it was in practice. Thus in 1469 Warwick and Clarence accused Edward IV's advisers of neglect of the common weal, charged them with harming the king's 'estate and the common weal of this land', and urged their own reform programme 'for the honour and profit of our sovereign lord the king and the common weal of all this realm'. In 1470, when Edward IV reasserted his authority, he in turn denounced the reformers as enemies not just of himself but of the common weal and identified as their objective 'the final destruction of his most royal person and the subversion of this his realm and the commonweal of the same'. So, too, at his accession King Richard III invoked 'the common and public weal of this land', and soon after declared 'his tender and loving disposition that he hath and beareth unto the common weal of this his realm' against those traitors, who sought among other evils the destruction of himself and 'the breach of the peace, tranquillity, and common weal of this realm'. Such instances could be cited indefinitely.

Moreover, the notion of the common weal was growing more important. Edmund Dudley, Richard's erstwhile subject and Henry VII's later notorious minister, who was imprisoned in the Tower and sentenced to death in 1509, wrote a treatise called *The Tree of the Commonwealth*. A few years later Sir Thomas More staged a fictional debate in his *Utopia* between the author, Cardinal Morton, the explorer Raphael, and a lawyer, in which all applied the concept of the weal public to assess English society. Their debate foreshadowed the work of the Tudor Commonwealth men, who made the ideal of the commonwealth into an instrument for their radical restructuring of Tudor society and economy.

'The Island of Utopia' by Ambrosius Holbein, a woodcut by Hans Holbein's older brother for the Basle version of Thomas More's famous work on politics, ethics and society.

In 1485, however, all that still lay in the future. It was not social and economic reform that medieval people saw primarily as the function of their king. As God's deputies, kings were obviously expected to promote God's wishes. They swore to uphold the rights of the Church and the Crowland chronicler thought it much to Edward IV's credit that he persecuted heretics. They had a duty to encourage virtue and to eradicate sin as Richard III tried to do. But their primary responsibilities were defence of the realm and the maintenance of law and order, as Aquinas made clear. Russell thought in exactly the same terms: a prince should 'give equal justice with pity and mercy and to defend his land from outward hostility'. Defence and justice were defined broadly to include foreign policy and covered the whole range of government business that he listed elsewhere:

> Thither are brought all matters of weight, peace and war with foreign countries, confederations, leagues and alliances, receiving and sending of embassies and messages, breaking of truces, piracies in the sea, routs and

riots, and unlawful assemblies, oppressions, extortions, contempts and abuses of the law…

Citing the Bible, Fortescue agreed: 'For the office of a king is to fight the battles of his people and to judge them rightfully'; and again, more succinctly and more famously, 'Lo! To fight and to judge is the office of a king.' These ideas were commonplace.

Kings were responsible for conducting foreign policy, for decisions about peace and war, and for the conduct of war itself. Ideally, therefore, they should be proficient soldiers and generals, able to lead their forces into battle, as Henry V, Edward IV and Richard III did and Henry VI could not. Defence of the realm was a king's most expensive responsibility and was one for which he could command financial support for the common weal from his subjects, which they could not refuse in time of necessity. In peacetime kings were expected to meet their general expenditure from their ordinary revenues without recourse to extraordinary parliamentary taxation. Edward IV invoked the doctrine of necessity for the last time in 1483 – 'it was just, he said, that these sums should be repaid by the public in whose benefit they were spent' – and Bishop Russell intended employing it on Edward V's behalf a few months later. Unlike government, which could be conducted adequately by a committee, the military responsibility of a king was his alone, and thus when kings were under age, as in 1422 and 1483, mad or simple, as in 1454, 1455 and 1460, the royal council appointed

> not the name of tutor, lieutenant, governor, nor of regent, nor no name
> that should impart authority of governance of the land, but the name of
> protector and defender, the which imports a personal duty of attendance
> to the actual defence of the land as well against outward enemies if
> circumstances require as inward enemies if there are any.

This was the office of Lord Protector to which Richard was appointed in 1483 and for which he declared himself admirably qualified. People had come to expect effective protection and glorious victories and anything that fell short of this aroused criticism and produced a reluctance to pay further taxes.

As well as defending society, government had been ordained to maintain order within it. In England the rights of each individual were defined and protected by the 'laws and customs granted to them by former kings of England', which Edward IV and Richard III swore to observe at their coronation and which were themselves considered divine. 'Law is a sacred sanction commending what is honest and forbidding the contrary,' observed Fortescue. 'All laws that are promulgated by men are decreed by God.' Justice was therefore the means of enforcing God's will and it was the king's duty to see that it did. This did not of course mean that he had to judge every case himself, for English kings had long since created an elaborate judicial system run by professional lawyers administering written law by delegation from the king. It did however mean that he was left with cases not covered by the law, with direct responsibility for offenders too powerful for the courts, and the effective administration of the judicial system itself. When local crime waves demanded the attention of the king in person and he presided over cases himself, so Russell observed, 'then the administration of justice is wont to be so terrible and precise in process that all the parties and people nearby quake and tremble in fear'. It was also the king's duty to see that justice was administered impartially, without fear or favour, and was not sold for money. A king swore at his coronation to be impartial and Richard III and Russell were typical in their concern for 'indifferent justice', which was also reflected in the elaborate oaths of office they required of royal judges and barons of the exchequer:

> You shall swear... that you shall do right to all manner people, as well to the poor as to the rich, and that you shall not disturb the right of the king or any other person against the laws of the land, neither for highness nor for richness nor for hatred nor for the rank of no manner person nor for any good deed, gift or promise of any person which is made for you.

It was here that the king's government touched his subjects in person and here that his reputation for good governance was won and lost. Henry VI in 1461 was held responsible for the 'unrest, inward war and trouble, unrighteousness, shedding and effusion of innocent blood, abuse of laws, partiality, riot, extortion, murder, rape and vicious living' of his reign, and Edward IV in 1469 for 'disturbing the administration of justice', condoning maintenance, and for many murders, rapes, robberies, extortions and much oppression. The same charges were made against Edward's regime by his brother Richard III in 1483, who declared his intention of doing better.

A king's justice extended beyond punishing criminals to the maintenance of that whole system of law and order on which the existence of civilized society depended. Justice, Lord Chancellor Stillington reminded parliament, was 'the root of all prosperity, peace and politic rule'. Consequently governments did have a responsibility for economic well-being and could be held to account if it decayed. It was the king's office, so Fortescue stressed, 'to make his realm rich'. His reputation suffered if his kingdom was poor, suffered more 'if he found the realm rich and made it poor', and became infamous if he reduced it from great wealth to poverty. In 1464 King Edward justified monetary regulation by his concern for 'the weal and prosperity of this land and the subjects of the same, whose welfare and increase is unto him the greatest comfort that may be'. This recalled his earlier denunciation of Henry VI's regime for the decline of overseas trade and its failure to create prosperity. Ironically in 1469 King Edward's own government was itself charged with letting the realm fall 'in great poverty of misery' and suffering 'great hurt and impoverishing' comparable to that of earlier kings who had been deposed. The charge was repeated in 1483, when Richard held Edward's government to account for the economic ills of the realm. Looking back, he recalled a golden age when, among other things, there had been good government, obedience to God, domestic tranquillity at home and victory abroad, and

> the intercourse of merchandise was largely used and exercised. By which things above remembered, the land was greatly enriched, so that as well the merchants and artificers as other poor people labouring for their living in diverse occupations had sufficient income for the support of themselves and their families, living without miserable and intolerable poverty.

Now prosperity diminished daily, there was misery and adversity, and 'it is likely that this realm will fall into extreme misery and desolation, which God forbid, unless a convenient remedy for it by duly provided in all goodly haste'. Note here that Richard III accepted responsibility for providing a remedy, as did Russell, who saw it as the task of the government to maintain wealth, to restore 'ancient prosperity', and who lamented the selfishness that had depopulated and impoverished parts of the realm.

Everybody shared in government through parliament. Parliament was the place of 'worldly policy' where 'the advancing of the common weal ... should be treated' and where all were represented: lords spiritual, lords temporal, and the commons. Parliament was supreme. It alone could make new laws and grant taxes. It brought the wisdom of the whole community together and what it did could not be corrupt since everyone had consented. As Henry VIII said, he was never more a king than when knit with his members in parliament. Naturally it was the king who directed the body politic:

> What is the belly or where is the womb of this great public body of England but that and where the king is himself, his court and his council? For there must be digested all manner of meats, not only common food but also delicacies and sometimes medicines, such as be appropriate to remedy the excesses and surfeits committed at large.

Russell stressed the role of the nobility. Their wealth gave them a vested interest in the common weal, in them stood 'the politic rule of every region', and thus on an everyday basis they could intercede for the people with the king. They were best suited to advise a king.

A sober and substantial council was needed, ideally – as Richard stressed – composed of lords 'of approved sadness, prudence, policy, and experience, dreading God, and having tender zeal and affection for the indifferent administration of justice and to the common and public weal of this land'. Ministers and councillors swore oaths to give their counsel to the king and to protect his interests if they could. It was their duty to give straightforward and honest counsel, however unpalatable, and it was the king's duty to accept it. It would take a long time, said Russell, 'to rehearse the manifold histories both out of scripture and of the acts of the Romans showing the fall of many noble men for that they despised such counsel and warnings as to them were given'. Kings, however, were free to choose their own councillors and were notoriously prone to choose insubstantial men whom they liked: the young and immature, the sinful, and even 'persons insolent, vicious, and inordinately avaricious'. Such men, often members of the king's household, were notorious for flattering him rather than giving good advice, putting their own interests before the common weal, feathering their nests at the public expense and abusing their authority. These were charges repeatedly made against the favourite advisers of such unpopular kings as Edward II, Richard II, Henry VI, and Edward IV in 1469 and 1483. Evil councillors were impeached, attainted, or merely eliminated in the interests of that common weal, which, of course, it was their duty to serve. The king they had advised badly could then seek better counsel from other sources.

If the criterion of a good government is that it exists for the benefit of the governed, then it follows that any government not concerned with the people is bad, and, indeed, a tyranny. The nature of tyranny was explored by such theorists as Aquinas and Marsiglio of Padua. 'Tyranny', the latter wrote, 'is a diseased government, wherein the ruler is a single man, who rules for his own private benefit apart from the will of his subjects.' And Fortescue, applying such principles to the English situation, observed that 'when a king rules his realm only to his own profit and not to the good of his subjects, he is a tyrant'. King Herod was within his power in murdering the Holy Innocents, but his action nevertheless was contrary to public interest and therefore constituted tyranny. Richard's supposed murder of Edward IV's sons was to be compared to Herod's Massacre of the Innocents. A tyrant, said another, 'does all things at his own pleasure and to his own personal profit and particular advantage and attends not at all to the honourable weal and profit of his land'. It was a tyrant also who broke the laws – such as the law of succession – and changed them at his arbitrary pleasure, who deprived his people of their rights or reduced them to poverty. If Edward IV had indeed impoverished his people by taxing them unnecessarily, as Richard alleged in 1483, it would have been a tyrannical act. It was the characteristic trait of tyrants to pretend, as Edward pretended, some worthy motive for his action. 'A real king is virtuous; a tyrant is not, but pretends to be.'

Kings, like ordinary mortals, were obliged by God to put the public interest ahead of their selfish desires. They were expected to follow God's teaching, to live virtuously and to eschew vice, and they were subject to God's judgement and His punishment for sin, like everyone else. No distinction had yet been made by Machiavelli between private and public morality and the standards expected of kings in their public capacities were still the same as those required of anyone else: *raison d'état* was no excuse for the sin of murder or theft. This was the teaching of those treatises called *Mirrors* that were written for princes. Henry VI's efforts to live up to such standards made it even harder for his nobles to depose him. Edward IV's exemplary deathbed repentance may not have compensated for his life as a worldly prince renowned for the deadly sins of avarice, pride, gluttony and lechery. Such sins were not a private matter for the sinner and for God, but were of public interest: they set an 'evil example' to the people and might prompt God to intervene to punish a sinful people. In 1483 Richard claimed God had so intervened because of the adultery of his brother Edward IV.

English kings were officials. They were obliged to share their power with the people, to place the public interest ahead of their own, to respect the will of the people, and to seek and accept counsel. They were liable to damnation both as tyrants and for sins committed in their public as well as private capacities. Why then did kings want to be kings? Leaving aside the material benefits, kings did stand at the pinnacle of human society below only God and the angels, they were the Lord's anointed and God's deputies, and were entitled to the respect and obedience due to God. There was an absolute obligation to obey a king. Russell cited Christ's rendering unto Caesar the things that were Caesar's in support of the duty of obedience to a king, and reinforced this with a saying of St Paul. Once mere suzerains, ultimate lords of the feudal system and first among equals, English kings were now sovereigns and different in kind from the great nobles. As sovereigns, they were entitled to allegiance – to loyalty that overrode and superseded the petty loyalties due to lesser men. The contracts that nobles made with their retainers reserved the prior allegiance owed to the king and the omission of such a clause could lay the offender open to a treason charge. So too could raising an army, 'no mention made of us', as Edward IV accused Warwick in 1470. The loyalty due to even the greatest nobles did not oblige retainers to follow their leaders into rebellion against their allegiance: even the great Warwick the Kingmaker himself found that he needed royal authority to recruit his army and in 1483 Richard as Lord Protector had to convince doubters of his loyalty at every step. To rebel against God's deputy was tantamount to rebellion against God and offended 'against God's law, man's law, and all reason and conscience'. Hence God's intervention on the side of his deputy – Edward IV regularly claimed that his victories were God's verdict on his cause – and hence the damnation that awaited traitors at the last judgement. Treason could not be condoned lest it encouraged others: the traitor was a rotten member of the body politic, Russell observed, and must be cut off for the benefit of all. In 1352 treason had meant levying war against the king and his assassination; by the Wars of the Roses, treason included seditious words and forecasting the king's death by sorcery. Treason was the direst of crimes and carried the greatest of penalties: not mere death, but the most horrible of deaths. Having been degraded from knighthood, the offender was hanged, beheaded, drawn, quartered and, in the 1460s, impaled. So foul was treason that it tainted or corrupted the blood not just of traitors but of their descendants, who were disabled by such acts of attainder from inheriting the offenders' lands in defiance of the otherwise sacred right of inheritance. Moreover, the treason laws now stretched beyond the king to protect his closest family, who in 1483 were singled out under sumptuary legislation to dress more splendidly than any other subjects.

Kingship was an office separate from the individual king. The concept of the king's two bodies – a public body and a natural body – made it possible to distinguish between respect for the office of king and for the character of the current incumbent. It was possible for the king to be under age, like Edward V, and for his functions to be performed by others, such as the council and Lord Protector, on his behalf. Although the office of king, like all offices of authority, was held by divine right, it was not the coronation in church that made a king but the law of the people that he ruled. In England kings succeeded the day after the death of their predecessor: Edward V was king from 10 April and not from the date of the coronation that never took place. A king's title had three parts: hereditary right; election or acclamation of the people; and conquest. Edward V, the son of Edward IV, was elected by the council the day his father died and was recognized everywhere. Usurpers lacking such incontrovertible rights, such as Henry IV, Edward IV, Richard III, and Henry VII, were careful to arrange elections in support of their titles. Title by inheritance was not precisely defined. Naturally sons took precedence over daughters and brothers over sisters, but when relationships were more distant it was not clear whether the male or female line was to be preferred. In 1399, when Henry IV became king, his election was facilitated by the abdication of Richard II, which released his subjects from their allegiance. In case Henry VI would not resign in 1460, Richard Duke of York asserted both that his hereditary title was irrefutable and that it conformed to divine and natural law. It thus sufficed by itself to defeat Henry VI's title by election, parliamentary confirmation, and the oaths of allegiance of his subjects. This message was remembered by Richard III. By making out a hereditary title for himself, he secured the acclamation and election that made him king and these in turn superseded the oaths of fealty formerly made to Edward V in ignorance of Richard's right. Rightly or not, a king *de facto* was a king, God's deputy on earth, and thus entitled to the allegiance and obedience of his subjects against all comers. But the hereditary title had to be made out first. Hence the prior claims of Edward IV's children had to be defeated before Richard III could establish his own.

The image of kingship

The obligations of allegiance and obedience by subjects to their king were ones that Yorkist kings could wholeheartedly encourage. They did not wish to be tyrants. They accepted the mixed monarchy and the ideal of the common weal and indeed were quick to exploit such ideals or claim credit for compliance when opportunities occurred. But what they needed most was respect and obedience to support their shaky authority, not scope for outspoken criticism by their subjects or the *coups d'état* of Warwick, Clarence and others. The Yorkist kings, after all, were usurpers. Edward IV, before 1471, and Richard III, throughout his reign, were confronted by rivals, two of whom – Henry VI and Edward V – had been kings and who enjoyed substantial minority (if not majority) support. They made the most of their status as kings. They were God's lieutenants on earth, the Lord's anointed. In parallel to other parts of creation, they were the head of the human body or the sun among the planets: Edward IV's badge was the sunburst or the sun in splendour. The Yorkists cultivated their hereditary claim. Yorkist genealogies tracing the York line back to Adam were published and circulated in many surviving copies. Such propaganda stressed the legitimacy, the prestige and the authority of the Yorkist line. It was such tactics that had been used to justify the Yorkists' usurpation of the throne and their continued occupation of it.

Kings needed to inspire respect, even awe, among foreign ambassadors and their own subjects. The greatest, the proudest and the wealthiest magnates could not fail to be impressed by a splendour that they could not emulate. Everything about the king must be better, bigger, grander and richer than among his magnates. King Edward stood out as a man even among noble men, a poet recalled. He was helped by his imposing height and impressive physique, but he left nothing to chance, as a panegyrist makes him lament.

> Where are my riches and my royal array?
> Where be my great coursers and my horses high?
> And where my great pleasure, solace and play?
> Where are my castles and buildings royal?

His clothes and horses, even his library and chapel-music, excelled those of any subject. So, too, his artillery and fortresses, as befitted a king. At the Tower of London, Dover, Nottingham and Windsor Castles, Windsor and Eton Colleges, and at Eltham, where his new hall remains, Edward had built lavishly and even pointlessly: 'I made the Tower strong, I knew not why'. Conspicuous consumption was much admired. Crowland tells the same tale.

> In the collection of gold and silver vessels, tapestries and highly precious ornaments, both regal and religious, in the building of castles, colleges, and other notable places and in the acquisition of new lands and possessions not one of his ancestors could match his remarkable achievements.

In his palaces Edward kept a 'royal rout', attended by lords, knights, and by a host of humbler servants clad in his livery, who together constituted the magnificent household *(domus magnificencie)* that constituted the outward face of majesty and Edward's own home. It was there he ruled and there he indulged himself. Even Edward's most sceptical historian, who saw the niggardly economy behind the display, believed him to be 'a very wealthy prince' and failed to recognize the way he maximized and focused the crown's limited resources.

Display, moreover, was coupled with elaborate ceremonial and etiquette. Its supreme expression, of course, was the coronation, at which Edward IV, later his queen, and Richard III were anointed with holy oil, solemnly swore oaths to their people, and wore all the insignia of majesty. On great occasions Edward wore his crown. In an effort to distance himself from the threadbare regime of the Lancastrian Henry VI, King Edward IV self-consciously upgraded the ceremonial and grandeur of his court, even attempting to emulate the elaborate etiquette and magnificence that made Burgundy the leading court of the time. A Hungarian visitor remarked on the

King Edward IV, from the Royal Window in Canterbury Cathedral.

splendour and arrogance of the queen. Edward's brothers and sisters-in-law were endowed more nobly than those of any previous king and in 1483 the whole royal family was set apart from the non-royal nobility.

Whenever artists depicted the royal court, they invariably show a formal scene. The king sits on his throne, richly attired, and bearing his insignia of majesty, surrounded by courtiers splendidly caparisoned; in front, on bended knee, there is some suppliant. He might be the king's brother-in-law Earl Rivers, his chamberlain Lord Hastings or the Burgundian chronicler Waurin; in the mural in Edward IV's own chantry chapel at Windsor, it was St Stephen. It could be a minister or foreign ambassador. In 1484 the Silesian knight Nicholas von Poppelau was formally received by Richard III in the company of the king's family, magnates, and councillors. Nobody was the king's equal, not even his relatives or favourites: all had to abase themselves. Richard dined in state even when in the North, where no palace could accommodate all his entourage. His chamber was a large temporary building or tent, in which von Poppelau saw both his bed, decorated with hangings as rich as those of the emperor, and his dining table 'covered all around with silk cloths embroidered with gold'. Princes and lords dined with the king. "When he had seated himself at the table, two princes of the royal blood and the earl of Northumberland, who is the most powerful man in England, [also sat down], but they sat very far away from the king, and almost at the end of the table'. We can visualize the scene from a contemporary drawing in *The Black Book of the Household* of Edward IV. King Edward sits in a canopied chair at a long covered table adorned with splendid salts. He alone is at centre, with a bishop and three laymen seated on the same side near the ends. All face from the dais down the chamber. Richard's invitation to von Poppelau, to sit with him at his table, was thus a remarkable honour. Unfortunately we lack descriptions of the formal ceremonial of the Yorkist royal chamber and chapel.

Besides such everyday display and ceremonial, special efforts were made on the major feastdays, such as Easter. The Crowland chronicler records the splendour, dancing, and other frivolity of Christmas 1483 and 1484. King Edward also made his rites of passage into great ceremonial occasions that were recorded at length by his heralds: the coronation of his queen (1465), the great tournament of Anthony Wydeville and the Bastard of Burgundy (1467), the marriage of his sister Margaret (1468), the betrothal of his eldest daughter (1469), the investiture of the Prince of Wales (1471), the entertainment of Lord Gruthuyse (1472), the reburial of his father (1476), the marriage of his younger son (1478), the christening of one daughter (Bridget, 1481) and the funeral of another (Mary, 1482); his own funeral and the coronation of his brother continue a sequence taken up by the Tudors. Such lavish and carefully staged events stressed the majesty and magnificence of kingship, presented the monarch as a rich and powerful prince and often served more immediate political purposes. That of 1467 cloaked the dismissal of Lord Chancellor Neville and that of 1478 gave the appearance of royal solidarity for the trial of Clarence. They played their part in the management of parliament.

Such events were as complicated logistically as military campaigns and just as expensive, in time if not money. A session of parliament by itself tied up the whole central administration for weeks and was extremely costly. So, too, the ceremonial re-interment of Edward's father and brother, killed at Wakefield in 1460, at the York family mausoleum at Fotheringhay in Northamptonshire. First of all, we may imagine, the College itself had to be completed, monuments constructed in the Lady Chapel, and decorations prepared. Someone set out the route in easy stages and timetabled the journey from Pontefract to Fotheringhay, laying on receptions, resting places, hearses, palls and candles at each nightly stop. The bodies of Richard Duke of York and his second son Edmund Earl of Rutland were exhumed on 21 July. Accompanied by heralds and the chapel royal, Richard Duke of Gloucester , six other noblemen and bishops, the cortège proceeded in short stages for ten days to Fotheringhay, where it was met by the king, royal family, ambassadors and everyone who was anyone. Nine bishops shared in the solemn obsequies. Meantime accommodation for many men and women, stabling for horses, and catering in tents was provided for 1,500 guests according to their rank, for the household itself, for 5,000 in receipt of alms, perhaps 20,000 in all. Fotheringhay can never have seen anything like it. What effort was required to collect enough meat, drink and fuel and to impress enough cooks, bakers, and brewers? Surely the routine business of government and administration was overshadowed for weeks and the private business of Gloucester and his fellow escort almost suspended? Intended to be a uniquely memorable event for all participants, it certainly worked for Duke Richard, who provided prayers for his father and brother at Queens' College Cambridge next year and dedicated a weekly Requiem mass for them at Middleham in 1478. Yet only two years later the regime girded itself up for another such set-piece occasion.

King Edward kept his last Christmas festivals in 1483 at his palace of Westminster. He was

> very often dressed in a variety of the costliest clothes very different in style from what used to be seen hitherto in our time. The sleeves of the robes hung full in the fashion of a monastic frock and the insides were lined with such sumptuous fur that, when turned back over the shoulders, they displayed the prince (who always stood out because of his elegant figure) like a new and incomparable spectacle set before the onlookers. In those days you might have seen a royal court such as befitted a mighty nation, filled with riches and men from almost every nation and (surpassing all else) with the handsome and most delightful children born of the marriage, as mentioned above, to Queen Elizabeth.

That was the intention: to distract attention from escalating diplomatic and financial crises. Although both the chroniclers Crowland and Mancini knew that the events were staged, both came away impressed, mistakenly, that Edward was a rich king with a full treasury, which was of course what he intended. Presenting the right appearance was always an essential part of government.

By holding parliaments at such times kings, assured a good attendance of well-dressed aristocrats. Those attendant at the king's audiences, at table, in chamber and in chapel were lords and knights, well-born, wealthy noblemen and gentry, even the knight of the Garter (often mistakenly identified as Duke Richard) featured in the foreground of Waurin's presentation of his chronicles to King Edward. A splendid court demanded first a magnificent royal household, ordained by the *Black Book*, and secondly a visiting nobility and gentry. Note the image that Richard chose to project when creating his son Prince of Wales:

> The clarity and charity of the sun's light is so great that, when it is poured on the other heavenly bodies, the sun shines with no less light and splendour, nor does it suffer any diminution of his strength, rather it is pleased to be seen, to shine as a king in the midst of the nobles and

to adorn the greater and lesser stars in the whole court of heaven with his outstanding light.

The nobility were satellites enhancing the prestige of the king and contributing to the image that kings wished to propagate. Both the symbolism and the reality it conveyed were intended to encourage conformity and to discourage sedition among nobility and their inferiors alike.

Practical politics

Neither the 'democratic' nor the 'monarchical' theories of government conformed precisely to reality. Political theory, as we have seen, derived directly from political practice and was propagated by practical statesmen and politicians. The exaltation of kingship, too, had direct practical applications and was indeed sometimes deployed for specific political ends. Yet inevitably there was a gap between theory and practice. No systems or procedures work always without a hitch: the phenomenon of Richard III is an obvious illustration. The system in practice was monarchical rather than democratic. The sharing of power and the obligations of the king to his people were highlighted only when parliament assembled, when lords and commons alike generally accepted the direction and detailed management of the king and his ministers. Even inside parliament, therefore, and always outside, the government was the king's government, its policy was *his* policy, and civil servants were *his* servants, who were bound to *him* personally by ties of loyalty more personal and immediate than mere allegiance and whose duty it was to implement *his* wishes. The king might seek advice, but he consulted whom *he* chose and *he* could reject their counsel. Decisions were *his* alone. It was *his* acts, *his* initiatives, that directed the great administrative machine over which *he* presided.

This was personal government. A king had not only to be virtuous but also to be effective. Kings had to be tough, authoritative and respected. The prestige of office, though valuable, was not enough: the qualities of the man were vital and shaped his reign. Ideally an English king was proficient at arms and a leader in battle. He was hardworking, for whatever was delegated, decisions were required of him daily. If he shirked them or took the easy course, he risked his throne. He needed to be physically impressive and proficient in public speaking: those audiences beloved of illuminators all transacted business demanding a royal response. He required the charm to win people's loyalty and devotion – Edward IV was notably affable – and the strength of personality to terrify even his most powerful subject into obedience. To a considerable extent, politics – even for kings – was a matter of personal relationships. After Clarence's death, so we are told, his brother Edward IV was strong enough to confront any evil-doer to his face with his offence. To support these personal relationships, he kept files in his signet office covering the favours of literally hundreds of protégés. He interviewed them all himself not once but twice in 1467, personally driving hard

The seal of King Edward IV in white wax shows the mounted, armed figure of the king, on a background of Yorkist roses and suns. (Carlisle Museum)

bargains with them, and he may have done the same in 1473. Behind his politically advantageous capacity to remember everyone, even the obscure, lay a devoted staff and good paperwork. As Richard's surviving signet registers show, the same was true of Richard III.

This was personal government. The essential functions – defence, foreign policy, and justice – were not reflected in its organization as they are today. There was no Ministry of Defence, no Foreign Office, still less any Department of Employment, Trade and Industry, or for Education. Instead the institutions of government reflected the king's needs for accommodation, food, drink, clothing, and transport, money, a secretariat and to do justice: hence his household, exchequer and chamber, chancery, privy seal and signet offices, and the common law courts. The king was the hub and the prime mover. Government departments were his agents, responding to his will. For the most part, they did not make policy, but implemented what he had devised. Much of their business was designed to maintain the king rather than to fulfil the duties outlined above. Thus the royal household with its 800 staff, the environment in which he actually lived, was much the most expensive institution – the equivalent of the great spending departments of today – even though Edward achieved good value for money by securing maximum magnificence for minimum waste. The exchequer, with its hundred staff, was primarily engaged in raising money to finance the rest of government. The writing departments issued perhaps 30-40,000 letters a year, many concerned with patronage, the remainder, perhaps principally, with law and order. Only the law courts were functional ministries in the modern sense that they catered for a recognizable duty of government. But the organs of central government were exceptionally highly developed for their time: bureaucratic procedures ruled and the staff were highly experienced and expert in the business that they handled. Business itself was immense and the records it generated were equally vast. Unfortunately the records which remain are mostly records of routine and cast relatively little light on the decision-making process – the actions of the king – which we most wish to understand.

The departments of state were administrative offices far from the centre of politics. Most decisions were taken outside departments and most clerks were never promoted. Members of the gentry often held key posts in the exchequer, but in chancery, the privy seal office and the signet office the senior administrators, the potential councillors and ministers, were generally recruited in middle life from the ranks of successful academics and ecclesiastical administrators. Such men took as their reward church livings and often treated them as mere sinecures. They brought to the post trained minds, a mastery of philosophical and legal subtleties, a proficiency in written and spoken Latin (the international language), an understanding of the principles of international law, and very often a cosmopolitan outlook gained from study abroad. Men like these did not write the duplicate and triplicate letters, writs, accounts, and memoranda that make up the genuinely vast bulk of surviving royal archives. Some of the decisions recorded there, those that lacked royal or ministerial authority, were certainly theirs. It was men like these who drafted the impressive state papers that now survive only for Richard III and are preserved in his signet registers in British Library Harleian Manuscript 433. They too were responsible for the recently discovered financial memoranda, which show them translating the raw data and impenetrable technicalities of the exchequer records into cash flow, solvency, and priorities for payment. The conclusions were then taken to the royal council, where it was ministers and bureaucrats rather than kings and nobles sat for long hours several days a week coping with dull administrative problems, co-ordinating the work of departments and implementing the policies that were decided by the king and his entourage.

Most of all we can see their work in the records of diplomacy, which have more often been preserved than the high-level working papers of exchequer or council. Foreign policy was primarily their concern. Many of them became diplomats, initially tackling the technicalities, later perhaps taking the lead. One such man, who had been a diplomat, wrote the best contemporary chronicle. A London-based clergyman, a senior chancery official and diplomat, he knew government and high politics from within, and treated events briefly, critically and precisely. Master Henry Sharp, doctor of civil law at Oxford and Padua, archdeacon of Bedford, a chancery diplomat well past his prime, could have written this so-called Crowland chronicle [henceforth called Crowland]. He is certainly more likely than his chief, the chancellor himself. Lord Chancellor John Russell, Bishop of Lincoln, doctor of canon law and privy seal official, was the leading diplomat of the 1470s and thereafter rose to ministerial office and a bishopric. Russell was reputedly both learned and pious, widely read in the classics and scriptures, and had pastoral interests quite foreign to Crowland. If the royal council included many Henry Sharps, ministers were more like Russell: Edward IV's chancellors Thomas Rotherham, Archbishop of York, and Robert Stillington, Bishop of Bath, were of this type. They were administrators and diplomats. Judicious and efficient, they ran the royal machine, but they did not play politics. Typically, however, they implemented decisions and observed events. Bishop John Morton, the future chancellor of Henry VII, who shaped events himself, was unusually partisan.

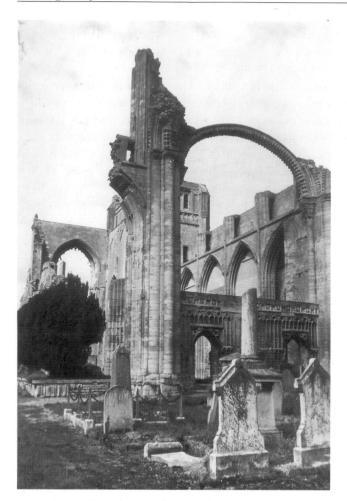

Yet Crowland (and doubtless the others) had strong prejudices and opinions that were concealed from his employers and to some extent, regrettably, from us too. Crowland was scathing about the results of Edward's invasion of France in 1475 and the Berwick campaign of 1483. They were a terrible waste of money, above all *his* money which his ecclesiastical superiors too easily voted in taxes, and an act of sacrilege: 'Wicked Ruin for the Church' was his marginal comment! King Edward's pillage, he strongly implies, was punished by the dynastic disasters that followed:

> O what a servile and pernicious ruin for the Church! May God turn away the minds of all succeeding kings from following up, in any way, an act like this, lest perchance they should be afflicted by these misfortunes, or worse if that can be imagined, which unhappily soon afflicted this king and his noble descendants.

While recognizing King Edward's exemplary deathbed repentance, he was highly critical of his self-indulgence and immorality. If Crowland was a career civil servant, he was very conscious that he was also a churchman. Initially he aligned himself with Hastings against the Wydevilles and perhaps with Gloucester, but he changed his view thereafter and ended up a Tudor partisan.

In theory the king held an office for the benefit of his subjects and was accountable to them. In practice he presided over an enormous central machine – no other contemporary institution was of equal size in the pre-factory era. He commanded literally hundreds of devoted servants and enjoyed the services in particular of the most highly qualified and experienced administrators in the country. No private individual, however overmighty, possessed more than a fraction of the resources and expertise available to the king. Kings could – and did – confront, overawe, and bring to heel a whole succession of great subjects. The king was far more powerful than the theorists suggested. And yet mixed monarchy was a concrete reality. Kings were in practice held to account at regular intervals, forced to modify their policies, and even dethroned – five times during the Wars of the Roses. Perhaps fear of the Last Judgement motivated them, as it did Edward IV on his deathbed, and perhaps they did seriously try to temper their policies to popular demand. Like Richard III, they were vulnerable to military attack and wished to forestall it.

Government and politics were the business not just of the king and his administrators but also of his greater subjects, the elites of town and country, and above all of the rural aristocracy. These comprised both the titled nobility, those with the hereditary titles of duke, marquis, earl, viscount and baron, and the landed gentry: knights, esquires and gentlemen. The distinctions in title recognized different levels of wealth and standing, but all had sufficient unearned income from land to support themselves without manual labour and to free them for participation in government and politics. The peerage dominated the House of Lords and the gentry the Commons, so it was with both groups that the king had to co-operate in parliament. The aristocracy dominated the localities and it was on the nobility that kings depended for the maintenance of order and the implementation of their wishes. At a military level the aristocracy deployed resources that no king could resist. Kings therefore had to tailor their policies to the purposes of the aristocracy if they wanted them implemented or if they wanted to avoid being coerced or even deposed.

Noble power stemmed from the income and tenants of their great estates, which bestowed standing and could be converted into manpower for military action. Even Chaucer's franklin, who could have called himself a gentleman a generation later, mirrored in miniature the lifestyle of a king. His house in its context was also exceptionally large, containing both a hall with service rooms for communal eating and his own personal chamber. Menial servants were decked out in his livery and financed from the unearned rents from his estates. He lived a life of conspicuous consumption, undertaking no physical labour and eating, drinking, dressing, enjoying himself, and being accompanied according to his rank. Doubtless the saints days regulated his diet too and the daily services that he followed in his primer, missal or breviary at his parish church. The greater gentry, like Thomas Troponell in Wiltshire or the East Anglian Pastons, with £20 or £300 a year, possessed private chapels or oratories, their own chaplains, altar-furniture, communion plate, vestments and alms-dishes. As proud of their lineage as any king, they too had fine tombs and mausolea, genealogical rolls and family chronicles, and placed their coats of arms and badges everywhere on the buildings, stained glass, tapestries, vestments and plate they kept for their own use or that they gave away. The lowliest gentleman was the squire of a village or parish. There were men at his call in his household and on his land that gave him political weight. Above him, a knight or baron ruled a district – like the Lords Berkeley over Berkeley – and an earl a county. At the top of the social hierarchy the greatest magnates, like the Duke of Norfolk in East Anglia or Richard Duke of Gloucester in the North, presided over whole regions. England was a federation of aristocratic spheres of influence, in which the smaller were contained in the larger as petty lords deferred to the great: thus, as we shall see, the northern earls and barons accepted Richard as their lord. Power rested everywhere with the local aristocracy. It could be used to frustrate the wishes of the king or even to wage war against him. It was noble retinues that formed the core of the armies of the Wars of the Roses.

Seldom, however, were such retainers in the majority. The people were in politics during the Wars of the Roses. From Jack Cade's Rebellion in 1450 the commons shared the expectations of their superiors, judged kings and governments by their contribution to the commonweal, backed demands for reform, and resorted to violence to secure it. A succession of noble leaders, from Richard Duke of York in the 1450s to Warwick the Kingmaker in 1470-1, identified themselves with reform, incited and orchestrated popular feeling with skilfully devised populist manifestos and directed the people into national politics. Crowland described such leaders as 'idols of the multitude'. Once raised, the people were an overwhelming force against which no regime could stand. Excited by Warwick, they swept away Henry VI's government in 1460 and Edward IV in 1469. It was against them and against the odds, as Crowland says, that Edward 'won a marvellous, unexpected and glorious victory' in 1471. His invasion of France in 1475, though costly, was popular, but not the treaty of Picquigny that he so rapidly concluded. However honourable he purported it to be, says Crowland, 'there is nothing so holy or proper that it cannot be distorted by ill report'. His royal brother Richard was one such critic. Edward feared that spin-doctors would inflame unemployed returning soldiers and fan those complaining about the bad management of the country's wealth into further campaigns of reform. Besides rigorously executed justice and quelled insurgency, he sought also to forestall future trouble by ceasing to exact taxation. Richard Duke of Gloucester, we shall see, was another noble demagogue, who posed as a reforming critic of the government and a protagonist of the commonweal, informed and inflamed public support, and directed and calmed it when he chose.

Kings were thus aware of their limitations. They knew that they could not withstand the people once they were up: hence the commons must be denied grounds to grumble and effective leadership. Kings knew themselves also to be weak in the localities, where their officers were neither respected nor effective. Hence they recruited to local office members of the local elite, who strengthened royal authority with their own standing and were able to enforce the royal will. As officeholders, the practical authority that such men already exercised was confirmed and made legitimate. They were allowed a free hand without royal interference, provided they did not exceed their powers or allow disorder to get out of hand. It was a genuinely reciprocal relationship.

Successive kings nevertheless used forfeited and escheated land and marriages in their gift to make their relatives and favourites into great magnates. Edward IV, for example, endowed his two brothers, arranged advantageous marriages for his Wydeville in-laws, and elevated others – like Lord Hastings – to the nobility. When Richard made himself 'Lord of the North' during Edward's second reign and the Wydevilles became rulers of Wales, whole regions were placed in reliable hands, to whom the king was happy to delegate unusual authority. Thomas Lord Stanley, steward of his household from 1471, was allowed to remain 'ruler' of Lancashire and Cheshire and indeed was protected against the expansionism of Richard and the Wydevilles alike. Other settlements of 1483 that did not take effect envisaged the dominance of East Anglia and the West Country by his second son Prince Richard and his stepson Dorset. These blocs are the provincial background to the events of 1483.

The division of power implied by mixed monarchy normally posed no problems. Initiative always rested with the king, parliaments could be managed, and the localities were ruled on his behalf. Kings and nobles shared a common upbringing, common tastes and a common outlook which made for harmonious co-operation. The aristocracy were bound to kings by allegiance and were reluctant to proceed to extremes. Any competent king could foresee difficulties and could ensure that he was never faced by the united opposition of the nobility. Many of them, moreover, had little interest in involving themselves in government. In the days before the London season, there was little incentive for most of them to come to London except for great councils and parliament, sessions which were in any case brief and intermittent, and many failed to attend even these. The more remote seldom if ever attended court or participated in government. Most of the time routine council business was handled by a mere handful of ministers, judges, and bureaucrats and court was dominated by the few noble and many gentry office-holders of the upper household. Day-to-day politics was restricted to this narrow group supplemented irregularly by visiting magnates and for the most part the provincial elites were content to leave politics in their hands.

Yet there was more to everyday politics than routine administration. It was these permanent politicians who made policy. Although less wide-ranging and fundamental than it is today, policy-making nevertheless embraced foreign affairs, decisions of peace and war, the management of commerce, finance and the maintenance of order. It was also those at court who determined the distribution of patronage: thousands of offices carrying remuneration or authority, grants and leases of land, grants of wards, appointments to church livings, custody of estates, and a host of other advantages. Politics was primarily about patronage. For royal dukes and the leading courtiers the spoils could be spectacular, but even backwoodsmen coveted the royal bounty in their own domains (or countries as they were called), royal office to justify their natural authority, the chance to advance their retainers, and the status that went with influence at court. The purpose of full-time politicians was to tap the king's patronage on behalf of themselves or their clients. Some of it was distributed by ministers or other officials: the Lord Treasurer was the man to approach for a customs post and the Lord Chancellor for many minor benefices. Most fruits, however, were directly in the gift of the king. It was he who had to be informed of the vacancy and persuaded to bestow it on a particular candidate. Access to him was crucial: those regularly in his company, like Lord Treasurer Essex with his daily audience with Edward IV or the attendants of his private apartments, were naturally best placed to put their case. While this most accessible of kings offered many opportunities for petitions to be slipped into his hands by some (though certainly not all) outsiders, those with such access could exploit it by getting in their petitions first and manipulating it, exchanging what they had for what they wanted, calculating on and anticipating future favours. Both King Edward's father-in-law and his brother of Gloucester were able to promise favours to their dependants months or even years ahead of the formal grants.

Those too far away or without the entrée had to use an intermediary at court. As Russell told the Lords in 1483, 'The people must stand afar and not pass the limits; you speak with the prince, which is like God on earth, mouth to mouth.' But petitioning alone was insufficient, for Edward IV was a king who was able to say no and often did. After the early 1460s, he kept records of his bounty and distributed it with care, weighing the qualifications, earlier rewards, and deserts of his suitors.

So persuasion was needed too. And persuasion demanded the continuous intercession of those about the king, particularly those he trusted and whose advice he accepted. All kings had favourites, often those who shared their recreation, and it was such favourites who were most likely to secure royal consent. It was to them that outsiders, many insiders, and even the great entrusted their applications for royal patronage.

The outstanding instance of such a man in Yorkist England was William Lord Hastings. A hereditary servant of the house of York, he knew Edward before his accession, shared his pleasures, and was his closest friend. Edward entrusted to Hastings the key post of chamberlain of the household, which carried authority over the king's personal apartments and staff, control over access to the king himself and considerable say in his decisions, some of which, indeed, were delegated to him. It was this office that made him so powerful rather than his barony, his noble connections or his Leicestershire estates. His capacity to help or harm encouraged many churchmen, towns and magnates, the future Richard III among them, to pay him retaining fees. It prompted town corporations and London livery companies to seek his intercession. One Yorkshire knight secured a place in Hastings' household for his son, while another sought his influence with his own master, the Earl of Northumberland. Hastings was the patron and they were the clients. Such services were paid for with annuities, sinecures, gifts, entertainment, expenses, straightforward payment and reciprocal favours. They were, for Hastings, a major source of profit. His clients presumed that Hastings had the capacity to deliver royal favour, which depended in turn on the trust and credit of the king. Hastings could not

The effigy of Thomas Cockayne at Youlgrave, Derbyshire. Cockayne was one of many northern and Midlands gentlemen indentured to serve Lord Hastings.

risk that credit for any client, whatever the rewards, since to do so could altogether destroy his influence. Hastings was outstanding, but not unique: Lord Herbert in the 1460s and Richard's William Catesby made comparable profits from their influence. There are many parallels to such men earlier and later in English history.

Hastings, Herbert, and Catesby were the established channels for individual aspirants, corporations, syndicates and pressure groups to solicit the king. They stood at the head of connections at court and in the localities that looked to them for advancement and served their patron's interests and wishes. They were bound together in factions by mutual self-interest. Usually there were several such factions of varying strengths and significance, headed by royal kin, ministers, household officers and intimates, who rose or fell in their master's estimation. Such factions, each with its front-men, backers and ramifications in the provinces, each represented on council and in the royal chamber, were the channels through which decisions of policy and patronage were brought to the king, debated and determined. They kept him informed of the options, offered him a choice of initiatives and candidates, and enabled him to control his agents.

Kings needed factions but they also needed to keep them in hand. A narrow circle of favourites vied for royal favours. It was essential that each had to be seen to be successful: setbacks, still less defeat, imperilled both one's purse and one's power. Not surprisingly, the higher the stakes, the higher the political temperature. Tensions mounted, animosities ran deep, and dirty tricks and

ELIZABETH · VXOR
EDWARDVS · IIII

A portrait of Queen Elizabeth Wydeville as foundress of Queens' College, Cambridge.

violence were invoked. It was the decisive defeat of the Warwick faction that provoked the bloodshed of 1469 and the titanic struggle for the Warwick inheritance of the royal dukes in court, council, parliament and the provinces that nearly threatened private war in 1472-5.The momentary alliance of all the factions destroyed Edward's second brother Clarence in 1478. The chain of minor misdemeanours that brought him to the Tower offered them their chance and his trial and execution for treason followed. Although condemned by due parliamentary process, the charges were vague and failed to convince then or now. 'Were he faulty were he faultless', one historian remarks. A majority vote was all that was needed and that was ensured by the prior division of the spoils, packing parliament, stage-managing proceedings and leading for the prosecution with the king, who could not be contradicted. Nevertheless, the verdict and sentence secured, Edward vacillated and had to be pressed to complete the execution, evidently against his better judgement and to his lasting regret. 'Oh unfortunate brother!', he allegedly complained. 'For whose life no man in this world would once make request!' Similar sorrows beset his grandson Henry VIII on the execution of Thomas Cromwell in 1540, again belatedly, as he too became the factions' instrument to eliminate their enemy.

The destruction of a royal duke not only benefited directly all the principal participants – the Wydevilles, Hastings, and Clarence's brother Richard – but it also offered the hope that other rivals could be similarly removed. So both Hastings and

Lord Hastings's step-daughter, Cecily Bonville, who was married to Thomas Grey, Marquess of Dorset, son of Elizabeth Wydeville, Astley church, Warwickshire.

the Wydevilles thought. Their enmity dated from at least 1464, when Lord Chamberlain Hastings had made his widowed kinswoman Elizabeth (née Wydeville) pay with her eldest son's marriage and inheritance for the access to the king that surprisingly made her queen. What was seen as an unequal match was given a virtuous respectability by the widespread publication of a romantic story that Elizabeth defended her honour against the king with a dagger and only yielded to him when they were married. Well-known later the same decade in Italy, it was retold to Dominic Mancini in London in 1483. Queen Elizabeth's understandable hostility to Hastings was repeatedly fuelled by his encouragement of the king's infidelity and by subsequent events; 'as well for that the king had made him captain of Calais, which office the queen's brother Lord Rivers claimed of the king's former promise, as for divers other great gifts which he received that they looked for', and the marriage of the queen's son Dorset against Hastings's wishes to the latter's heiress-stepdaughter Cecily Bonville. Each tried dirty tricks to defeat the other. For example, Earl Rivers, so we are told, persuaded the king that Calais was to be betrayed to the French by Hastings, and Hastings's Calais council engineered charges by torture from one John Edwards against Dorset and Rivers. What these charges were we cannot now know, but they were serious enough for Edwards' retraction on 8 August 1482 to be witnessed by the king himself, his principal ministers, three bishops, six peers and many others, and for multiple copies to be circulated by the Wydevilles. Such divisions were mere irritants to the king himself, who was always master, but what was their explosive potential when he was gone? No wonder that he strove to reconcile the contenders on his deathbed.

The last parliament of Edward IV early in 1483 was a public triumph for the queen's family, the Wydevilles. When first she became queen in the 1460s, King Edward had promoted three of her brothers and made countesses of all her sisters. During the 1470s, her eldest son, Thomas Grey, had twice been found heiresses and raised first to an earldom and then a marquisate, and her eldest brother, Earl Rivers, had been made tutor of Edward Prince of Wales and effectively custodian of his estates and ruler of Wales. Now in 1483 Rivers and Elizabeth's younger son Lord Richard Grey strengthened their hold over Edward Prince of Wales, his estates – now to include Pembroke – and hence the whole of Wales. The Greys were to share the important Exeter inheritance. On behalf of her youngest son, Prince Richard, Duke of York, the Wydevilles were confirmed in control of the great Norfolk inheritance that he had held in right of his deceased child bride. They had been exempted from the effects of financial retrenchment and they had been amongst the beneficiaries of a new law that allowed the royal family to wear particularly splendid clothes. They were thus exalted above the ordinary – now drabber – nobles and above others who had better legal claims, even such trusted royal councillors as Lords Berkeley and Howard, who later had good cause to want the Wydevilles scotched. Here is some justification for the charge made later the same year that

> the queen ennobled many of her family. Besides, she attracted to her party many strangers and introduced them to court, so that they alone should manage the public and private business of the crown, surround the king, and have retainers, give or sell offices, and finally rule the very king himself.

A monopoly of access, policy-making and patronage was the ultimate aim of all factions. It was achieved by Henry VI's favourites in the 1440s and 1450s and was alleged against Elizabeth I's Earl of Leicester in the scurrilous libel *Leycester's Commonwealth*. That charge was false and so too is a similar charge against the Wydevilles in 1483. It was to counter their influence in 1469-70 that their enemies sought to discredit the king's marriage by charges of sorcery against the queen's mother. The slur was revived in 1483.

Doubtless the Wydevilles wished that their control was complete, but it was not. Edward was never the prisoner of any faction. Even in 1483 others still had influence over the king: notably Hastings himself; the king's brother Richard, who could also dress in purple under the sumptuary law and who secured vice-regal powers on the western borders; the king's uncle, the octogenarian Lord Treasurer Essex, the political implications of whose death immediately before Edward's can only be guessed at; and probably others as well. Edward was never stronger than in his last years and remained in control until the end. When he wished, that is, for there were certainly occasions when he turned a blind eye.

Those immersed in such factional struggles could easily imagine that this was all

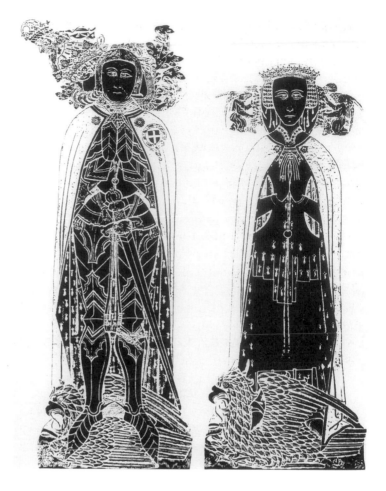

The brasses of Henry Bourchier, KG, 1st Earl of Essex and Lord Treasurer to Edward IV, and his countess, Isabel Plantagenet, at Little Easton, Essex.

there was to politics and could forget that England was a mixed monarchy in which power was shared. It was not those gathered at court, but those scattered in the provinces who could coerce. Government and politicians were ultimately answerable to the provinces and the people and periodically were held to account by the community of realm and/or those in power in these localities. In 1478 the outsiders had played the courtiers' tune. Again in 1483 their compliance was encouraged by the carefully orchestrated splendour of the Christmas celebrations, by the enhanced status given to the royal family, and by the exaggerated praise of Richard and his fellow commanders in the Scottish war. The loss of Berwick, which been surrendered by the Lancastrians in 1461 and which Edward could never afford to recapture, had long been a blot on the king's reputation that he felt deeply. Its recapture by Gloucester symbolized much more to Edward than its actual military value. These celebrations, however, disguised the collapse of the king's foreign policy, actual war with Scotland and potential war with France, a shortfall in revenue and the urgent need for new taxes which he still dared not yet request. Edward vacillated between economic and expensive policies towards Scotland. He issued a printed summary in English of the treaty of Picquigny that the French had broken, the first known propaganda printed in English, to put the French firmly in the wrong and to justify the aggression that he contemplated in vengeance for the jilting of his daughter Elizabeth, fiancée of the dauphin. In life he hesitated and his death forestalled any action. Royal financial policy was criticized by churchmen, suppliers and apparently many others and Edward had to reorganize his household to ensure prompt payment of his bills in future. While still embroiled in

> the inextricable cures, pensiveness, thoughts and charges wherewith his wise and forecasting mind was hugely occupied and encumbered, … seeing the crafty and fraudulent dealing of the foreign princes with whom he was allied and how untruly they disregarded the marriages, payments, sureties and other great and noble treaties that they had approved by their oaths and seals,

Edward died, leaving the problems for his successor to solve. Despite the extent of the problems and the criticism by the country of the court, the two dominant factions nevertheless expected and intended to continue governing and indeed hoped to eliminate their hated rivals by invoking outside support which, it emerged, they could not control. The countrymen asserted themselves and both factions were destroyed.

The Wydevilles fell first, at which 'bursting with joy over this new world', Lord Hastings 'asserted that this had been accomplished without any killing and with only so much bloodshed as might have come from a cut finger'. His death followed. And yet it is true that only a handful of individuals had to be removed by death, custody, sanctuary or exile to cripple both factions and place the government in other hands. Their superficial pre-eminence had rested on the pleasure of the king, but they had also been the principal beneficiaries of that decentralization of authority in Edward IV's second reign to which reference has already been made. Their estates and retainers, their status and respect in the localities, the obligations and loyalties due to them were not so easily scotched. The political establishment was rooted more deeply than the favour of any king – for kings could not choose their greater subjects – and it could not be defeated by the elimination of its current leaders. Once the initial shock was passed, it reasserted itself.

2 Richard III as Duke of Gloucester

Upbringing and early life

Few aspects of Richard's life are more controversial than his birth and deformity. His birth was merely noted at the time. It was after his death that it was first declared unnatural by enemies who tried to denigrate him. Actually it is not unnatural for a mother to have a difficult labour, for a baby to be in the breech position, for an episiotomy or a Caesarean section to be required, or for the infant to arrive with hair; less common, but not unheard of, is birth with teeth; but a two-year pregnancy is not merely unnatural but impossible and quite unbelievable. If there is any truth in any of this, it did not cause Richard congenital weaknesses or hunch his back. Probably he was short of stature, delicate of build and with uneven shoulders, as those who knew him said, but he was certainly neither a cripple nor incapable of bearing arms.

Richard was born at Fotheringhay in Northamptonshire in 1452. His father was Richard Duke of York, Earl of March and Ulster, his mother was one of the well-connected Neville clan, and through them Richard traced descent in three lines from Edward III. He was the youngest of four sons at a time when only the eldest inherited. Edward was destined to be the next duke and Edmund was already an earl, but nothing could be guaranteed for the younger sons, George – the later Duke of Clarence – and Richard. In merely recording his continued existence the *Clare Roll* may faithfully represent Richard's significance to his father! The dynastic revolutions of 1460-1, which destroyed their father and brother Edmund, made Edward king and made Richard abruptly into a royal prince, a knight and Duke of Gloucester. At sixteen he was of age and at thirty the premature deaths of his remaining brothers brought him the crown.

Richard's conventional aristocratic education made him proficient in the use of weapons, pious according to the standards of his day, and literate in English and probably Latin. In 1480 a large cannon (great bombard) was a welcome gift and one of his favourite saints was the patroness of artillerymen. He could be enthusiastic about the crusade. Richard was *particularly* devoted to no less than thirty-nine saints in 1478, an extraordinary total. He expressed a clear preference for the services and ordinal of Salisbury over their York counterparts and ordained that his college at Middleham should celebrate particular masses on three weekdays and specific collects and psalms within them. His capacity to discriminate arose from first hand knowledge of the services which he could have followed in his breviary or missal. Since his surviving primer was evidently for private use, it is probable that he could read Latin. When von Poppelau addressed him at length in Latin in 1484, Richard replied through an interpreter: perhaps he could understand spoken Latin, but lacked the

Richard Duke of York, father of Edward IV and Richard III, from a stained-glass window in Trinity College hall, Cambridge.

confidence to speak it himself. Whether he ever read his thirteen surviving books is uncertain, but he certainly signed them and could not have valued them purely for their illuminations, which are unexciting or altogether lacking. Among other things they could have acquainted him with a range of history, fabulous and actual, from the Old Testament, the Fall of Troy, and King Arthur almost to the present day.

Immediately after Edward's accession, Richard was housed with his brother Clarence and sister Margaret at the new palace at Greenwich, whence he moved in about 1464 into the household of Warwick the Kingmaker. Where better could Richard learn to be an aristocrat than in the household of the greatest nobleman of the time? Richard Neville (1428-71), Earl of Warwick and Salisbury, enjoyed estates, revenues, expenditure and a standard of living greater than those of any contemporary duke. Warwick conducted England's diplomacy and dominated the English marches towards Scotland, Wales and Calais. He wanted to rule England too. He may have viewed Richard as the prospective husband of his younger daughter Anne. Richard could have learnt a great deal: about how to behave and about places and people who bulked large in later life. We know only that in 1464-5 Richard was with the earl, his countess, and two brothers-in-law, when all made offerings at the high altar of St Mary's, Warwick, that he was in or near York in 1468-9, and that the king paid Warwick for Richard's keep with the wardship of young Lord Lovell. Only from this time can Richard have been attracted to the North which, to our knowledge, he had never before encountered. All else, regrettably, is conjecture.

Fotheringhay Church, mausoleum of the House of York, and the River Nene, Norhamptonshire.

Richard's development must also have been influenced by tenants and companions, about which, again, little is known. His financial affairs – and those of his siblings – were handled at first by old servants of the house of York and of the king himself. Whereas one such, John Peke, passed into Clarence's service, another, John Milewater, the attendant of his brothers Edward and Edmund in the 1450s, joined Richard. Such 'servants and lovers' could have reinforced that loyalty to the Yorkist dynasty that is often seen as one of Richard's distinctive features. All were older men. Nearer in age if not in rank were Thomas Huddleston and Richard's esquire Thomas Parr, younger sons of leading Cumbrian families retained by Warwick, whom Richard must surely have met in the earl's household. Perhaps he encountered others of the same kind there, such as Richard Ratcliffe of Derwentwater and James Tyrell of Ipswich, both of whom later served him well, respectively from at least 1478 and 1473. He certainly encountered Francis Lord Lovell, heir of a major baronial family. Warwick's ward and later husband of Warwick's niece, Lovell is usually regarded as Richard's friend. He was to serve him when duke in Scotland and as chamberlain when king, was created a viscount and knight of the Garter, and died while still resisting Richard's conqueror. We know of Milewater, Huddleston and Parr because they fell at Richard's side at Barnet in 1471 and because, much later, he ordained prayers for their souls. Certainly proof of service, this points also to friendship, a strong emotional attachment, and a sense of responsibility on the part of the young duke, which extended beyond the grave and did not fade with time. Conspicuous loyalty to and generous treatment of his retainers was an enduring feature of his career.

The most important figure in shaping Richard's career was his brother Edward IV. It was he who represented the *status quo* – the political framework within which Richard had to operate – and he initially shaped that career. Edward it was who took the crucial early decisions. Thus it was he who late in 1468 declared Richard's majority at the age of only sixteen. Young though he was, Richard was soon sitting on a commission of oyer and terminer, which condemned Lancastrian traitors to death, and electing his brother-in-law Duke Charles the Bold of Burgundy to the Order of the Garter. The surviving offer to Charles of 13 May 1469 bears Richard's signature. A royal progress to East Anglian shrines was followed by Warwick's rebellion, the king's brief incarceration and retreat, and Gloucester's despatch to Wales as the royal figurehead. The next three years were crowded with practical experience of justice, government, and warfare. Richard shared in Edward's exile in 1470 and in his victories in 1471, when Warwick was slain. He himself was slightly wounded and lauded in verse as the new Hector, the Trojan hero. Victory was completed by the deaths of Henry VI in the Tower and his son at or after the battle of Tewkesbury. If Richard had any share in their deaths – and probably he did not – he acted at the king's command and in the interests of public peace. As constable of England, however, it was his duty to summarily try and despatch captured Lancastrian leaders; although initially pardoned, the bastard of Fauconberg suffered the same fate.

Twice Richard had been endowed with lands in the 1460s that ultimately went to others. He lacked the endowment appropriate to a royal duke, still less to Edward IV's notion of what was fitting. In 1467 Edward had intended his next brother Clarence to have £4500 a year, three times the qualifying income for a duke. In 1471 at last Richard's services gave him priority among those deserving royal bounty and Edward gave him most of the possessions forfeited by his defeated enemies. Scattered throughout England and Wales and often contested by others, they required great determination to secure. From 1471-4 Richard was at odds with the Stanleys, his brother Clarence, the Earl of Northumberland and the Countess of Oxford. At some risk to public order, he emerged with an estate equal to that of any magnate and as the dominant figure in the North of England.

For much of Edward's second reign (1471-83), Richard was preoccupied by the acquisition and consolidation of his estates, the recruitment of a retinue, and, somewhat prematurely, planning the good of his soul. As a royal duke and king's brother he was a public figure. He had succeeded Warwick as constable and admiral of England, royal offices that required exercise. We still possess his seal as admiral of England and some records of suits before his court of admiralty. As constable he had to update the rules for English tournaments. Later he was Great Chamberlain of England. Not even the Kingmaker held together such a constellation of prestigious offices. However often in the North, he attended the sessions of parliament of 1472-

A brass plaque inlaid into the chancel floor of Tewkesbury Abbey, marking the presumed resting place of Edward of Lancaster. It reads 'Here lies Edward, Prince of Wales, cruelly slain while but a youth. Anno Domini May 4 1471. Alas the savagery of men. Thou art the last light of thy mother, the last hope of thy race.'

5, 1478 and 1483, appeared in the royal council at Westminster and at the Garter chapter at Windsor when available, and featured in ceremonial state occasions. He was at court as often as was compatible with his other commitments; his frequent inclusion as a witness to royal charters on other occasions however is without significance. He supported other family projects. We have already witnessed him as chief mourner at his father's reburial at Fotheringhay. His brother Edward, however, intended interment at Windsor, where he had St George's Chapel rebuilt and re-endowed. Gloucester contributed. His sister-in-law Queen Elizabeth patronized the existing Queens' College at Cambridge. Again, Gloucester was a contributor. He went on Edward's expedition to France in 1475 with a retinue second to none and publicly stood out against the treaty that brought the war to an inglorious, if profitable, end. In short, Richard developed a national role.

Yet increasingly Gloucester gave priority to the wardenship of the West March – defence of the borders west of the Pennines against Scotland – and it was in the North that he came to see his future. Public and private careers combined in the Scottish war of 1480-1483. Richard was appointed lieutenant of the whole North in 1480 and was Commander-in-Chief of a royal army 20,000 strong in 1482. The Scots proved no

Richard's seal as admiral of England.

opposition. Richard advanced to Edinburgh, which he briefly occupied, and recaptured Berwick-upon-Tweed, which had been in Scottish hands for twenty years. Dunbar was occupied soon after. As ambitious as most younger sons and brothers of kings, Richard saw on the borders an opportunity to carve out a brilliant future for himself and his heirs. He petitioned to be granted Cumberland as a palatinate (a county in which he held all the rights of the Crown and his authority replaced that of the king); for the hereditary wardenship of the West March; and for as much land on the Scottish side of the borders as he could conquer. King and parliament agreed. There were only three English palatinates, the last granted to John of Gaunt, and none were in noble hands. It was a remarkable distinction elevating Richard above all the rest of the nobility.

From 1468 to 1483 Richard's career is one of continuous and conspicuous royal service and fidelity to the crown. Historians have repeatedly contrasted it with the faithlessness, the perjury and treachery of Warwick the Kingmaker, the Duke of Buckingham, and especially Richard's own brother Clarence. They are right to do so. Their mistake is in treating Richard as an honourable exception to a dishonourable norm. The Yorkist nobility was a nobility of service. Loyalty was not a virtue but a duty. Noblemen might have many loyalties but only one allegiance – the allegiance due to the king, which overrode all other ties. Richard himself swore allegiance to Edward IV's heir in 1471 as Prince of Wales and in 1483 as Edward V. To be disloyal was treasonable, shameful, and even damnable. Did Richard have an option to be disloyal or was he never tempted? Of course he was right to remain faithful but he was neither unique nor unusual. Bar a few individuals, the English nobility changed their allegiance seldom, reluctantly and only when defeat was irretrievable. Earl Rivers and Lord Hastings, who had shared Edward's exile in 1470-1, each maintained their loyalty until death. Some of Richard's own men fought on after 1485.

The heir of Warwick

Richard was a younger son who had no inheritance of his own to support to status as a great nobleman and a royal duke. During the early 1460s King Edward had tossed him spare lands of the proscribed Lancastrian peers Somerset, Oxford, and Hungerford, but Richard had actually managed to secure very little. Providing for him became more urgent in 1468-9, when he came of age. Of the Somerset lands, he still had the lordship of Chirk in the marches of Wales and Corfe castle in Dorset; from Margaret Lady Hungerford he wrested Farleigh Hungerford Castle in Somerset; and Edward added Sudeley Castle (Gloucestershire). In Farleigh and Sudeley he possessed two of the most sumptuous and up-to-date palaces, the products of the wealth of two fifteenth-century Lord Treasurers. Despite his title, he was never interested in Gloucestershire. There is no evidence that he ever visited any of these estates. Even taken together they were insufficient for a royal duke. What was to be done? Edward no longer had confiscated properties to give away. His duchy of York was in the hands of his mother and his father's creditors. There remained the duchy of Lancaster. It was permanently vested in the crown by act of parliament, but Edward had already raided it twice, granting lands in the south to the queen and in the North Midlands to Clarence. Now therefore he bestowed the two Lancastrian honours of Halton in Cheshire and Clitheroe in northern Lancashire on Richard.

Probably Edward had nothing more in mind than to provide for his brother. It was however a serious mistake. Though nominally the particular domains of the king and his eldest son, the two palatine counties of Lancashire and Cheshire had over the preceding half-century come under the sway of the Stanley family whose head, Thomas Lord Stanley, was the brother-in-law and political ally of the Earl of Warwick. Richard was thus an unwelcome intruder in another's sphere of influence. Having suffered frustrations in the past, the teenage duke was determined to make his control effective and to maximize his gains. Stanley was summarily directed to hand over any revenues that he had received. Although Richard was despatched in November 1469 to Wales to restore order as a temporary royal figurehead and appointed to major offices throughout the principality, he did not stay there, nor indeed did he obey Edward's urgent summons against the Lincolnshire rebels in the spring. Instead he proceeded to Lancashire, where he presumably took control of his new possessions and immediately embroiled himself in local politics by intervening in a major inheritance dispute. He backed Sir James Harrington, a younger son who claimed the Harrington family estate and Hornby Castle, against his nieces, the daughters of his elder brother, who were backed by Thomas Lord Stanley. When the dispute was investigated, the court of chancery had found in favour of the nieces and subsequently arbitrators including Warwick had awarded their guardianship to Stanley, who had promptly married them to his own younger son and a Stanley cousin. Sir James Harrington, however, refused to give way, clung on to Hornby Castle, and found in Richard a new patron prepared to back him against all comers. On 25 March 1470 the king referred to a variance between the duke and Stanleys,

Effigies of Thomas Lord Stanley, Earl of Derby, and his wife, Ormskirk church, Lancashire.

perhaps the 'fond fray' between their tenants near the Ribble mentioned in much later Stanley verses, and Richard was certainly at Hornby Castle next day, 26 March 1470. While it was perfectly permissible for lords to back their retainers in their *just* cause, here Richard had done quite otherwise. He had allowed his new-found client Harrington to suck him into an existing dispute in which he was in the wrong, to bring him into conflict with another lord, and potentially with the regional magnate too. There was a danger that a minor local dispute would blow up into a regional conflict between great noblemen. Perhaps it had. Inadvertently, however, Richard may have done his brother some service, since his intervention may have deflected Stanley from joining Warwick in his rebellion in March 1470. The wardenship of the West March, to which Richard was appointed on Warwick's exile, might have complemented these duchy lands given time. Richard himself was in exile with his brother in 1470-1 and on their return King Edward cancelled Richard's patents and substituted other properties for Halton and Clitheroe. Henceforth Edward backed Lord Stanley in the North-West, appointing him steward of his household, and commissioned Richard to take Hornby for the nieces. Richard did not. It was not in fact until 1475 that concessions to Harrington settled the dispute.

This neglected episode reveals unfortunate traits in Richard's character. His acquisitiveness, his impatience with opposition, his aggression, his over-commitment to his client, his tenacity and his unwillingness to accept the king's ruling recur later in his career, fortunately never again in such an unbridled manner. He was never so inexperienced again. His acquisitiveness emerges in his search for profit, through piracy and the quest for mines, and through the extension of his estates. Where possible, he relied on legal means, such as purchase or royal grant, but where these failed, as we shall see, he was not averse to fraud, threats or force. His aggression and his unwillingness to give up occurs many times. His patronage of retainers in future was more measured and discreet.

Of course Richard benefited enormously from his royal birth. King Edward was generous to him, was repeatedly persuaded to be yet more munificent and was induced to make grants in lieu of paying arrears of wages due to Richard as warden, to exchange property to the duke's advantage, and to reward him for further services done or to be done. A long wish list was fulfilled in 1478 in return for Richard's support against Clarence. The presumption that Richard had access to royal favour for himself and his clients, which is actually quite difficult to demonstrate, was repeatedly exploited by the duke. The promise of royal licences that Richard made to Lady Hungerford in 1469 was probably not honoured. Even though their agreement was sealed on 14 May 1469, one day after a Garter Chapter at Windsor attended by Richard and his brothers, King Edward's signature of approval, which the indenture states was appended, was never added and the promised licences materialized only three years later. Undoubtedly it was the king who set Richard up in the North in first place, but his intentions were more limited than those of Richard, whom he sought to restrain. Richard, however, was impatient of such constraints, which he circumvented, achieving what Edward had not intended and what the easy-going king, averse to conflict, ultimately accepted. The king was persuaded, to quote Rosemary Horrox, that 'what was good for Gloucester was good for royal authority'. The qualities displayed in 1469 foreshadow those Richard employed for the rest of his life. To an extent that is wholly exceptional among his contemporaries, Richard shaped his own estate and his own career. Richard is unique in this period for taking a strategic overview of his estate and career, for developing and implementing a plan. It makes him strangely modern.

But 1469 had been a false start. Richard lost Halton and Clitheroe which he had hoped to keep. He had hoped to retain his Welsh offices, but these were restored to their rightful holder. What he gained, instead, was much more valuable. It comprised three sets of estates in different parts of England: in the North, where he became Warwick's heir; in south Wales, where Warwick's Beauchamp and Despenser lordships made him the most powerful marcher lord; and in the Essex area, where he was granted the forfeited lands of the Earl of Oxford and his retainers. In the fifteenth-century it was normal to hang on to the miscellaneous properties that one inherited, however geographically dispersed. Richard's own father had estates in Ireland and Wales and important estates at Sandal in south Yorkshire, Fotheringhay in Northamptonshire, Berkhamsted in Hertfordshire, Clare in Suffolk, and much else elsewhere. Aristocrats felt freer to dispose as they chose of what they had acquired themselves, but seldom did. Richard, who had inherited nothing, was freest of restraint and acted decisively, logically, unfettered by restraint. This began early, immediately after the Yorkist victory in 1471, when he discriminated between those of the vanquished whose estates he kept and those allowed to pay him instead.

Sandal Castle, part of Richard's inheritance from his father, modelled as it appeared in the fifteenth century.

Several strategic choices were open to him. If consolidation was thought desirable, Richard could have chosen to focus on Wales, where he was already lord of Chirk, or in the Home Counties. In fact, he chose to become a great northern magnate. If perhaps initially the decision was made for him by the king, it came to be a deliberate policy. At first, Richard relied on Edward's generosity. When this dried up, as the 1470s progressed, so Richard built up his estates by exchange, liquidating his resources elsewhere to enhance those in the North. He chose to surrender Chesterfield (Derbys.), Bushey and Ware (Herts.) in 1474 in return for the town of Scarborough and lands in Cottingham (Yorks.). In 1478 he exchanged Farleigh Hungerford and Sudeley Castles in the South for Richmond and the reversion of Helmsley in Yorkshire. He chose to surrender, sell or alienate to the Church most of the Oxford lands that he held in the South-East. Even more strikingly, in 1475 he chose to exchange Chirk with Sir William Stanley for Skipton-in-Craven in Yorkshire. Richard had other lands and aspirations in Wales, while Skipton was near the Stanley's Lancashire heartlands. In each case, there was a re-ordering of priorities, as Richard and the Stanleys focused their attention towards the North and Cheshire/ North Wales respectively and, of course, away from Wales in Richard's case and the North for Stanley also. These exchanges did not involve, as has been suggested, the exchange of less valuable properties for more lucrative ones.

The gatehouse of Skipton castle, which passed to Richard, Duke of Gloucester, in 1475.

There is no reason to suppose that Farleigh Hungerford, Sudeley, Chesterfield, Bushey, Ware or Chirk brought in less revenues than Richmond, Helmsley, Scarborough, Cottingham and Skipton; indeed the reverse is most probably the case. They were, however, less highly *valued*. Richard looked at his whole estate strategically. Viewed in that light, Richard evidently placed a higher estimation on possessions in the North and in South Wales and was prepared to dispense with others elsewhere to achieve that result. Instead of hanging onto everything, there were properties that Richard was willing to abandon, sell, or give away. He was even prepared to spend his capital. Hence, perhaps, he was constantly looking for more.

In retrospect the most important of the lands confiscated from erstwhile Yorkists that Richard was given in 1471 were some that belonged to his erstwhile guardian, Warwick the Kingmaker. Warwick had two daughters, Isobel and Anne. As Warwick's daughter Isobel had married Richard's brother George Duke of Clarence, whose good service to the king meant that he could not be disinherited, Richard was given only those Neville lands entailed on Warwick's nephew George Neville to which Isobel had no rights. These were the Neville lordships of Middleham and Sheriff Hutton in Yorkshire and Penrith in Cumberland. They had underpinned Warwick's authority as warden of the West Marches and as king's lieutenant of the North. A contest between the royal dukes produced in settlement the rest of Warwick's lands in the North, notably the lordship of Barnard Castle on the Tees.

As warden of the West March Richard based his authority in the borders on these lands just as Warwick had done. Again like Warwick, his home territory was Richmondshire – that upland area of North-West Yorkshire as large as the whole county of Northumberland. Richmond in Swaledale was the traditional capital, but Richard like Warwick substituted his own town of Middleham. He resided in the old castle of Middleham whose keep Warwick had converted into lofty well-lit apartments to the highest contemporary specification. Richard also acquired what remained of Warwick's battered retinue. But he needed other retainers too. He recruited so extensively in Richmondshire that by 1474-5 most of the revenues of the lordship of Middleham were being spent on fees to the Conyers, Metcalfes and other dalesmen. He spread his net more widely, into Tynemouth and the county of Northumberland. In 1472 he supplanted the Earl of Northumberland as chief justice of the royal forests north of the Trent. He secured the stewardship of the archbishop's lordship of Ripon, asserted his patronage over the city of York, and intruded himself into County Durham. He enhanced his land-holdings in the region: he added the lordship of Barnard Castle in County Durham, a stream of Yorkshire towns, lordships and castles in 1474-8, and the whole county of Cumberland in 1483.

To his office of warden of the western Marches (1470), Richard added the posts of sheriff of Cumberland, constable of Bewcastle, custodian of the northern forests, steward of the north parts of the duchy of Lancaster and commissioner of oyer and terminer, array and the peace throughout the North. Ultimately in 1480 Richard also became the king's lieutenant and warden-general of all the marches. His northern retainers were his agents in this aggressive forward policy and its principal beneficiaries. The destruction of the northern Lancastrians in 1461 had enabled Warwick and his brothers to rule the North. After 1471 the Percies, Dacres, and Nevilles of Raby recovered their estates and rebuilt their retinues. These lords rivalled Richard and Richard's forward policy imperilled them. All competed for retainers and retained one another's. The scene was set for the escalating spiral of competitive recruiting and violence that had culminated in private war in the 1450s. Richard coveted the fees and offices of other lords. When Richard retained John Wedrington, undersheriff of Northumberland and the Earl of Northumberland's right-hand man in his home country in 1473, he upset the natural order and equilibrium whereby the two wardens and the leading magnates 'ruled' their own home areas, coexisting and co-operating with one another. Richard again appeared a disruptive intruder. Private war loomed. Accordingly King Edward and his royal council intervened. Gloucester was forbidden to recruit Northumberland's men. Each was to content himself with what he had.

This should have halted Richard's advance and reduced him once again to merely one of the northern nobility, albeit the most powerful. Instead he resolved the difficulty by establishing his supremacy and extending his sway over the whole North. The council's ruling was followed next year by Northumberland's submission. The second greatest magnate in the North forgave the hereditary rivalries with Richard's Neville forebears that had been sealed with the blood of his four predecessors and his three uncles. He accepted Duke Richard as his lord. In 1475 they

A model of Middleham Castle as it may have appeared in the reign of Richard III. By Ian Weekley of 'Battlements'.

Middleham Castle from the south.

Ralph Neville, 2nd Earl of Westmorland, and his first wife, Margaret Percy. Neville co-operated with Richard when he was Duke of Gloucester, and the Yorkist collar around his neck formerly carried Richard's white boar badge as a pendant. The effigies at Brancepeth church, Co. Durham, were destroyed by fire in 1998.

visited York together with 5,000 men. Similarly Ralph Lord Neville, nephew and heir of the Earl of Westmorland, hereditary rival of the house of Middleham, quitclaimed his rights and entered Richard's service. Lady Scrope of Masham committed her under-age son to Richard's 'rule and guiding' and her retainers and tenants to faithfully attend on him. Richard was thus able to persuade the northern nobility to accept him as their lord, to enter his service and to include their retinues in his own. His connection thus embraced the whole region. Lords FitzHugh, Greystoke, Scrope, Neville, Dacre and even the Earl of Northumberland complied. We can only guess at Richard's charm and the blandishments that he employed.

The evidence shows that henceforth he did respect their authority in their home areas: he ceased to intervene directly in Northumberland, the East and Middle Marches, or the East Riding, home territory of the Percies, or in the Lancashire stronghold of Lord Stanley. In his home area, Northumberland was the only avenue to favour for Percy retainers; there was no longer any point in Sir William Plumpton asking Gloucester to pressurize the earl. Whereas Bishop Lawrence Bothe of Durham had preferred the service of the Nevilles of Raby, from 1476 his successor, Bishop William Dudley, deferred to Richard and the Nevilles followed his lead. It was sufficient that without cost to himself Richard could count on the service of themselves and their men when required. From now on they shared in his advantages: some through fees and employment, like Dacre, his deputy warden; some through leases and access to royal favour; some through wardships and advantageous marriages; some as his councillors, like Greystoke; others via redress of grievances, which Gerard Salvan of Croxdale in County Durham chose to seek from Gloucester rather than the Lord Bishop himself or the Nevilles; and all in his victorious campaigns against the traditional enemy, the Scots, in 1482. It was northerners above all whom Richard honoured by appropriating royal prerogatives as his own when he dubbed thirty-one knights and thirty-seven bannerets on his campaigns against Scotland in 1481-2. Some of those already knighted by Northumberland and Stanley were elevated further to banneret. It was Richard's need for patronage that caused him retain the feudal rights and ecclesiastical presentations that might have brought in wardships and livings to bestow on his retainers and his clerks when he leased back the Scrope of Masham estates to Lady Scrope in 1476.

Nor was it merely a cold and calculating alliance of convenience and mutual advantage. Richard and Northumberland, Richard and Neville, worked together to common ends, to exploit mines and mediate disputes, to control the citizens of York and to defeat the Scots. When their retainers quarrelled and appealed for support to their 'good lords', as inevitably they did, Richard and Northumberland firmly refused to take sides and arbitrated the disputes together. It is significant that both Northumberland and FitzHugh gave Richard books: not formal presentation copies but personal gifts, which they knew he would read and appreciate. And, as we shall see, he trusted them.

Sentiment was an element in the transfer of Richard's attention to the North. His sojourn in Warwick's household had familiarized him with that area. Perhaps it had also acquainted Warwick's men and the northerners with Richard. He had been a part of Warwick's household and Warwick's connection, he had rubbed shoulders with his retainers and enlisted some of them himself. Probably he already knew Middleham, Sheriff Hutton, Barnard Castle and the West March. It had been a combination of generations of service and the Kingmaker's own charisma that had made his military following so remarkable. Richard now wanted to revive it for himself. The obstacles were formidable. He himself had helped suppress Lord FitzHugh's uprising in 1470 and to destroy Warwick and his retinue at Barnet in 1471. Heirs and survivors had good cause to resent him. Sullen, reluctant, obedience was all he could expect. Richard could appeal only to the self-interest, not to the sentiment, the traditional fidelity, of potential retainers. They took his fees but what was the quality of their service? If he could present himself as Warwick's heir, he could channel the old loyalties to himself. The grant of Warwick's lands to Clarence and Richard had left the Kingmaker's widow Anne Beauchamp and younger daughter Anne Neville unprovided for. Richard knew them both. He removed the Countess Anne from sanctuary in Beaulieu Abbey and her daughter from kitchen service into sanctuary at St Martin's-le-Grand in London and thence into his protection. He married the younger Anne, who was then able to make good her claims as her father's co-heiress to half his estates. With the help of the king and queen, Richard wrested a larger share

Richard Neville, Earl of Warwick, immortalized as a bronze 'weeper' on the tomb of Richard Beauchamp in St Mary's Church, Warwick.

of the Kingmaker's possessions from Clarence and thus strengthened his hold over what he already had. Inheritance by Anne offered more security than did royal grants of forfeitures.

His marriage enabled Richard to step into her father's shoes, to claim to represent continuity, to reveal himself to the Neville retainers as their natural lord, and hence to inherit their loyalty instead of merely commanding their obedience. By marriage Clarence and Gloucester had made themselves heirs of the ancient houses of Beauchamp and Despenser, Montagu and Neville, of their estates, castles, and retainers, above all the traditions associated with each.

Though Clarence took the title of Earl of Salisbury, it was Richard who then became patron of Bisham Priory, that now-vanished Berkshire monastery founded by the first Montagu Earl of Salisbury, where he and his Montagu and Neville successors were buried. *The Salisbury Rolls of Arms* trace the title back to William Longsword and chart the ramifications of the house of Montagu. The rolls consist of a series of miniatures of Bisham Priory itself and of each successive generation of the family, husband and wife connected by a chain. The last portraits are those of Richard and Anne. It was Clarence who had secured the West Midlands estates formerly of the Beauchamp Earls of Warwick and the Despensers, but Gloucester, as Anne's husband, was the co-heir. Chantry chapels stand between the pillars of the choir of the great Gloucestershire abbey of Tewkesbury to remind us that the church was the mausoleum in successive generations of the De Clares, their heirs the Despensers, and ultimately of Clarence himself. The *Tewkesbury Roll* records the family tree and the deeds of the abbey's patrons. The abbey chronicles depict each patron in miniature. Although Warwick the Kingmaker is the last portrait, the arms of Clarence and Gloucester are included. After a lengthy description of the obsequies of the Duchess of Clarence and a briefer notice of the duke, the chronicle ends with the birth of Richard's son.

Still better known are the traditions of the Earls of Warwick, because they were collected and published by the family chaplain John Rows in 1483. His history consisted of potted biographies of each earl to accompany portraits of successive generations. Rows began with the legendary King Guthelin and such mythical heroes as Guy of Warwick, 'flower and honour of knighthood', and his son Rainbrun, and continued to his own day. The earldom existed continuously for four centuries and successive earls developed Warwick and its locality and earned renown on the national and international scenes. None was greater than Earl Richard Beauchamp (who died in 1439), the 'flower of courtesy' and model knight; his distinguished military and political career had culminated in appointments successively as tutor to Henry VI and as lieutenant – effectively regent – of Lancastrian France. Rows had much to retell with pride. He was not the creator of the tradition but its recorder. Several fourteenth-century earls named their sons Guy and Rainbrun and Earl Richard was particularly anxious to keep the name of Beauchamp alive. He remarried after his first wife had borne only daughters, he founded a chantry at Guyscliff 'that God would send him heirs male' and when his prayers were answered he charged his son always to keep Warwick in his title

71

Richard Neville, Earl of Warwick, ('The Kingmaker') and his wife, Anne Beauchamp, drawn from the English version of the Rows Roll.

however much he was promoted – a promise that Henry (who died in 1446) honoured when he was created Duke of Warwick. In his will Earl Richard had ordered building at Guyscliff and the construction of his Beauchamp Chapel at St Mary's Warwick, where he himself was buried. His monument is lined with statuettes of his descendants, some of whom were interred there before it was finished. These lavish projects took fifty years to complete, outlasting the devoted executors who directed them and successive generations of his descendants, who had assisted the executors and fostered the tradition. Earl Richard Beauchamp was commemorated by an illuminated biography written about 1483, *The Pageant of Richard Beauchamp, Earl of Warwick* and by lengthy treatment in *The Rows Roll*. An Oxford graduate and a considerable antiquary, John Rows was remarkably well qualified for a chantry priest; his thirty years at Guyscliff had committed him to the family and he had made himself extremely knowledgeable about it. He knew personally Earl Richard's daughter the Countess Anne, her husband the Kingmaker, their daughters Isobel and Anne and their husbands Clarence and Gloucester. The final entries of his *Roll* celebrated the accession of Anne as queen, Richard as king, and their son Edward as Prince of Wales. Born at Warwick, Anne never forgot her origins nor allowed Richard to do so, apparently signing herself Anne Warwick in

Warwick Castle, with (foreground) the Bear and Clarence towers, part of Richard III's projected 'Great Tower' defence but never completed.

her books. It was she – or possibly Richard – who commissioned the *Pageant* of her father. Richard could hardly fail to have imbibed the Warwick traditions. He was determined to exploit them.

A perusal of *The Rows Roll* tells us what Rows looked for in his lord. He presented the earls in the chivalric image to which they aspired. He depicted each earl in the armour and heraldry peculiar to his day. The text stressed their martial prowess, loyalty and services to the crown: what might be categorized as their national importance. Similarly he had a churchman's natural approval for piety and generosity to the Church. To dwell on the earls' sins was not appropriate. He attached great importance to the earls' roles as local rulers, listed their activities in and around Warwick and judged them by the extent to which they benefited the local community. In a cruder and more provincial way he shared Bishop Russell's concern with the social function of the nobility. His information reflects the intimate knowledge arising from residence there. The great Richard Beauchamp had endowed the chapel at Guyscliff, founded his chapel at St Mary's Warwick, established St Bartholomew's fair, and had intended to build town walls, provide piped water, and make the Avon navigable up to Warwick. His son Henry Duke of Warwick had meant to enlarge commons and to give new maces to the bailiffs. The Kingmaker himself planned more priests and an almshouse at Guyscliff on the model of Cardinal Beaufort's hospital of St Cross by Winchester that he had despoiled and had wanted burial at

Warwick, presumably in the Beauchamp Chapel. George Duke of Clarence continued the tradition, organizing the consecration of the Beauchamp Chapel, and similarly planned to 'have done many great things' as his predecessors had intended: walling the town, creating an outer ward to the castle and enlarging the foundation at Guyscliff. A great builder and almsgiver, he laid out a park before the castle and sought great privileges for Warwick. King Richard, in his turn, was 'special good lord to the town and lordship of Warwick', building in the castle

> in the which his most noble lady and wife was born and at great instance of her he of his bounteous grace without fee or fine granted to the said borough freely by charter great privileges like King William the Conqueror his noble progenitor before him.

Even when king, Richard was happy to be represented with his consort Anne on *The Rows Roll* and *The Salisbury Roll*.

What Warwick and Tewkesbury were to Clarence, so Middleham and Barnard Castle were to Gloucester. That his surviving letters, accounts and charters show him most frequently at Middleham may be pure accident. Barnard Castle, where he planned a large college, may really have been the centre of his power. Alternatively, perhaps, it had to be larger to outshine Staindrop College nearby, the mausoleum of his near neighbours the Nevilles of Raby Castle. Most of the rents of the lordship of Middleham were spent on fees for Warwick's old retainers and his own, all local men naturally dependent on his estate. Richard offered them honourable employment, military opportunities on the West March and good lordship in their quarrels. He kept them in order and arbitrated in disputes of all kinds, always 'according to the king's laws'. He patronized local monasteries such as Coverham and joined the fraternities of Corpus Christi at York and the cathedral priory of St Cuthbert, Durham. His support for the corporation at York and intercession with the king for 'the weal of the city' was much appreciated. His accession brought concrete benefits to the city, to Scarborough, and to Pontefract. He knew Middleham itself well enough to plan for its improvement. Like Clarence at Warwick, he founded two annual fairs, while masonry boars at Barnard Castle identify his work both at the castle and church. At Barnard Castle and at Middleham he intended founding chantry colleges, neither to be completed before his premature death. Unlike those of so many earls of Warwick who lived their allotted span, Richard's projects were much more than wishful thinking. At Middleham at least he had already elevated the church into a college, earmarked the endowment and had embarked on the construction of the conventual buildings. Such colleges were to be his equivalent of Fotheringhay, Bisham, Tewkesbury, and Warwick, the spiritual heart of his connection.

Richard chose to found his colleges. He need not have done so: there was space and good reason for him to lie beside his father and brother at Fotheringhay, with King Edward at Windsor, or with his wife's ancestors at Bisham or elsewhere. Former Nevilles had been interred at Coverham and Jervaulx Abbeys and in

Barnard Castle, County Durham, where Richard, Duke of Gloucester, established a college.

Durham Cathedral. Licences for both colleges survive. Presumably Barnard Castle, much the larger of the two, was to be his mausoleum; the 'Duke of Gloucester's College' at Middleham was a spare. Where one college had sufficed for Beauchamps, the Nevilles, or the house of York. Richard wanted two. At a time when endowments to the Church were limited and most commonly recycled former church land, Richard intended granting new land worth 600 marks (£400) a year. Nor was this pious aspiration: he actually conveyed Oxford estates to Middleham College and had earmarked others for Barnard Castle; other properties were alienated to Coverham Abbey, Queens' College, and St George's Chapel Windsor. Richard's pious aspirations and benefactions were truly princely and dwarfed those of his contemporaries. There were to be twelve priests at Barnard and seven at Middleham; once king, plans for a hundred at York took priority. The royal mausolea at Westminster and Windsor were not for him. Richard, it seems, wanted his own foundations, not to share with others, and wanted them bigger and more splendid than anyone else's. The primary purpose, as in all such colleges, was to celebrate mass for the good of the founder's soul, his parents, and siblings, but by this date few colleges confined themselves to this function. Schools and almshouses were commonly included. They were lacking at Middleham and Barnard Castle. Devoid of educational or charitable attributes, Richard's colleges were thus of an outmoded type. The statutes reveal in meticulous detail how carefully Richard had

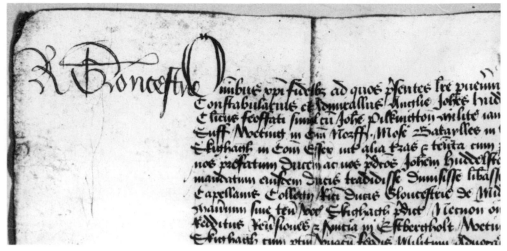

The signature of Richard, Duke of Gloucester, endorsing one of the foundation documents for Middleham College. (North Yorkshire County Record Office)

selected the patron saints, the services and the prayers. The votive mass for Friday in honour of the Name of Jesus was the only modern devotional cult to be mentioned: interestingly, it was the dedication of foundations by two Yorkshire bishops at Rotherham and Cambridge. There is no trace of northern mysticism or the Netherlandish devotions of his mother Cecily or his sister Margaret of Burgundy. Jesus was omitted both from Richard's seven favourite saints and the other thirty to whom he was particularly devoted. Headed by St George, an appropriately nationalist and military choice for a commander and Garter Knight, they are a traditional blend of apostles, martyrs and virgins. Among them were only four distinctively northern saints: St William of York and St Wilfrid of Ripon, St Cuthbert – the patron saint of the North-East – and St Ninian of Whithorn in Scotland, Apostle of the North. Their presence alone gives a northern tinge to services and saints that could otherwise have been located anywhere. That construction had hardly begun by his accession indicates the long-term planning and intended permanence of Richard's northern connection to which these colleges were the symbols and the intended seals.

Gloucester fitted in. What he did in Richmondshire corresponded to Rows' expectations of a lord. In 1483 the historian Mancini reported that Richard self-consciously 'set out to acquire the loyalty of his people through favours and justice. The good reputation of his private life and public activities powerfully attracted the esteem of strangers' and his people alike. He brought renown not just in war but also in peace, becoming king as no previous lord had done. Both *The Rows Roll* and *The Salisbury Roll* depict Richard and Anne together. He conformed to Rows' ostentatious standards of piety. He respected and fostered family traditions and set about creating new ones. He continued the line with his son Edward, who was born at Middleham and who took the Kingmaker's title of Earl of Salisbury in 1478. Richard made the Neville retinue into his own. He founded his power on it and his achievements depended on their support, as they pointed out when he was king. If such conduct was politic, there was more to it than that. Richard's self-identification with his wife's traditions continued after his accession. It was not just that he was depicted as heir to the Beauchamps and Montagus in the rolls of arms, which he may have commissioned, not just that he self-consciously furthered family tradition as advantageous to himself, but that he saw himself that way. Witness his patronage of Warwick and his building operations there *after* he had become king. Witness his nomination as his heir, according to Rows, of Clarence's son Edward Earl of Warwick. The Neville retainers were those northerners whom he used to rule the rebellious south. And some of them, in turn, remembered him beyond his grave and fought on against his conqueror.

A lion under the throne and model of nobility?

Richard Duke of Gloucester was an essential element in the image of royal unity projected in 1478 and 1483. He had justified his status as the greatest of subjects by his service against foreign and domestic enemies and had fulfilled all that could be expected of him. He had created a great inheritance for himself and united the North behind him. By 1483 he was ready for a new challenge. The Scottish war of 1480-3 had been the consummation of his career as Duke of Gloucester both in the North and on the national stage.

A warden of the West March policed the less important part of a distant border. French provocations and Scottish infringements of the truce justified the outbreak of war in 1479, yet it appears that English aggression was the real reason. Edward's financial inability to attack Scotland and to recover Berwick had long been a stain on his reputation. Now he could afford war. He demanded the return of Berwick, Roxburgh and Coldingham, the restoration of the exiled Earl Douglas, and sought simultaneously to ensure the marriage of his daughter Cecily and the Scottish Prince James. The ultimatum was a negotiating ploy: he was ready to settle for Berwick and the marriage alone and apparently expected the Scots to give way. Edward miscalculated. The Scots did not comply. The English were unprepared when their ultimatum expired on 1 May. It was the Scots who were effective, sacking Bamburgh in Northumberland at once. On 12 May 1480 Richard was appointed lieutenant of the North, the king's official deputy, an office held hitherto – only briefly – by Warwick the Kingmaker himself. No successes are recorded. Next year, in 1481, the king planned to campaign himself; in his absence, again, nothing concrete was achieved. Northumberland raided only the 'main of Sefford', while Gloucester reached Jedburgh and Hutton Field by Berwick. In May 1482 Richard was at Dumfries in Galloway. Another campaign by the king was scheduled for later that year, but again Edward did not come. Edward's war treasury, it appears, had been drained to very little purpose, certainly not the achievement of any of the original war aims. At this point, however, the circumstances became more propitious. The Scottish warden of the West March, Alexander Duke of Albany, allied himself with the English. At Fotheringhay on 10 June 1482 he promised to surrender Berwick and the western dales; Edward would make him Alexander IV. Moreover his brother James III was arrested by his own Scottish nobles. Fine though Richard's army was, his triumph was achieved with Scottish help and without resistance. It was also strictly limited. Only Berwick fell. Albeit the only war aim to be achieved, it was better than nothing and the full publicity value was extracted. Richard's reward was the palatinate of Cumberland, which raised him above other northern nobles, sealed as permanent his dominance of Cumbria and the West March, and committed him forever as spearhead of the northerners against the traditional Scottish enemy.

The campaign confirmed Richard as Edward's right-hand man and first in precedence among the nobility. Since Edward had hoped to campaign in the North himself, Richard's forces were worthy of a king in their numbers, the quality and expense of the preparations, and in the rank of the divisional commanders. Richard's own northerners, Northumberland and the rest, were of course prominent and gave Richard weight, but they were supplemented by other levies from further afield. Albany was there. The men of Lancashire and Cheshire were led by Lord Stanley, steward of the royal household, the fleet by the veteran East Anglian John Lord Howard and the Wydeville levies by the queen's eldest son Thomas Marquis of Dorset and her brothers Earl Rivers and Sir Edward Wydeville, all distinguished jousters. John Elrington, the king's household treasurer, was treasurer of war and handled the logistics. Pleased to command such distinguished and experienced company, Richard was surely even more pleased to oblige many by creating them knights and knights banneret, notably Wydeville and Elrington. Several Scots were included. All worked together harmoniously under his command.

Richard's campaign was presented as a national victory by a beleaguered government which otherwise had only bad news to report. Edward while alive, and his funeral laments once dead, made much of the defeat of the Scots and the recovery of Berwick. Richard's supreme distinctions of the Cumberland palatinate and the hereditary wardenship of the West March should be seen as part of this public relations exercise. Unusually the 1483 parliament publicly congratulated Richard, Northumberland, Stanley and other unnamed barons and knights for 'their noble deeds, acts and services done and to be done for the lord king in defence of the realm in the Scottish war'. Richard, moreover,

> late by his manifold and diligent labour & devoir has subdued great part of the west borders of Scotland, adjoining to England, by the space of 30 miles and more, thereby at this time not inhabited by Scots, and hath got and achieved divers parcels thereof to be under the obedience of our said sovereign lord, not only to the great rest & ease of the inhabitants of the said West March, but also to the great surety & ease of the north parts of England.

It was so that he might continue such work that parliament confirmed his acquisition of the palatinate and the wardenship. The publicity exercise was successful and convinced even such later historians. The recovery of Berwick was listed by Sir Thomas More among Edward's achievements.

This campaign made Richard's military reputation. 'Thank God, the giver of all good gifts,' wrote Edward to Pope Sixtus IV in August 1482, 'for the support received from our most loving brother, whose success is so proven that he alone would suffice to chastise the whole kingdom of Scotland'. The 1483 parliament praised him. Bishop Russell intended reminding its successor of the 'martial cunning' of Richard, 'protector of this realm', in whose hands 'rests at this season the execution of the defence of the realm'. The same year the historian Mancini took Richard's prowess for granted: 'Such was his renown in warfare that whenever a difficult and dangerous policy had to be undertaken, it would be entrusted to his discretion and generalship.' Similarly *Titulus Regius* – the formal instrument that declared Richard to be king – referred to his princely courage and to 'the memorable and laudable acts in divers battles, which we know by experience you heretofore have done for the salvation and defence of this same realm'. It was to his own face in 1484 that Archibald Whitelaw, a Scottish ambassador, praised Richard as 'the embodiment of military skill' and of 'all qualities [to] be sought in the best military leader'. Richard's prowess was already a commonplace and was so well established – and indeed reinforced by his heroic death at Bosworth – that later, hostile, historians felt obliged to acknowledge it. 'For all that, let me say the truth to his credit: that he bore himself like a noble soldier and despite his little body and feeble strength, nobly defended himself to his last breath' . Sir Thomas More was another who acknowledged Richard's reputation, although he sought to belittle it by writing in a negative way. Richard was, he stated,

> such as among noblemen is called warlike, in other men otherwise… None evil captain was he in war, to which his disposition was more suited than for peace. Sundry victories had he, and sometimes overthrows, but never in default of his own person, either of courage or generalship.

That was how Richard appeared early in 1483. All our informants say so. That was the image that he had chosen for himself and how the government presented him. But was this image more than a veneer – the result of careful packaging and publicity? Certainly there is much that contemporary writers omit.

There can be no doubt about Richard's courage, his interest in and knowledge of military affairs and his experience of military administration. But what about his prowess and his generalship? It was an unusual chivalric hero that never jousted. 'The proven capacity in the arts of war' referred to in 1480 are hard to substantiate. Certainly he was at the great battles of 1471, when he had been slightly wounded, but his experience otherwise comprised only the clean-up operations of 1470, the inglorious parade to Picquigny in 1475 and the policing of England's north-west frontier. He believed in the military use of artillery, for which he adapted his greatest fortress using the most modern material, brick. He may have been deficient even as warden in 1475, a time of peace with Scotland, when his failure to hold regular days of the march, to redress infringements of truce, and his own implication (though Lord Admiral!) in illegal piracy caused the king to intervene directly, to assure James III of remedies, to rebuke Richard for past failings, and to galvanize him into appropriate action in future. It is unclear whether Richard was merely negligent or refused to implement a peace policy with which he may not have agreed. If Richard was hostile to Scotland, as has been speculated, he was unable to prevent negotiations for closer ties in the years that followed. Mancini was wrong to identify him as Edward's military troubleshooter. In 1477 the projected despatch abroad of the king's brothers did not happen, for on such occasions Edward preferred Lord Hastings, his Wydeville kinsmen, and the Blounts Lords Mountjoy as the most professional soldiers amongst an increasingly civilian nobility. There were many with military records longer and more distinguished than Richard's, even in his army of 1482. What happened in 1480-3 only deserved remembrance once the Scots ceased to resist. Did Edward deliberately surround his brother with a staff of longer experience and proven competence?

Richard's military reputation rests overwhelmingly on a campaign that was deliberately projected as a triumph. But did even the result deserve its hyperbolic treatment? That well-informed civil servant, the Crowland chronicler, thought not:

> What he achieved on this expedition [was] amply demonstrated by the result of this business. Thus, having got as far as Edinburgh with the whole army without meeting any resistance, he let that very wealthy town escape unharmed and returned through Berwick.

Edinburgh fell not because of Richard's prowess, generalship nor even overwhelming numbers, but because the Scots were elsewhere eliminating James III's favourites. Once at Edinburgh, without opposition to defeat or anybody to negotiate with, Richard could conceive of no plan to make the Duke of Albany King Alexander IV, his ostensible objective, or do better than retrace his steps. He had not brought victory, for the Scots would not have Albany, still less had he brought peace. He had not secured Roxburgh and Coldingham, part of the official war aims, or the western dales that Albany had promised in 1482. Edward IV himself, so Crowland says, was 'grieved at the frivolous expenditure of so much money', totalling £100,000, and with the expense of continuing the war. Admittedly Lord Stanley's 'recapture of Berwick alleviated his grief for a time' and produced some positive result to show parliament, but it was a 'trifling gain, or perhaps more accurately, loss, for the maintenance of Berwick costs 10,000 marks a year'.

Since Crowland seems to have disapproved of wars, their cost, and consequent taxation, perhaps here he is not the most trustworthy commentator. However there can be no doubt that any financial reserves that Edward had managed to accumulate were drained by the Scottish war. In his last months he was strapped for cash and obliged to levy forced gifts. In 1482 Edward had contracted to pay Richard's army for only one month. Berwick at once became his most pressing financial commitment. No wonder he wanted to offload the burden of the West March on Richard and that he was prepared to give up to Richard everything that Albany had promised the previous year. What is perhaps surprising is that Richard was willing to take on the defence of the borders and English claims to the debatable lands. Was he suffering from misplaced ambition and an uncritical euphoria about his last campaign? Was he confident if necessary of his capacity to extort support from the king if the opportunities or risks demanded it? No sooner than the grant was law, after all, Edward agreed further financial backing for Albany, admittedly for only six weeks. As for the debatable lands, there seems no evidence to confirm parliament's belief that Richard was actually in occupation. Richard was neither committed to defending them, nor indeed to make war to secure them, merely entitled to keep them if he were to conquer them. Richard, as we have already seen, was a proven collector of claims and a bider of time until the appropriate moment to make them good. A hereditary claim ensured that his dominance would endure and limited royal interference, which, despite everything that he had gained, Richard may have found constraining. However that may be, Richard's military reputation was unearned and was not even believed by those projecting it.

So, too, with Richard's status as Warwick's heir. John Rows, *The Salisbury Roll*, and the Tewkesbury chronicler wrongly present Richard at his own estimation. The Kingmaker's daughters were entitled only to his Salisbury lands. The whole Beauchamp and Despenser inheritance in the West Midlands belonged to Warwick's countess, Anne Beauchamp, and the Neville lands in the North to his young nephew George Neville, Duke of Bedford. Had Warwick been attainted in parliament for his treason and his lands confiscated, King Edward could have distributed all these properties freely except those of the countess herself, but this did not happen. Forfeitures offered only an insecure title that could be reversed and rather than entering as conquerors both dukes wanted to benefit from continuity. Moreover Richard and Clarence were not prepared to limit themselves to what did not belong to the countess and to George and endeavoured to deprive them of their rights. By rescuing and marrying Warwick's daughter Anne Neville, Richard could wrest more of her parents' lands from Clarence. Richard refused to take her without her lands. The eventual division, as Crowland observed, 'left little or nothing at the disposal of the Countess, the true lady and heiress of Warwick to whom, during her lifetime, the noble inheritance of Warwick and Despenser belonged'. She 'had in her days great tribulation for her lord's sake', Rows observes, and many powerful people refused to help her recover her inheritance. When Richard responded, whisking her away to the North, he did so not to restore her inheritance but to deprive her of it permanently. Parliament in 1474-5 divided her lands between the royal dukes as though she was 'naturally dead' and gave George Neville's inheritance to Richard for life and to his heirs for as long as George and his unborn

The carved pulpit at Fotheringhay Church, a gift from Edward IV, showing his arms flanked by the badges of his brothers, the black bull for George, Duke of Clarence, and the white boar for Richard, Duke of Gloucester. The dukes' closeness to the king gave them, at least in the early years, considerable influence.

heirs survived. Though property thereby passed wholesale from Clarence to Richard in 1474-5 and again in 1478, it was not sufficient or on satisfactory terms, so Richard seized more than his due while Clarence lived and grabbed yet more on his death. Since the parliamentary settlement was hardly secure given fifteenth-century mortality and life-expectancy, Richard secured George's wardship and had him degraded from the nobility to prevent him from recovering his lands. Richard also sought custody of George's next heir Richard Lord Latimer for the same purpose. Custody was a first step, though young Latimer's guardian Cardinal Bourchier could not be moved; it could have opened the way to persuasion, inducements, and menaces when the young man came of age. If Richard could have persuaded George or his heir to give up his rights, the title of his own line would have become secure. Of course guardians, even in the fifteenth century, were normally expected to protect not to pillage the interests of their wards.

Richard knew exactly what he was doing. Since what they wanted was legally impossible, he and Clarence had to argue most ingeniously to secure it. 'As a result,' wrote Crowland,

> so much disputation arose between the brothers and so many keen
> arguments were put forward on either side with the greatest acuteness

in the presence of the king, sitting in judgement in the council-chamber, that all who stood around, even those learned in the law, marvelled at the profusion of the arguments which the princes produced for their own cases.

Influence at court enabled the two dukes to dispossess their friendless victims. The countess, as Rows puts it, 'fled to him as her chief refuge and he locked her up for the duration of her life'. The death first of George Neville's father in 1471 and then his mother in 1476 provided further opportunities for the duke. His treatment of those inadvertently in his power offers precedents enough to justify the 'sinister rumour' in 1483 that Richard as Protector of Edward V 'had brought his nephew [Edward V] not under his care, but into his power'. Moreover, Richard had not obtained the dispensation necessary for his wedding to Anne, his cousin and sister-in-law, so he was never properly married to her nor was he really Warwick's heir. Probably Rows did not know that. It may also have been at this stage that Richard procreated the two bastards whom he acknowledged on his accession.

The old and feeble countess of Oxford also suffered from contact with Richard. He was granted the lands of her rebel sons, which did not include her own inheritance, took her into custody to prevent her from helping them and then terrorized her into surrendering her inheritance to which he had no legitimate claim. She wept when Richard wrested her from Stratford Priory, seized her valuables and bore her off to Stepney (Middx.). There, one witness recounts,

> he saw the same lady weep and make great lamentation divers times, but what cause he cannot say, but he saith that [there was] a rumour then amongst the household of the said duke that her weeping was for as much as she was desired and entreated by the said duke to make a conveyance to him of certain of her lands.

Under duress the Countess succumbed. 'I thank God heartily [that] I have these lands, which now shall save my life,' she told one trustee. No physical violence was required. Richard merely menaced that if she declined

> he would send to her to Middleham there to be kept. Wherefore the said lady, considering her great age, the great journey, and the great cold which then was of frost and snow, thought that she could not endure to be conveyed there without great jeopardy to her life .

This was an effective threat for an old lady who was to die naturally within the year, though only after publicly protesting to the Lord Chancellor and privately expressing her regrets. Some of her trustees also had to be coerced: 'False priest and hypocrite!' shouted Lord Howard at her unfortunate confessor. Richard himself claimed that he had bought her estate amicably, argued his case in court and succeeded in persuading the Lord Chancellor to back him up. Even Edward knew his case to be false. Asked by a third party if he should buy part of the countess's estates, the king advised against it. The title was bad, since the countess had been coerced, and 'though the title of the place be good in my brother of Gloucester's hands', a less powerful man might not be able to keep it. Edward knew but turned a blind eye. It was because he 'thought in his mind that it was not to the profit of the said lady to be brought to the said place' that one of Richard's own northern retainers, William Tunstall, chose not to accompany him to Stratford. Later when talking with the tearful countess in London, Tunstall consoled her 'that the said duke was a knight and a king's brother and he trusted that he would do her no wrong'. How wrong he was! Richard failed to live up to the standards of chivalry not only of Tunstall, the king, and Rows, but also of Crowland: 'I pass on readily without further inquiry into this hopeless business [of Warwick's inheritance], leaving these wilful men to exercise their will.'

These are the most unambiguous instances of Richard's high-handedness, but there are similarities in his backing of Sir James Harrington, his treatment of the Hungerfords and his contest for South Wells in Romsey in Hampshire. Such conduct was not unusual at the time, but Richard stands out because he acted thus so frequently, because his cartulary [book of charters] reveals how systematic and wholesale he was in pursuit of such advantages, and because of his contempt for legal titles. Several times he exploited weaknesses normally protected by the law. And having extracted what he wanted, to the loss and fear of his victims, he felt free to sell, grant, or exchange it with his brother, his retainers, or religious houses. Always he took the lead in person.

Richard was a hawk rather than a dove. He opposed peace with France in 1475 and favoured aggression against Scotland. What is called warlike in the great, More reminded us, may in others be regarded as combative, unruly, disorderly and disruptive. Richard may have fanned border and naval disputes, certainly poached retainers and offices, and undoubtedly molested the weak. He did not flinch from using force or from potential conflict. His struggle with Clarence for Warwick's inheritance had national repercussions, promoting disorder, threatening private war, and embroiling king, council and parliament. His disputes with the Stanleys and Percies had similar implications. Not content with his own country, Richard expanded into those of others, prompting further conciliar intervention. There are several well-documented cases of disorder involving his retainers, perhaps with his support. Richard was a fighter, not a temporizer or a peacemaker. Impatience, aggression, and ruthlessness prevailed over caution, diplomacy, and conciliation. Victory against Clarence and the two countesses brought peace only in the sense of a cessation of conflict. Settlements were not permanent but the basis for future gains. Peace came in the North only because Richard's rivals owned him master.

Richard's quarrels did not escalate out of hand because Richard achieved his objectives and because the intervention of crown and council worked to his advantage. Richard was no more willing than Clarence to be his brother's passive instrument. Edward had to push him to do his duty as warden and admiral in 1475 and to restrain his assaults on the Stanleys, Northumberland and Clarence, and observed his treatment of Countess Elizabeth with disapproval. If Richard's domination of the North was indeed 'the outstanding success of Edward IV's policy of establishing regional hegemonies', it was achieved by disregarding the king's attempts at restraint and by extracting more from him than he intended to give. Richard's services were not unconditional but had to be bought and rewarded, sometimes at a high price. Richard was an egotist whose own interests took priority over those of his brother, consort and son. It is not merely hindsight that questions whether such regional supremacy in a subject was desirable or that provokes qualms about its inheritance in future by less able or less trusted successors. However if Richard really intended to create permanently a dominant northern house, as his hereditary estate, wardenship and colleges suggest, he failed in the short-time available to him to assure continued possession of the Neville inheritance.

Repeatedly reality departs from Richard's chosen image. The more we know, the more Richard, as duke, resembles his traditional reputation. He was not a great soldier, general or chivalric hero, not a peacemaker, not even a northerner. The great estate he assembled, the North he united, and the local traditions he fostered, all resulted from a judicious mixture of violence, chicanery and self-publicity. Though many could dispute parts of his image, it was widely accepted at the time. Yet he also was sincerely religious, loyal to his friends, and evidently quite charming. There was a genuine warmth in some of his relationships and several of his followers remembered him affectionately in their wills. He was intelligent and able, a man of large schemes and attention to detail, and a natural leader.

The sheer complexity of his character is brought out by the patronage that he solicited in return for his support – or, at least, acquiescence – in the trial of his brother Clarence in 1478. In most cases his petitions to their brother Edward IV survives. Three demonstrate him strengthening his hold on the Warwick inheritance and on the North: in the first his rival George Neville was degraded from the peerage; in the second, he secured Clarence's rights to the lordships of Richmond and Hemsley; and in the third Clarence's Salisbury earldom was transferred to his son. Richard himself added Clarence's great chamberlainship of England to his other dignities. Two related to Wales, where he wrested the marcher lordship of Ogmore from the duchy of Lancaster and secured a favour for a client Welshmen. A further three licensed him to found his two colleges, to give away lands worth £400 to them, and specifically to give away parts of his duchess's Warwick inheritance. At the same time as he sought to enhance his worldly prestige, to round off his power both in the North and Wales, to fend off a rival, and to reward a client, he was focusing on the good of his soul and giving away much more than he gained, giving away what he had fought ruthlessly to obtain. To do this, he had to amend three acts of parliament and to override Edward's strong prejudice against alienations in mortmain. Obviously he was not satisfied with the original Warwick settlement and still did not obtain all that he wanted, which he had to seize. Moreover Ogmore, Richmond and Helmsley were not freely granted, but were paid for by exchanges. Even for his services in 1478, he wanted more than Edward was willing to give, yet prevailed once again.

The obvious parallels to Richard are his brother Clarence and his father-in-law Warwick the Kingmaker. Though close, parallels with Clarence are unfashionable because unflattering: Clarence failed. Warwick, in contrast, succeeded. Richard's northern hegemony matched Warwick's, which Richard knew at first hand, and was most probably modelled on it. Successful though Richard's Scottish campaigns were, they are less illustrious than Warwick's Herculean labours. Before 1483, however, Richard was neither the national or international figure that Warwick had been. He did not dominate the war against the Lancastrians, government, and diplomacy as Warwick had done. Yet even Warwick needed the opportunity to take centre stage and to control events. For Richard that opportunity came only in 1483.

3 Richard III's usurpation of the throne

The usurpation story

In January 1483 Richard had apparently decided his future lay in the military conquest of southern Scotland. In June he was diverted to the crown of England. The death of Edward IV on 9 April 1483 began a process completed by Richard's own accession on 26 June. Between these two events are less than three crowded months obscured by a dense fog of controversy. Was Richard's accession a criminal usurpation or was he rightfully king? When did he decide to accept the crown? Was his accession premeditated or accidental? What were his motives? Was he the prime mover or was he pushed? For Richard's earliest, hostile, historians, the answer was too obvious to need support, and so to us their case appears unsubstantiated. The gaps cannot easily be filled. As Professor Ross observed:

> By definition, this was a period of a struggle for power, carried out in an atmosphere of rumour, suspicion, propaganda exercises, plot and counter-plot. Only those at the centre could be fully aware of what was going on, certainly not contemporary or later chroniclers, with the possible exception of Crowland, who, however, chose not to reveal all he may have known.

It is not freedom of interpretation but licence that reigns. Conjecture jostles with evidence and almost as many answers have been offered as there are historians. Charting Richard's course to the throne has become a game that everyone can play.

It is difficult to establish precisely what happened. Facts, it has been said, cannot lie, but they can be interpreted differently. Here our facts do not come to us unvarnished, but are loaded, slanted, and embedded in narratives that attach particular significance to them and from which they can be extracted only with difficulty. Almost every so-called fact comes with its accompanying bias. These events have been assessed and reassessed repeatedly in search of answers to the crucial questions. Precise details of chronology, such as when the council made this decision or to what date the coronation was deferred, too often depend on arguments that themselves presume a particular interpretation. There is little common ground. Yet some must be found if meaningful discussion is to take place. Hence the narrative below, which seeks to avoid bias by minimizing detail and by avoiding comment and explanation. Cursory though it is, it provides the essential basis for further discussion.

9 April. Edward IV died during the night at Westminster. Among those present were the queen, her son Thomas Marquis of Dorset, and the king's chamberlain Lord Hastings.

10-11 April. The royal council took control and arranged the coronation of Edward V, probably settling at once on 4 May as the date. Two lords were sent to the corporation of London to instruct them to keep order and the corpse was displayed in the chapel royal.

14 April. The news reached the Prince of Wales, now Edward V, at Ludlow.

16 April. Edward V wrote to King's Lynn corporation informing them of his impending coronation at Westminster.

16-18 April. The funeral cortège travelled from Westminster to Windsor, where Edward IV was interred on 20 April. Both archbishops, eight bishops and nineteen lay peers were in attendance.

23 April. By this date Richard Duke of Gloucester had started to journey south from York.

24 April. Earl Rivers and hence Edward V were still at Ludlow.

26 April. Gloucester was expected at Nottingham.

29 April. Gloucester was at Northampton.

30 April. Gloucester and Henry Duke of Buckingham met Edward V's maternal uncle and guardian Earl Rivers at Stony Stratford in Northamptonshire and spent a convivial evening together.

1 May. The first *coup d'état*. Gloucester and Buckingham arrested Rivers, the king's half-brother Richard Grey and his chamberlain, Thomas Vaughan, who were sent to Yorkshire, disbanded the young king's household, and took custody of Edward V himself. They protested their loyalty and explained their actions as a pre-emptive strike against traitors plotting their own destruction. Probably it was on this same evening that his mother the queen took sanctuary at Westminster Abbey with Dorset and her youngest son Richard Duke of York.

2 May. Edward V wrote from Northampton to Cardinal Bourchier in London.

4 May. The day originally designated for the coronation, which was deferred. Edward V was escorted to London by the dukes and housed in the

bishop's palace. He moved to the Tower between 9 and 19 May.

By 8 May. The council appointed Gloucester as Lord Protector.

10 May. Bishop Russell replaced Archbishop Rotherham as chancellor. Then or soon after the decisions were taken that resulted in action against Sir Edward Wydeville (14 May), the summons of parliament for 25 June (13 May) and the convocation of clergy (16 May), and the setting of 24 June (later 22 June) as the date for the coronation (18 May). Parliament, originally summoned for 22 June, was later rescheduled for 24 June.

23 May. Gloucester, Buckingham, and the archbishops made an unavailing attempt to persuade the queen to leave sanctuary.

10-11 June. Gloucester wrote to York, Hull, and Lord Neville for military support. York corporation was informed of a plot organized by the queen. The troops were to muster at Pontefract on 18 June. The letters arrived on 15-16 June.

13 June. The second *coup d'état*. Lord Hastings, Archbishop Rotherham, Bishop Morton and perhaps Lord Stanley were unexpectedly arrested at a council meeting at the Tower by Gloucester, who had Hastings executed at once without trial. He charged him with treasonable conspiracy with the queen. The others were imprisoned.

16 June. Cardinal Bourchier removed the Duke of York from Westminster sanctuary to the Tower. On 16-17 June both parliament and the coronation were put off until November.

19 June. A new proclamation against plotters was received from Gloucester at York, which the levies had not yet left.

22 June. Ralph Shaa preached the bastardy of the princes at St Paul's Cross, London. At Pontefract Earl Rivers made his will in expectation of execution.

24 June. At the London Guildhall Buckingham urged Gloucester's title to the crown. At Pontefract, Rivers, Grey and Vaughan were executed.

25 June. Edward V's reign ended.

26 June. A meeting of estates elected Richard as king, which he accepted. The reign of Richard III commenced.

6 July.   The coronation of Richard III at Westminster.

Because Richard usurped the throne, it is easy to believe that this was always his intention. Hindsight revealed all, not only to modern and Tudor writers, but also to contemporaries, to whom a confused or inexplicable chain of events suddenly made sense. Half-remembered occurrences were reshuffled to fit the new explanation. There is therefore no easy distinction between later writers and contemporaries. We know that people disagreed at the time. Even the most reliable eyewitnesses, such as Crowland, like most contemporaries, seem to have changed their minds as they lived through events. There is no single contemporary interpretation, rather a succession of rival interpretations. This chapter therefore starts with the well-established traditional interpretation, the ***case for the prosecution***, which is hostile to Richard, and then investigates whether a ***case for the defence*** was made for Richard at the time. From such data it seeks to establish the series of verdicts – ***contemporary verdicts*** – that people reached in turn at the time as events unfolded. However, we cannot allow them the final word. It is obvious sometimes that they were mistaken or deliberately mislead – spin-doctoring is not a twenty-first century novelty! Today we have an oversight of the whole picture, what was happening in Ludlow *and* York *and* Westminster *and* Pontefract, which none of our informants possessed, and we have access to records that contemporaries were denied. The contemporary consensus is therefore interrogated and tested against record evidence. From that emerges a more authoritative interpretation – the ***verdict of history***. Whether the ***verdict of history*** eventually confirms or corrects ***contemporary verdicts*** is not really material here. To be genuinely historical, it cannot fall outside the range of possibilities passed down to us by contemporaries, but it is more soundly based. The evolution of contemporary perceptions is identified, particular elements in the story are traced to their origins, and what people thought can sometimes now be verified or disproved. Contemporaries, right or wrong, could not do this and subsequent historians have not.

The case for the prosecution

Richard's usurpation has traditionally been regarded as a crime. Normally Richard is seen as directing the whole course of events. He was wrong to take the throne and did so not from principle but self-interest. He was ruthless in eliminating all obstacles in his path. Everything was planned in advance, even before Edward IV's death and perhaps as long ago as 1471, and he carried his schemes through with the most subtle dissimulation. Everything that happened was planned. Intervening events mark stages in the implementation of Richard's plan.

Essentially this was the viewpoint shared by all Richard's historians from 1483 onwards. The threads were drawn together into a coherent narrative and substantiated some thirty years after these events. ***The case for the prosecution*** was thus the achievement of the historians Polydore Vergil and Sir Thomas More. It was then

THE
HISTORIE
OF THE PITIFVLL
Life, and unfortunate Death
of *Edward* the fifth , and
the then Duke of *Yorke*
his brother :

With the troublesome and
tyrannical government of Usvr-
ping *Richard* the third,and
his miserable end

Written by the Right Honor-
able Sir *Thomas Moore*
sometimes Lord Chanc-
cellor of England.

LONDON,

Printed by *Thomas Payne* for
the Company of *Stationers*, and
are to be sold by *Mich: Young*,
at his shop in *Bedford-street* in
Covent-Garden, neere the
new Exchange.1640.

Left: Statue of Sir Thomas More by L. Cubitt Bevis, 1969, outside Chelsea Old Church, London. Right: The frontispiece of the 1640 edition of More's history, which clearly signals its attitude towards Richard III.

unforgettably dramatized, publicized and stamped on the consciousness of the English public by William Shakespeare.

All three thought that Richard had contingency plans in case Edward died and was ready to exploit the opportunity when it occurred. They considered that his first priority was to secure control of the young king and the government. There were problems here, for the queen's family (the Wydevilles) wanted a speedy coronation. On the precedent of 1429, a coronation was tantamount to a declaration that a young king was of age and could rule himself, without a regent or protector. In practice, aged 12, Edward V could not have coped, and would naturally have depended on those maternal relatives whom he knew and trusted. So the Wydevilles supposed. Fortunately for Richard, the dominance of the Wydevilles threatened Edward IV's erstwhile chamberlain Lord Hastings, who saw alliance with Gloucester as the only hope and kept him informed of proceedings. It was fortunate also that Gloucester secured the committed support of Henry Stafford, Duke of Buckingham, his only equal in wealth and power among the nobility. On 1 May the two dukes intercepted

Edward, Prince of Wales, later Edward V, from the Royal Window, Canterbury Cathedral.

the young Edward V at Stony Stratford and removed from effective politics his Wydeville escorts, namely, his uncle and governor Earl Rivers and his half-brother Lord Richard Grey, and his household.

With the king in his custody, Richard was able to take control of the government, becoming Lord Protector, and his remaining Wydeville opponents took refuge in sanctuary or flight. This was his first *coup d'état*. The next month could be spent in consolidating his hold on government and in defeating the naval threat posed by Sir Edward Wydeville.

That achieved, so the prosecution argue, Richard could remove those identified as irreconcilable opponents to his accession. These were Lord Hastings, chamberlain of Edward IV's household, the late king's chancellor Archbishop Rotherham of York, and John Morton, Bishop of Ely. The date was Friday 13 June. More tells us how all three attended a meeting of council at the Tower of London to plan the coronation. Richard attended briefly, apparently in good humour, illustrated by his famous and perhaps apocryphal request for strawberries from Morton's palace-garden in Holborn. Returning later in a rage, he charged Hastings with plotting treasonably with the queen, had him executed forthwith without trial, and had the others imprisoned. The whole proceedings were carefully stage-managed to conceal the element of planning. This was Richard's second *coup d'état*.

Even with possession of the king and his principal opponents neutralized, so the prosecution argue, Richard still could not safely take the throne while the younger prince was at liberty. He was too obvious a focus for opposition. The next step therefore was to secure possession of the younger prince. This was achieved on Monday 16 June, when Cardinal Bourchier fetched Prince Richard from sanctuary which, it was alleged, protected offenders and not the innocent. With both princes in his hands and a northern army available to overawe potential opponents, Richard's usurpation could be completed. The claim was concocted, falsely, that Edward IV and his queen had never been properly married, for the king was already indissolubly contracted to Lady Eleanor Butler, and thus both princes were bastards. This justification was published in a sermon at St Paul's Cross on Sunday 22 June. Buckingham secured grudging approval from the citizens of London on 24 June for Richard's accession in their stead. An attenuated meeting of lords and MPs offered Richard the crown, which he accepted with outward signs of reluctance. This reluctance and the apparent initiative of others was feigned, for Richard was the prime mover in his own accession to the crown.

This interpretation held sway for four centuries. If More and Vergil were not actually eyewitnesses (More being too young and Vergil abroad at the crucial time), both moved in the same circle as surviving participants and had interviewed at least some of them. They did in fact possess first-hand information, as shown by the precision and accuracy of much of their data, which cannot really be dispensed with even when listing the course of events.

Yet nowadays their unsupported testimony is no longer accepted. Vergil, More and Shakespeare, so Richard's supporters (the Ricardians) argue, were writing literature and shaped their data to that end. The lengthy speeches beloved of Renaissance historians have gone out of fashion and serve only to blur the line between fact and fiction. Their informants were unduly influenced by knowing the end of the story, which they understandably wished to explain, and their testimony was slanted to conform to Richard's unpleasant reputation. Inevitably anything in Richard's favour was winnowed out, events were rearranged in a more comprehensible sequence, and Richard's character was deduced from his crimes rather than described from personal acquaintance. Worst of all, they wrote far into the Tudor period, were devoted to the Tudor dynasty and accepted the hostility to Richard current in their own day. They were mouthpieces of Tudor propaganda. So runs the charge. It exaggerates somewhat, for much that the Tudor authors wrote is unexceptional and can be confirmed elsewhere, but a great deal of it is valid. The analysis that follows dispenses with their services.

Such Ricardian arguments fail against Crowland, as Professor Ross showed. No Tudor propagandist, he was an independent eyewitness as events unfolded. As we have seen, he owed his presence on the royal council to technical expertise, owed allegiance to no faction, and was critical of them all. Reporting on that first council meeting at Westminster immediately after Edward IV's death, he recorded that all including himself wanted the young Edward V to succeed. In the disagreements that arose, he aligned himself with 'the more far-sighted members of the Council' who 'thought that the uncles and brothers on the mother's side should be absolutely forbidden to have control of the young man until he came of age'. Fearing that Edward's Wydeville escort would overawe proceedings, with adverse implications for those in disagreement, Crowland and others of this opinion favoured Hastings' demands that the royal entourage be restricted to a more reasonable size. The Wydevilles, by implication, would then be insufficiently powerful to override other opinions. Crowland accepted Edward's majority, but hoped for a regime more broadly based than the Wydevilles. Once the queen agreed to limit her son's escort, he was satisfied. 'Everyone', he reported, 'looked forward to the eagerly desired coronation day of the new king'. Richard's coup was a surprise, but Crowland was persuaded that it was all for the best. When an oath of fealty to Edward V was tendered by Richard to all the lords, the mayor and aldermen of London, 'it was performed with pride and joy by all', said Crowland, 'because this promised best for future prosperity'. After Richard's appointment as Lord Protector, 'he exercised this authority with the consent and goodwill of all the lords'. Although Crowland does not explicitly state whether he shared in this decision or himself took the oath, he clearly included himself in 'everyone [who] hoped for and awaited peace and prosperity in the kingdom'. Most probably he did not go as far as Lord Hastings in exulting at the discomfiture of the Wydevilles, since he wanted more respect for the queen and may perhaps be numbered among those who thwarted the execution of the Wydevilles for treason. He did not foresee Hastings' fall, when 'grief completely took the place of joy', ascribes Cardinal Bourchier's removal of Prince Richard from sanctuary to compulsion, and records that 'from that day forth both these dukes showed their intentions, not in private but openly'. Henceforth no source is more antagonistic to Richard, not even More or Vergil, and none more alienated by the northern character of his regime. Crowland traces the evolution of public opinion, his own perceptions and how he was deceived. He does offer us a succession of verdicts rooted in the actual passage of events. That he alone puts Hastings' death and Prince Richard's capture in the correct order is a testimony to his reliability. Yet even Crowland was writing after 1485, under Henry VII, whose comparison to an angel he reports, and after the battle of Bosworth which brought the peace he yearned for. Crowland was also capable of rationalizing events with hindsight and he too has been identified as a Tudor propagandist, whose testimony should be rejected. If this seems unjust to such a measured and nuanced account, it still means that he cannot be allowed the decisive voice.

Hence the importance of the discovery this century of a history composed by a strict contemporary before the end of the story was known. He was Dominic

Mancini, an Italian visitor. His version agrees particularly closely with the account of Sir Thomas More and this fact has been used to argue that the charge of Tudor propaganda levelled against More is unfounded and that Tudor tradition was right to condemn Richard for his usurpation.

The discovery of Mancini's history could have revolutionized Ricardian studies. It has not because it agrees so well with those later accounts that were already known. Like Sir Thomas More, Mancini thought Richard had been aiming for the throne from the start and saw his motives as entirely selfish. Richard's explanations for arresting Edward V, for executing Hastings, and the precontract story were all untrue; each coup was a stage in Richard's premeditated usurpation of the throne. Instead of becoming the basis of a new interpretation, Mancini has been used to supplement and substantiate the traditional story. Only very gradually has Ricardian criticism of traditional sources brought out his true significance. As Dr Hanham pointed out in 1975, Mancini's history

> demolished the view that Richard's accession was welcomed by contemporaries as right and just and that he was a most popular king until his reputation was destroyed by the cunning propaganda of the Tudors and their paid historians.

Similarly for Professor Ross in 1981:

> The importance of Mancini's narrative lies in the fact that he provides direct contemporary evidence that Richard's ruthless progress to his throne aroused widespread mistrust and dislike, to the extent that at least some of his subjects were willing to believe, within a fortnight of his accession, that Richard had disposed of his nephews by violence.

That every chronicle believes Richard to be guilty makes for a formidable prosecution case. That a strictly contemporary source – and one of such quality – says the same appears decisive. The case for the prosecution rests.

The star witness

The strength of the prosecution case now depends largely on its star witness – Mancini – and his history. Both seem exemplary. Mancini the man was respectable, painfully fair and objective. His history is a complete, rounded and accurate narrative. Born into a well-known Roman family, he was a clergyman of high-minded principles, probably an Austin friar, and a Renaissance humanist. He was steeped in the language and literature of the ancient world, certainly Roman and quite possibly Greek. He wrote original works in Latin in the purest of classical styles, was famous for his Latin verses and appropriated to himself the title of poet laureate. When writing his history, he modelled it on – or at least echoed – such classical predecessors as Sallust and Suetonius and his own contemporary Politian. We do not know precisely when or why he visited England, except that it was before Edward IV's death and thus for reasons unrelated to the usurpation. Most probably it was at the behest of his fellow-countryman Angelo Cato, a noted astrologer, physician to the French king and archbishop of Vienne; certainly it was Cato who recalled him in July 1483, Cato to whom Mancini recounted his experiences and Cato who later made him set those experiences down on paper, which Mancini was apparently reluctant to do. Their relationship was that of literary patron and client.

The history is not a Renaissance masterpiece, but it has much to commend it. The classical influence can be seen in his determined effort to write a complete and rounded history rather than to recount a single thread, in the explanations Mancini provided whenever he could and in his conscious archaisms. On the other hand, he ignored other conventions of Renaissance history such as the invented speeches so characteristic of Sir Thomas More, and limited himself to recording events in sober prose. Nevertheless, his history is far more than a list of events and is the fullest and most accurate narrative that we possess. The factual content, particularly his descriptions of London and the English soldiery, are reminiscent of diplomatic newsletters and reveal him to be an intelligent and accurate observer. Apparently he strove to be objective, wrote of what he knew, and rigorously excluded subsequent insights and conclusions more appropriate for discussion orally than on paper. He frankly admitted his ignorance and doubts. To John Armstrong, his brilliant and learned biographer, he was entirely successful. Apart from Mancini's hostility to Richard III, Armstrong could uncover no other bias either when first editing the text in 1936 or when returning to it in 1969. Nor, despite assertions to the contrary, have historians writing since.

It is because Mancini took account of all the alternatives – and, indeed, faithfully records Richard's own self-justifications – that his condemnation of Richard is taken all the more seriously and his history is accepted at its face value. Yet Mancini could hardly have been more forthright in his conclusion. He entitles his history in Latin *Concerning the Occupation of the Kingdom of England by Richard III*, which, it has been suggested, is neutral and undamnatory. Such a pro-Ricardian point, however, is invalidated in his first sentence when Mancini declares it his intention 'to put in writing by what machinations Richard the Third, who is now reigning in England, achieved the high dignity of kingship', and by such comments as 'Therefore the protector rushed headlong into crime' that intersperse his text. If not a literal translation of his Latin title, *The Usurpation of Richard III* faithfully reflects Mancini's purpose and achievement. He believes Richard's usurpation was premeditated from the start. It is Richard's single-minded and self-interested pursuit of power that binds the whole story together.

Given the crucial importance of Mancini to the prosecution, it is hardly surprising that Ricardians have sought to discredit his evidence. He is invulnerable to the charge of Tudor propaganda and southern bias levelled against More, Vergil and Crowland, but other chinks in his armour have been exploited. To Richard

The remains of Fotheringhay Castle, birthplace of Richard III.

Richard's father, Richard, Duke of York, (left) and brother Edward IV. Stained glass by Thomas Willement, St Lawrence's Church, Ludlow.

Elizabeth Wydeville, wife of Edward IV and mother of Edward V. Figure in stained glass from the Royal Window, Canterbury Cathedral.

The remains of the Great Hall at Sudeley Castle, Gloucestershire, which was granted to Richard by Edward IV in 1469 and exchanged by him for Richmond Castle, Yorkshire, in 1478.

The ruins of Sheriff Hutton Castle, Yorkshire, seat of Richard's 'Council of the North'.

More of Richard III's widespread possessions: (above) Kenilworth Castle, Warwickshire, and (below) Helmsley Castle, Yorkshire.

Richard III's boar on the carved pulpit given by Edward IV to Fotheringhay church.

The arms of King Richard III above the door of the 'Gloucester Arms', Penrith, Cumbia.

A Yorkist collar with a Richard III boar pendant adorns the effigy of Ralph Fitzherbert, Norbury church, Derbyshire.

Richard III's arms with boar supporters and motto, from the Wax Chandlers' charter of 1483.

Above: Richard III (right) and his son, Edward, Prince of Wales. Below: Richard's wife, Anne Neville. Details from the Richard III Society Memorial Window, 1934, Middleham church.

Richard III and Queen Anne in a stained glass by William Burges, Cardiff Castle.

Richard III's friends and foes. Above, left to right: Lords Stanley and Hastings, Viscount Lovell, the Earl

of Northumberland; below: the Dukes of Clarence and Suffolk, Earl Rivers, the Duke of Buckingham.

Memorial tomb attributed to Henry Stafford, Duke of Buckingham, Britford church, Wiltshire.

Richard III's standard flying over Ambion Hill, Bosworth Field.

Richard III's charge at Bosworth, painting by Ernest Kruger, 1908. Also included are the figures of Lovell, Ratcliffe, Norfolk, Scrope and Berkeley.

Richard III falls at Bosworth. Detail from the Shakespeare Window, Southwark Cathedral, London, by Christopher Webb, 1954..

The Tudor version of the royal line: Henry VII (left) , Edward V (uncrowned) and Edward IV. From the painted screen of the Bishop Oliver King Chantry, St George's Chapel, Windsor.

Memorial stone in 'King Richard's Field' near the traditional site of his death, the 'Sandeford',
Bosworth Field.

III's modern supporters, Mancini was a prejudiced partisan, an ignorant Italian – 'our foreign correspondent', as he has been unkindly dubbed – and a purveyor of literature rather than history. In reply to the last point, it is sufficient to point out, as some modern historians have done, that Mancini missed many opportunities for literary and dramatic embellishment, that he did not prepare his work for publication and indeed seems to have been only too conscious of its defects, that he possessed the knowledge and experience to produce something much more literary had this been his aim, and to note that it is the factual core – and above all Richard's activities – that give the history its unity and make it resemble the self-conscious literary life by Sir Thomas More. Mancini can hardly have wished to write a moral discourse on over-ambition and tyranny that left the tyrant in unpunished possession of his spoils! The other criticisms are more serious and do demand an answer.

How could a foreigner and an outsider like Mancini obtain so much accurate information? Particularly if, as seems likely, he did not understand English. He may have picked up a little data from personal observation in London. He may have met Edward IV and other principal characters in his history, but he cannot have been present in the royal council or at the Stony Stratford coup, of which he includes full and apparently accurate accounts, and clearly he had no access to the inner circle of Richard's advisers. Again, his lack of English must have meant that he could not converse with the public at large or comprehend the numerous public proclamations and open letters that are now so irretrievably lost and which he nevertheless summarizes. Most of his information must have been gleaned at second hand. Who told him? Generally we do not know: 'men say', Mancini frequently writes; 'they say', 'it is said', 'it was said', 'it was commonly believed', and 'I have learned', he continues. Such comments offer little clue and tempt us to reject the whole account as unsubstantiated, but the sheer quality and precision of his knowledge prevents us. Where then can he have gleaned it?

To this several historians, notably Armstrong and Pollard, have attempted to give answers. One name only was cited by Mancini himself. This was Master John Argentine, a distinguished academic later to be provost of King's College, Cambridge, whose brass in the college chapel depicts him in full doctor's array. Argentine was of unimpeachable respectability. Significantly he was a clergyman like Mancini, a physician like Cato, a man learned in Italian and thus able to speak Mancini's own tongue, and hence, almost certainly, a fellow humanist. A whole series of shared interests could thus have drawn him and Mancini together. As Edward V's doctor, so Mancini tells us, Argentine was the last of the young king's household still attendant on him. He passed on his final impressions to Mancini. No doubt he also supplied the information for Mancini's famous portrait stressing the intellectual attainments of the young Edward V:

> In word and deed he gave so many proofs of a liberal education, of polite, nay rather scholarly, attainments far beyond his age … [and] his special knowledge of literature, which enabled him to discourse

elegantly, to understand fully, and to declaim most excellently from any work whether in verse or prose that came into his hands, unless it were from among the more abstruse authors.

Nothing could have appealed more to both Argentine and Mancini and better commended Earl Rivers – the prince's governor – to them. Although Argentine's name occurs only at the end of Mancini's story, he could have also informed him of much else that occurred or is described earlier, such as the young Edward V's spirited defence of his maternal kinsfolk at Stony Stratford and Mancini's eulogy of Rivers. He *could* have done so. Mancini cites him specifically and *only* as source for Edward V's imprisonment. Professor Pollard is indeed 'too fanciful to suggest that the shape of the story derives from Argentine'! The Italian community in London has been suggested as the probable source of a naval story. So has another Italian visitor to London, Pietro Carmeliano, as his introduction to the royal household, provided, of course, that he and Mancini had met, which has not been proved, and provided he had direct access to the information suggested.

Such specific identifications by modern historians of informants who are not named arise from a serious misapprehension that needs to be corrected. To take the speculative role proposed for Carmeliano, it arises because he too was a humanist and an Italian, and Mancini, as we have seen, may not have understood English. It is assumed that this linguistic defect confined Mancini's conversations to the tiny handful of Englishmen fluent in Italian. If true, this would be a most serious limitation and one that seriously discredited his work. But it is a mistaken presumption and completely unsubstantiated. Mancini's everyday medium of conversation, in England as in France, cannot have been Italian but Latin, the international European language in which he was particularly well versed. Latin was the tongue of the clergy, of learning and of diplomacy. Mancini was a clergyman, member of a religious order, the client and perhaps the envoy of an archbishop. He must have had access to the highest ecclesiastical circles, recruited from successful academics and employed as civil servants, diplomats and even ministers. He could have conversed with that minor diplomat and chancery official, the Crowland chronicler, and could have met Cardinal Bourchier, Archbishop Rotherham, Bishop Russell or Bishop Morton, all characters in his story and for whom he expresses respect. Moreover they may have wished to meet such a celebrity. Mancini the distinguished humanist had much to offer the small coterie of English Renaissance scholars, who numbered not just Argentine, but Earl Rivers and Lord Chancellor Russell. Direct personal acquaintance may explain why he depicted them so favourably. Moreover Mancini almost certainly could converse in French and there are hints in his account, as Pollard says, that actually he could understand English too. However, the precise source of his information matters less than the fact that Mancini could seek it not only from the tiny minority of Italian speakers but from all those literate in Latin or French, including all the clergy and all the aristocracy. Literally thousands of people could have told him what was happening. And probably the newsletters that he cites, like those during earlier and later upheavals, were flyposted and broadcast everywhere for Mancini to collect, read, or have translated to him.

Much of this, indeed, is suggested by a close reading of the history itself. Armstrong long ago remarked on the noticeably more favourable interpretation Mancini placed on the characters and motives of the bishops in comparison to a lay nobility activated by cynical self-interest. His account is too balanced and judicious, insufficiently black and white, to be the product of a single faction. Undoubtedly he had access to Wydeville sources, yet his treatment of the queen's family is often critical and sometimes hostile. It cannot be solely attributable to the last supporters of Edward V! If Hastings receives a good character reference, Mancini also notes his faults, and amongst his denunciations of Richard there appear observations favourable to him and perhaps emanating from him that can have come from no Wydeville source. Mancini's informers were in the plural, probably primarily clergymen resident in London, and were not restricted to a single faction. Buried in his work are facts, attitudes, and opinions that can have come from no single quarter. He may have been hostile to Richard, but his history records what Richard wrote, said, and explained. He disapproves of Edward V's deposition but does not advocate a Wydeville government. Dominic Mancini was not the tool of the Wydevilles or Hastings or anybody else.

It was because Richard seized the throne and because Archbishop Cato was intrigued by the story that Mancini wrote his *Usurpation*. That Mancini recounted the story several times contributed to the refinement and definition of his shapeless memories into what became a finished composition. When writing Mancini knew that Richard had become king, presumed that usurpation was always his intention, and thus imposed this retrospective interpretation on his evidence. At the time of Edward's death, for instance, he cannot have supposed that Richard was aiming for the crown, yet he later came to believe it. He rationalized the order of events. His portrait of Richard as a consummate planner and dissembler could have arisen in this way: unless it was true. Although writing so closely to events, Mancini was as exposed to hindsight and as guilty of it as any of the Tudor historians. There remain several crucial differences. He actually lived through the events he described. He was the prisoner of his sources and recorded what they actually said. He wrote much closer to events and was unable to add to his information after the episodes described. And within this hostile framework are buried Richard's own justifications and explanations of events.

Mancini's history ends before Richard III's coronation on 6 July. He had fulfilled the task that he had set himself. He may well have left England before the coronation. His account was not set down until somewhat later, on 1 December 1483. Quite a lot happened between those dates, but it is not mentioned in his history. Richard was crowned, plots were laid against him, the princes were believed to be dead and another claimant was raised up, Buckingham rebelled and was executed. None of these developments are recounted. They were no part of Mancini's story. But they are not mentioned, alluded to, nor even implied. Could Mancini, a clergyman supposedly telling a moral tale, have failed to mention how the dukes fell out, that Richard suffered treachery or that Buckingham, his evil genius, betrayed him, or indeed that

Richard III with the crown in his grasp, a statue by James Butler, RA, in Castle Gardens , Leicester.

Buckingham had his come-uppance if he knew of it? That he does not even refer to such matters indicates that, at Beaugency, he was out of touch with subsequent developments. He could not add to his information and explicitly denies that he did. He could not verify names, places or dates, which had to stand. He could not correct bias, misinformation or errors, or otherwise improve his story. He was limited to his memories from his time in England.

Neither Mancini (nor any other impartial observer) can have known that Richard would usurp throughout the whole period of 9 April – 26 June, certainly not before 1 May. Even Mancini's personal conviction about Richard's intentions may have developed only after Richard's accession. Precisely when Mancini became sure is not material here. What matters is that he cannot always have been aware that he was living through a revolution, that he was not yet actively researching his version of events, nor yet imposing his anti-Ricardian interpretation on them. Nor had he even been asked to write a history at all. His informants could not have served him his facts in pre-packed anti-Ricardian form, for they, too, cannot have known the outcome of the story. His facts did not come to him loaded but in their raw state, as events happened and as his informants explained them.

Mancini tried to write a balanced account of Richard's revolution. He recorded letters, speeches, and proclamations emanating from all sides, Hastings, the Wydevilles, Richard and Buckingham alike. He set the scene as it was before the usurpation story commenced. He told of Elizabeth's wooing by King Edward, including the dagger story, of Edward IV's store of treasure and its appropriation by the Wydevilles, of Richard's sorrow at Clarence's death and the revenge that he vowed on the perpetrators. Though strongly disapproving of Richard, he nevertheless praised his high moral reputation and military achievements and identified him as Edward's military troubleshooter. Some of this material is untrue and the rest may be mere hearsay and gossip, as Pollard has claimed. However all these are contemporary stories that can be demonstrated to have been current in 1483. Here Mancini is faithfully recording what was circulating during his stay. Why should we not credit other stories for which we lack such substantiation? Moreover they may not be mere hearsay: they may be what Elizabeth and the Wydevilles, Edward IV, and Richard wanted to be believed and had deliberately disseminated to shape the public opinion of which Mancini was a part. In some cases this seems clear enough. Suspended in Mancini's narratives, therefore, is material current at the time, emanating from all factions, available for modern historians to use.

Given that he was writing a narrative that he had not self-consciously researched, it is not surprising that he is vague on names (to him, of course, they were all foreign names), on chronology, and on English geography. His disclaimers are wholly comprehensible:

> I had not sufficiently ascertained the names of those to be described, the intervals of time, and the secret designs of men in the whole affair... Wherefore you should not expect from me the names of individual men and places, nor that this account should be complete in all details; rather shall it resemble the figure of a man, which lacks some of the limbs, and yet a beholder delineates for himself a man's form.

It was not the details that Mancini expected us to rely on, for he could not have known how limited are the surviving narratives of England in this era! It was his interpretation, his account of the course of events, that he certified as reliable. Pollard has argued that this too is undermined by the faults that Mancini admits and by other defects, such as the location of Richard's estates, of which he was unaware. He is mistaken. Mancini's account of events is precise and much of it can be demonstrated to be accurate. It is fuller and superior to any other narrative, even that of Crowland. Moreover it is the evidence that he recycles that we should be treasuring. Mancini evidently possessed a remarkably capacious memory. He remembered things as they happened. His data is specific to particular times and places and possesses an immediacy that he would doubtless have removed had he had access to more orthodox sources, if he could have checked it or criticized his sources, or indeed if he had planned his history in advance. One cannot easily discriminate between one's memories. Mancini's are not necessarily consistent with his overriding interpretation or indeed compatible with it. They remain raw and undigested, not unlike the fleeting impressions recorded in letters written at the time. Below the smooth and sophisticated surface there lie archaeological deposits crying out for excavation and forensic analysis if we are to approach closer to the truth.

The case for the defence

For four hundred years Mancini and his successors condemned Richard for his usurpation. Nowadays it is commonplace to deny that he was to blame. Wishful thinking plays a part, the desire to defend the indefensible and to protect the underdog. So does the application of modern standards of proof which no distant history can satisfy. But there is more to Richard's vindication than mere present-mindedness. Several different approaches are possible. Two have already been considered. Partially successful attempts to discredit the prosecution witnesses have already been noted. Historians have now generally discounted the charges that Richard committed earlier crimes and have shown the whole idea of a plot beginning before Edward IV's death to be incredible. While undoubtedly useful in rebutting the charges made against Richard, such negative tactics go little way towards justifying what Richard actually did. This is not because we do not know Richard's own point of view, for we do. While Richard's historians have generally been hostile, it is not sufficiently appreciated how much we know about the events of 1483 through Richard's own utterances and publications. The document known as *Titulus Regius* sets out Richard's reasons for taking the crown. Although hostile and sceptical, the chroniclers have recorded Richard's arguments at frequent intervals and in some cases these can be confirmed by reference to original letters by Richard and others still extant today. Finally we may compare this material with what actually happened. Defenders of Richard III are not restricted to discrediting the witnesses of the prosecution. They can also advance the case for the defence that Richard presented himself and this indeed is much their most effective course of action.

Richard's title to the crown is set out most fully in the document called *Titulus Regius*, which was incorporated in a statute enacted at Richard's parliament early in 1484. This statute describes it as a parchment roll or petition presented by the estates of the realm outside parliament before his accession and asking him to take the crown. That dates it to 25-26 June 1483, when such a meeting certainly took place.

It has recently been suggested that the text we possess is not authentic but was actually drafted for the 1484 parliament. This, however, is scarcely credible.

Opposite: The offer of the Crown to Richard, Duke of Gloucester, 26 June 1483. Mural by Sigismund Goetze in the Royal Exchange, London.

OFFER OF
THE KINGSHIP
TO RICHARD
DVKE OF GLOVCESTER
AT BAYNARDS CASTLE
JVNE 26TH
1483

Although the original copy is lost, we know that it existed, for Richard himself refers to it explicitly on 28 June 1483, only two days after the petition was supposedly presented: 'whose sure and true tide is evidently declared and showed in a bill of petition which the lord's spiritual and temporal and the commons of this land solemnly presented unto the king's highness at London the 26th day of June'. He ordered that a copy of this petition should be sent to Calais and read to the garrison to persuade them that they now owed obedience to Richard. Not only was there such a petition, therefore, but it was issued by a public gathering and published. Too many people knew about it to permit tampering with the text, which none of his enemies allege. The text is anyway in close agreement with the testimony of Mancini and other contemporaries, most notably in its attacks on the Wydevilles as evil councillors of Edward IV. While evidently carefully drafted, there remain nevertheless many defects that any editor working at leisure at a year's remove would surely have corrected. Neither are there any improvements to discredit decisively the claims of Henry Tudor, which was the immediate imperative by January 1484. In short, there can be no doubt that what we possess is the authentic text, and no doubt either that it represents Richard's point of view. If he did not compile it in person, he most certainly determined its contents, and furthermore accepted them publicly and promulgated them.

Titulus Regius justifies Richard's accession by invalidating the marriage of Edward IV and Elizabeth Wydeville and thus bastardizing their sons Edward V and Prince Richard. Many grounds were advanced:

> [The marriage was] made of great presumption, without the knowing and assent of the lords of this land, and also by sorcery and witchcraft, committed by the said Elizabeth and her mother Jacquetta Duchess of Bedford, as the common opinion of the people, and the public voice, and the same through all this land… It was made privily and secretly, without reading of banns, in a private chamber, a profane place, and not openly in the face of the Church, after the Law of God's church, but contrary thereunto and against the laudable customs of the church of England.

None of these charges were new and none sufficed to bastardize the princes. That result was achieved by the charge that Edward had not been in a position to marry Elizabeth, because he was already betrothed [precontracted] to another woman, Lady Eleanor Butler. It followed that Edward and Elizabeth were never validly married but living 'together sinfully and damnably in adultery, against the law of God and his Church'. All their children, including the two princes, were therefore illegitimate. Given that Clarence's children were disqualified by their father's attainder, Richard alone remained as 'true inheritor to the said crown and royal dignity and as in right king of England by way of inheritance'. *Titulus Regius* cites no source for the betrothal, merely asserting it 'in very trouth' to be true, and we do not know what justification was produced at the time. 'It was put about then that

Old St Paul's Cathedral, in a reconstruction by H. Brewer. In the foreground is Paul's Cross, from which Ralph Shaa preached the bastardy of the princes on 22 June 1483.

this roll [justifying Richard's title] originated in the North', wrote Crowland, 'although there was no-one who did not know the identity of the author (who was in London at the time)'. Sadly Crowland does not name him. It could have been Edward IV's former chancellor Bishop Stillington, who was certainly well-placed to know and to whom the Frenchman Philippe de Commynes much later attributed the story. Whether he was right we cannot tell.

Titulus Regius also presents Richard's succession as conducive to good government and to the benefit of the common weal. It harks back to a golden age of good rule by kings with public-spirited and God-fearing councillors, who were committed to impartial justice, the common good and obedience to God's commandments, to a time of law and order at home, glorious victories abroad and flourishing commerce that provided adequate livings for all the poorer people. Now felicity was changed to misery. Prosperity, politic government and 'the Law of God and Man' were alike confounded. The root cause was a decline in morality of those in government, whose liking for flattery, sensuality and concupiscence caused them to prefer advice from 'people insolent, vicious, and inordinately avaricious' rather than 'good, virtuous, and prudent' councillors. Things became even worse after the marriage of Edward IV and Elizabeth Wydeville, when law and order, Christian morality, rights of property and civil rights collapsed. Not only was Edward IV's

The Richard III Society Memorial Window in Fotheringhay Curch demonstrates some of the noble bloodlines of the Yorkist kings. Top left are the arms of Edmund Langley, 1st Duke of York, impaled with those of his wife, Isabel of Castile. Below are the 2nd Duke's arms and those of Philippa Mohun, his wife, while at centre right a shield bears the arms of Richard's father and mother, Richard, 3rd Duke of York, and Cecily Neville.

government not in the interests of the common weal, but it had actually operated against it, failing most notably to offer impartial justice and acting sinfully against his subjects. Richard, in contrast, was king by inheritance and was thoroughly kingly in character. In appearance he resembled his father Richard Duke of York, whence the Yorkists' title stemmed. In Richard's veins flowed the blood royal of France, England and Spain. He had been born in England, which assured parliament both of his parentage and his natural inclinations towards prosperity and the common weal. Parliament commended the intelligence, prudence, justice, virtue and princely courage which he had already deployed in battle for the public good. Clearly transfer to Richard's rule was highly desirable.

Titulus Regius thus invoked in Richard's support the deplorable nature of Edward IV's rule, the vicious degeneracy of the Wydevilles and Richard's own exemplary character. None of this was new, for here *Titulus Regius* continues themes touched on earlier in April and May, when Richard was not the rival of Edward V but his loyal subject. Albeit misled by evil councillors and personally deficient, Edward IV is presented as a legitimate king, to whom Richard was the rightful successor. Hence Richard represented dynastic continuity. The story simultaneously circulating that Edward himself was a bastard, not the son of Richard Duke of York, does not feature in *Titulus Regius*: while it served to further discredit the princes, it was incompatible with Richard's claims to continuity. We have already seen that Richard's enemies presented his actions during these weeks as systematically clearing the ground for his usurpation, but this is not how Richard explained his actions then or how many Ricardians do today.

Alternatively Professor Wood has argued that Richard was not in control of events, but was reacting to them as problems arose. He did not look ahead, reacted pragmatically, stumbled from problem to problem and was panicked on occasion. That view demands respect but underestimates both Richard's ability and his consistency.

A third alternative is that Richard was not the prime mover but the victim, a man pressurized by his enemies – first by the Wydevilles and then by Hastings – into acting as he did: he was motivated throughout by high principles, and ultimately persuaded by the revelation of Edward IV's betrothal into taking on the onerous burden of kingship himself. This interpretation has to be taken more seriously, not least because it dates from the time and can be attributed directly to Richard himself. Ironically it is Mancini, the prosecution's star witness, who here contributes most to the defence case, and the equally hostile Crowland who assists. Richard evidently saw political mileage in keeping the citizens of London and York informed of his case, in enlisting their support, and in disarming their opposition. Hence the flow of open letters, proclamations and apparently also rumours that he circulated at the time and which were duly recorded in Mancini's history. Other letters sent to his supporters in the North, surviving in the original or as copies, preserve particular moments in the course of events. If Mancini did not believe Richard's protestations, almost certainly after Richard's accession rather than at the time, this does not reduce his value for Ricardians arguing Richard's case. The favourable admissions of a hostile witness are doubly valuable to the defence.

Mancini set the scene in terms reminiscent of *Titulus Regius,* but in far more circumstantial detail. Edward IV and his government were discredited and unpopular and his court was torn by the warring factions of Hastings and the Wydevilles, the latter having the advantage. Edward's deathbed efforts to reconcile those factions were unsuccessful. The Wydevilles also controlled the young king. Queen and prince stood in pride of place behind the king when Earl Rivers – the queen's brother and the prince's governor – presented his printed edition of his *Sayings of the Philosophers* to Edward IV. Richard meantime was devoting himself to the good government of the North, where he had withdrawn because he was alienated from the court. Edward's nomination of Richard as Lord Protector thus involved supplanting those in control by an outsider known to be hostile to them. While all wanted Edward V's peaceful accession, therefore, not surprisingly the Wydevilles determined on advancing his majority so that the protectorate of their enemy could be avoided. 'We are so important', declared the queen's son Dorset, 'that even without the king's uncle we can make and enforce these decisions.' This plan frightened Hastings into an alliance with Richard as his most powerful potential ally.

Mancini's account thus far is wholly critical of the Wydevilles and thus can hardly derive from Argentine and the circle of the young Edward V! It agrees closely with

Crowland's inside view. Richard, on the other hand, was doing everything right. Both Crowland and Rows report that he made northern notables take an oath of allegiance to the new king, presumably in York Minster:

> He therefore came to York with an appropriate company, all dressed in mourning, and held a solemn funeral ceremony, full of tears. He bound, by oath, all the nobility of those parts in fealty to the king's son; he himself swore first of all.

Richard was addressing a variety of audiences: the northern nobility and populace and his own retainers, who were reassured, whose alarm and potential unrest was assuaged, and whose respect for him was reinforced. Moreover it was a public act for national consumption, certain to be passed to the queen, council, and the prince, and to prevent any misunderstandings, friction, or hostility.

Similar functions were served by his letters. Crowland records that Richard wrote to the queen and reassured her of his loyalty. Mancini recites another letter from Richard to the council that declared his own loyalty and sought recognition of his rights in the most restrained terms:

> He had been loyal to his brother Edward, at home and abroad, in peace and war, and would be, if only permitted, equally loyal to his brother's son, and to all his brother's issue, even female, if perchance, which God forbid, the youth should die. He would expose his life to every danger which the children might endure in their father's realm. He asked the councillors to take his deserts into consideration, when disposing of the government, to which he was entitled by law, and his brother's ordinance. Further, he asked them to reach that decision which his services to his brother and to the State alike demanded; and he reminded them that nothing contrary to law and his brother's desire could be decreed without harm.

Although the letter was addressed to the council, Richard also had it published more widely. It had, as undoubtedly intended,

> a great effect on the minds of the people, who, as they had previously favoured the duke in their hearts from a belief in his probity, now began to support him loudly and aloud; so that it was commonly said by all that the duke deserved the government.

Thus it came to Mancini's ears. All authorities and classes in London and Westminster were being addressed. The government had no monopoly on information and had henceforth to take account of public opinion which could not safely be denied.

As the council was unmoved by this appeal and evidently intended not to recognize the duke as protector, Richard staged his first coup. Edward V was

A Victorian stained-glass panel by Thomas Willement at St Lawrence's Church, Ludlow, showing Edward V and, right, Prince Arthur, son of Henry VII.

persuaded to meet him on his way to London 'that in their company his entry into the city might be more magnificent' and his Wydeville escort was disarmed without bloodshed. Crowland also reports Gloucester's protestations of loyalty: he 'did not put off or refuse to offer to his nephew, the king, any of the reverence required from a subject such as bared head, bent knee or any other posture'. As justification for his action, Richard 'said that he was only taking precautions to safeguard his own person because he knew for certain that there were men close to the king who had sworn to destroy his honour and his life'. In Mancini's version, they were evil councillors, who had led Edward IV astray and would do the same to Edward V; conspirators 'preparing ambushes both in the capital and on the roads, which had been revealed to him by their accomplices'; and opponents of his protectorate.

In contrast, Richard himself was a loyal subject to the young king and was best fitted to rule on his behalf both by Edward IV's designation and by his own experience and popularity. The same themes of loyalty to the king and concern for his welfare appear in an open letter addressed to the council and corporation of London again reported by Mancini:

> He had not confined his nephew the king of England, rather had he rescued him and his realm from perdition, who, since the young man would have fallen into the hands of those who, since they had not spared either the honour or life of the father, could not be expected to have regard for the youthfulness of the son. The deed had been

necessary for his own safety and to provide for that of the king and kingdom. No one save only him had such solicitude for the welfare of King Edward and the preservation of the state. At an early date he and the boy would come to the city so that the coronation and all that pertained to the solemnity might be more splendidly performed.

Again, the duke was appealing for support beyond the council and government. Richard's charge of treason was supported by cartloads of weapons with the Wydeville arms that he brought to London and which everyone could see. No Wydeville denial or alternative explanation was allowed. A month of relative calm then followed.

On 10-11 June Richard wrote urgently to the cities of York and Hull and to Lord Neville asking for military support. The oral credence registered at York states that this was required against the queen. Three days later, on 13 June, he charged Hastings with complicity in this plot and executed him. A herald, so Mancini reports, proclaimed at once that 'a plot had been detected in the citadel and Hastings, the originator of the plot, had paid the penalty'. Richard's justification for the death was that Hastings and the queen were plotting against him. Not against the king, to whom Richard continued to protest his loyalty, showing, for example, every reverence to Prince Richard on his departure from sanctuary on 16 June.

The final stage – the bastardization of the princes and Richard's accession – marks a break in Richard's avowed intentions and explanations, for which *Titulus Regius* is the justification. Up to 20 June all Richard's actions were those of a subject loyal to Edward V, who was regrettably compelled to scotch repeated plots by members of the corrupt old regime who resented his reforms. His coups were forced upon him. His usurpation was prompted by the revelation that his nephew's claims were invalid and the consequent realization that the crown was his by right. His principled decision to assert his own right was in the public interest because he was undoubtedly the individual best suited to rule.

Contemporary verdicts

The defence can present a highly plausible case based on Richard's own explanations for his actions recorded by contemporary chroniclers. It is an entirely *contemporary* defence. But dare we accept it? After all, none of these chroniclers believed what he had to say at the time of writing and all interpreted his conduct in a wholly hostile way. Mancini is quite explicit about this. Can we legitimately accept their testimony on what Richard said, while rejecting the constructions that they place upon his words? Are we not obliged to give as much weight to the use they make of the facts as we do to the facts themselves?

There are three answers to this. First, we must not assume that the chroniclers themselves were consistent. All were guilty of hindsight and all reshaped events to fit their subsequent beliefs about what happened. This applies to individual events as well as to the sequence as a whole, and can be most strikingly illustrated by the error that almost all of them made in locating the removal of Prince Richard from sanctuary before Hastings' execution rather than afterwards. This order made best sense if Hastings' death was an obvious step by Richard towards his own accession. Without this presumption, so natural after Richard's usurpation, there is no problem in placing events in the correct order, with Hastings' fall first and York's removal second. Secondly, the chroniclers do not give us one verdict but several. They were themselves credulous and impressionistic, subjected to imperfect information and deliberate propaganda, that was designed to influence and mislead them in particular ways. As we have already seen, Crowland honestly records how his responses changed. We are concerned not with one, but with a succession of contemporary verdicts. Thirdly, we should consider not just what the chroniclers say people thought at the time, but what they actually thought. This is much more difficult, not least because the chroniclers purport to tell us both. Mancini and More, for instance, assert that many saw through Richard's plans at an early stage and at least some must have shared Queen Elizabeth's fears from 1 May. Perhaps Mancini himself did, as he claims. But it is not credible that all or even a majority of people realized all along that Richard was out to become king: if they had, their combined opposition would have prevented him from achieving his objective. It follows that the chronicles must be used sparingly here, that their comments on public opinion need to be treated particularly sceptically, and that even greater reliance than usual should be placed on documents produced at the time, combined with logical common sense.

All Richard's actions before his first coup presented him as a loyal subject concerned both for the good of the king and kingdom and for his legitimate rights. He maintained this stance when arresting the king, protesting his loyalty and treating him with reverence. We know that the two dukes treated the young king well, sought his goodwill and indeed secured it, from the existence of a famous parchment dating from this time on which Edward V, his uncle Richard, and Buckingham each wrote their signatures and mottoes.

When the first news of the coup reached London public reaction was evidently hostile. Mancini reports that everyone there was horrified. In fact, on his own evidence, the horror seems to have been restricted to a relatively small group. It was those most threatened, Queen Elizabeth and the Marquis of Dorset, who sought to raise forces to rebuff the dukes and to rescue the king; when this failed, Elizabeth and her children took refuge in sanctuary. Those whose support they sought, proved to be 'not only irresolute, but altogether hostile to themselves. Some even said openly that it was more just and profitable that the youthful sovereign should be with his paternal uncle than with his maternal uncles and uterine brothers.' In short, the nobility even in London saw the coup from the start as a blow by the dukes against the Wydevilles, not against the king, still less as the first move in Richard's usurpation. The Wydevilles' attempt to mobilize, albeit unsuccessful, gave support to Richard's charges that they would use force to maintain their privileged position.

While Richard's letters were designed to allay any fears that he meant to usurp, actions speak louder than words. At this juncture his conduct was very well judged.

He sent letters both to council and City and allowed his letters to have their effect before proceeding. He expressed concern to Cardinal Bourchier concerning the safety of the great seal, the Tower and the royal treasure. With control of all three, the Wydevilles could overawe London, issue commands supposedly on the king's behalf, finance their machinations, and deny all three to duke and/or council. Richard's warnings were certainly justified if Lord Chancellor Rotherham did indeed hand the great seal to the queen, as More relates. Next Richard demonstrated his commitment to Edward V as king: by organizing a state entry to London in which the young king took centre stage and he personally showed a proper reverence; by housing him not in a fortress but in the Bishop of London's palace; by dressing himself and his men in the 'coarse black cloth' appropriate as mourners for his late brother; by arranging for all the lords including himself and the mayor and aldermen of London to swear allegiance to Edward V; and by setting a new date (24 June) for the coronation and young king's majority. He placed responsibility for the coup firmly on the Wydevilles, which he illustrated by exhibiting their weapons, and brought only a modest force with him to demonstrate that he himself did not intend imposing his will by force.

The fruits of this approach emerged in the behaviour of the royal council, shorn now of the queen and Dorset, but decidedly not packed with Ricardian partisans. Clearly it accepted his version of events and, like Crowland and Hastings, the loyalty that he professed. By 8 May it had appointed him as Lord Protector in the knowledge that his term of office was temporary and would cease with the coronation. In the meantime Richard was the legitimate head of the executive. He could command the obedience of servants of the crown, formerly retainers of Edward IV, and employed them to implement his decisions. The fact that the chancellor was changed, other appointments were renewed, parliament was summoned and diplomacy resumed are all signs of the new initiative that Richard brought to government and of the confidence that the councillors felt in him. If to Crowland he now appeared as authoritative as another king, Richard exercised this authority extremely circumspectly, reassuring Londoners about the text of his oath, conceding on representations that the customs should cease to be levied until parliament had met and renewed the government's mandate, and accepting the royal council's refusal to allow the trial or execution of Rivers and Grey for treason. He was careful not to impose his will by force and was rewarded by a relaxation of tension, a return to stability and acceptance of his explanations for his first coup. As Dr Horrox has observed, 'by mid-May contemporaries had recovered from any anxieties prompted by the seizure of the prince and were prepared to accept Gloucester's protectorship at face value'.

Evidently the council accepted Richard's analysis of the political situation. It came to acknowledge that Sir Edward Wydeville was an enemy of the king as well as of Richard himself and authorized military action and expenditure against him. The Wydevilles' fleet deserted to the crown. The Wydeville faction was no longer a threat. Nevertheless Crowland was in good company in distinguishing between them and the queen herself, who was entitled to more honourable treatment.

Two of Richard's 'enemies' appear on the frontispiece of the Luton Guild Book: Thomas Rotherham (centre) and Elizabeth Wydeville (right). On the left is Edward IV, while immediately behind Queen Elizabeth is Cecily Neville, his mother.

Accordingly on 23 May guarantees were offered to her to come out of sanctuary. Those involved were not just her principal enemies, Richard and Buckingham, but the two archbishops, Cardinal Bourchier, the king's great-uncle, and ex-chancellor Rotherham, who had earlier committed himself to her. Elizabeth was uncompromising. On 9 June it was reported that council had met at Westminster, but that nobody had spoken for or with the queen. The extent to which the Wydevilles had been discredited emerges first in the extension of Richard's protectorate beyond the coronation, agreed about this time, and, second, in Lord Chancellor Russell's commendation of the 'surety and firmness' of lords and noblemen against the tempestuous Rivers and his praise for Richard's 'great puissance, wisdom and fortunes at this recent execution of the defence of this realm as well against open enemies as against the subtle and faint friends of the same'. This was in the sermon he drafted for Edward V's parliament.

Preparations for both parliament and the coronation were interrupted by the second coup. Again, it was Richard's version of the events of 13 June that was initially believed. Hastings was executed and Rotherham and Morton were imprisoned for plotting with the queen against Richard. Sir Thomas More claims that the herald's proclamation was disbelieved from the start, but this is untrue. 'At first the ignorant crowd believed,' writes Mancini. 'And in the mean time there was divers [who] imagined the death of the Duke of Gloucester,' observed a Londoner without apparent scepticism. 'And it was espied and the Lord Hastings was taken in the Tower and beheaded forthwith.' Hastings' fate 'was deserved, as it is said', noted the St Albans Abbey register. Almost all the other chroniclers deny the plot, but almost all are guilty of hindsight. The events that follow are a better guide.

Hastings' death did not stir fears amongst the political leadership that Richard aimed for the throne, but, if anything, served to reinforce fears of the queen and the Wydevilles and to strengthen trust in Richard. On Monday 16 June Cardinal Bourchier fetched Prince Richard from sanctuary in Westminster Abbey. The queen conceded 'graciously, as far as words went'. The cardinal's action was entirely consistent with earlier attempts to persuade Elizabeth herself to leave sanctuary. If Duke Richard had taken the prince by force, as Mancini says he intended, he would have indelibly blackened his reputation and taken a step from which there was no withdrawal. It would have been out of character, for throughout these months he was extremely careful to carry public opinion with him. The boy was fetched by his great-uncle and primate. This shows that Cardinal Bourchier did not see Richard as the threat. The cardinal would hardly have broken sanctuary to deliver the boy to a usurper and a murderer, nor could a cardinal-archbishop have been *compelled* to do it. He had already refused, as we have seen, to surrender his great-nephew Latimer to the duke. The cardinal was not alone in his perception. Canon Simon Stallworth wrote in a letter of 'the deliverance of the Duke of York', described Prince Richard's ceremonial and affectionate reception in Westminster Palace by the two dukes, and reports his departure with the cardinal to join his brother at the Tower 'where he is, blessed be Jesus, merry'. Even the queen was willing to hand Prince Richard over to his great-uncle, the cardinal. Confiding him to Bourchier served to disarm any opposition. It seems that contemporaries accepted the explanation that the prince was needed at his brother's coronation to make it as splendid as possible and to reinforce the otherwise implausible impression of family unity. Hastings' fate was not yet seen as altering Richard's plan to achieve the untroubled majority of Edward V.

It has been suggested that Prince Richard's transfer was preceded by a council meeting, yet the decisions taken suggest that the meeting came afterwards. It is agreed that Richard's main argument for removing Prince Richard from sanctuary was so that he could attend his brother's coronation. Such an argument would not have been possible had the coronation already been postponed. By next day, 17 June, it had been. Parliament was also put off. Perhaps it was at this stage that it was agreed to prolong

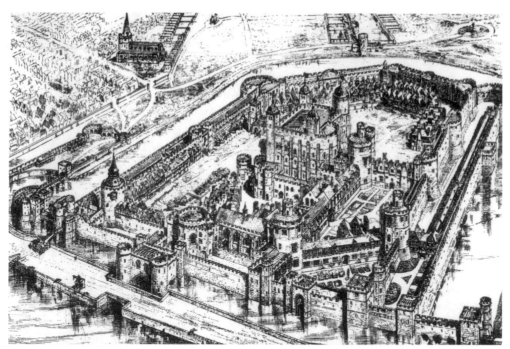

The Tower of London as it appeared in the fifteenth century. Reconstruction by H. Brewer.

Richard's protectorate beyond the coronation. These actions indicate uncertainty that such great events could be conducted peacefully and are thus further testimony to the atmosphere of crisis recorded in the letters. Perhaps the strong hand of Richard as Lord Protector was seen to be essential by uncommitted councillors to cope with a crisis for which Richard himself was largely responsible. It is clear that there was indeed an atmosphere of crisis. Rumours flew around and not all could be true. Mancini speaks of a panic on Hastings' death, as townsmen seized their weapons, but Richard's proclamation was sufficient 'to calm the multitude'. In the week before 21 June Stallworth records the arrests of 13 June, that the conspirators were still in prison, that their release was imminent, and that they were still confined. 'With us', he wrote, 'there is much trouble and every man doubts other'. On 19 June the City corporation posted an overnight watch of 227 armed citizens in Cheapside and Cornhill ward against an unspecified threat. George Cely's notes of the same time, cryptic and incoherent as they are, were also full of rumours and fears:

> There is great rumour in the realm. The Scots have done great [damage] in England. The chancellor [Rotherham] is deprived and not content. The Bishop of Ely is dead. If the king, God save his life, were to die; the Duke of Gloucester were in any peril. If my Lord Prince, whom God protect, were troubled. If my Lord of Northumberland were dead or greatly troubled. If my Lord Howard were slain.

It was not only the princes for whom he feared, but Richard himself and his allies Northumberland and Howard; he had no fears for the queen. Whoever Cely saw as the threat, it was not Richard. It was not only Prince Richard's removal from sanctuary that Stallworth presented favourably. He had heard of the approach of Richard's northern army: 'to what intent I know not but to keep the peace'. This favourable interpretation was written not sooner than 21 June, the day before the St Paul's Cross sermon about the bastardy of the princes. Clearly Richard's interpretation of Hastings' death had carried the day. If Richard was indeed riding around dressed in purple and was feasting men in his house, it was not yet to the accompaniment of curses, as Mancini says, except possibly Mancini's own.

And so to the precontract. Here we have no independent testimony to balance the chroniclers. Richard's northern army, though anticipated, was still at Pontefract, a latent threat rather than an immediate resource. Without it, Richard could not override by force the substantial groups of commons and lords present in London even though parliament had been postponed. There are strong grounds here for supposing that Richard acceded with consent. Although obviously inspired by Richard, the petition of the estates that offered him the crown nevertheless enjoyed some support. Richard was allowed to take the throne and was crowned king. The procedure for his election and coronation was as formal as that of previous usurpers and replaced earlier oaths of fealty to Edward V. There is a strong case here for supposing that the precontract story was believed, that it did shock those who heard of it and was initially accepted as grounds for deposition. Modern historians are now inclined to the view that the precontract offered sound grounds for Richard's accession if the story was true. Undoubtedly events were orchestrated; but the open hostility claimed for the Londoners was probably invented after the event, either by More himself or by Londoners, who had every wish to re-evaluate their part in Richard's accession and found it impossible to suppose that the usurpation had not been predicted at the time.

In April to June 1483 Richard's actions were supported by much more than a faction. Buckingham was with him always, but most of his northern retainers remained in the North and became important only towards the end. His retainers were deliberately limited in number and restrained in their actions. Richard committed himself to persuading the royal councillors and Londoners to support and believe in his course of action, and he seems to have succeeded. Had he not managed this after the first coup, he could not have become protector except by force. If he had not used his position to neutralize and discredit the Wydevilles, he would have been in no position to take the throne except by force. At each stage alternatives existed. Force was evidently ruled out. But Richard could always have drawn back. Before 1 May he could have accepted the decisions made by council without penalty. After the first coup and even after Hastings' death, his protestations of loyalty were believed and he was not committed to usurpation. He could have permitted the coronation, Edward's majority and the end of his own protectorate to have taken effect. His decision to put off the coronation the moment that Prince Richard was in his power looks at first conclusive, but even here Richard allowed

Pontefract Castle, in a painting by Alexander Kiernick.

himself an escape clause. The coronation was not cancelled but postponed to November. For a few days longer, proceeding with the coronation remained an option. He could have disowned the precontract story and blamed it on its author, on Dr Shaa or on Buckingham. Of course, Richard's forceful actions had permanently changed his position. He had fanned the enmity of the Wydevilles towards him and had he withdrawn from his road to the throne he could not have been sure of his long-term security. It was only on 26 June, when he accepted the throne, that he was committed. In short, it was always possible for Richard to draw back and not to take the throne. It is even possible on this evidence alone to argue that usurpation was not his objective until the very end. The chroniclers did not reject his case until the usurpation or afterwards.

Cross examination

For April, May and the first half of June most contemporaries found in favour of the defence. They took Richard's protestations at their face value. Their acceptance of his version of events enabled him to succeed peacefully. It is a satisfactory explanation of the usurpation. Yet we cannot leave the case there. Our verdict cannot be assumed to conform to theirs. Our evidence differs. Our longer perspective, even our hindsight, can be made into advantages. To admit that Richard's declarations of loyalty convinced people at the time cannot erase the inconvenient facts that he *did* subsequently renounce his allegiance, *did* seize the throne for himself and *did* lose the faith of many (perhaps even most) of his former supporters. However widely believed in 1483, the betrothal story enjoyed little credit until recently, for the only possible Lady Eleanor Butler seemed too old to be credible and no confirmatory evidence of any kind has been found. Even now that a credible candidate has been found, it does not make the story true; it still depends, as it has always done, on the partisan testimony of *Titulus Regius*. Crowland complained that only an ecclesiastical court could judge. Even if Edward's sons were bastards, William the Conqueror was not the only bastard to be a medieval king: illegitimacy and kingship were not incompatible. Bastardy could not dispel the recognition of Edward V as king by the whole political nation, including Richard, and his entitlement to the allegiance that all had sworn. Richard's usurpation and his execution of Hastings, Rivers and Grey, however politically justified, were all illegal acts and were, moreover, sins – a consideration more important in Richard's own day than our own. We need to cross-examine our star witness rather more closely before we acquit Richard on evidence recycled from his unwilling admissions. We also need to recall that even when they are telling the truth, contemporaries recounted what was believed at the time, which may not necessarily be accurate.

Mancini's analysis of the situation at Edward IV's death is highly favourable to Richard because it highlights the difficulties that Edward left behind him and because it presents a complex web of long-standing problems calling for drastic solutions. It was a situation which threatened to become a disaster, even without a self-interested usurper. Mancini identifies as 'an important factor in this revolution' the dissension between Hastings and the Wydevilles. We must agree. But Edward IV's difficulties, although severe, did not threaten his throne: if short of money, he was not bankrupt; if the war in Scotland was expensive, it was under control; and the dangers of conflict with France were to recede sharply in August with the death of Louis XI and the succession of his young son Charles VIII. Edward was in no danger of being deposed and was indeed as secure as he had ever been. His problems were not on the scale presented by Mancini and *Titulus Regius*, and certainly did not call for the drastic solution of a usurpation.

Moreover, we need not accept that the council was as riven with divisions in April 1483 as Mancini and indeed most other historians assert. For Mancini, a key issue arousing heated – and apparently prolonged – debate was whether the king would be crowned or whether there would be a protectorate. If true, however, this issue was decided very early, against a protectorate. By 16 April at Ludlow Edward V already knew of the decision to crown him forthwith, having presumably been informed of it with news of Edward IV's death on 14 April. The key decision must therefore have been taken at once by the council in London, on 11 April or even earlier. It seems unlikely that this was a Wydeville victory in council, since Crowland, as we have seen, was opposed to their dominance and reconciled to the result. The suggestion of a Wydeville victory at this stage is not supported by the membership of key commissions of 27 April on which Hastings was also well represented. Crowland reports that the debate related to the size of the young king's escort, which the queen conceded should be modest. That compromise achieved, the council willingly authorized Sir Edward Wydeville to take command of the fleet and the expenditure associated with it. If Hastings was indeed scheming to

A detail from the screen of the Oliver King Chantry, St George's Chapel, Windsor, showing Edward V, the king who never wore his crown.

overthrow the Wydevilles, as all the chronicles suggest, he was doing so not because Wydevilles in the ascendant were threatening him, but because he saw scope for decisive victory with Richard's help *after* the coronation. He cannot have intended the first coup.

We must also reject Mancini's account of the animosity between Richard and the Wydevilles dating back to 1464. Certainly they were at odds in May/June 1483, when Richard, after all, arrested Rivers and Grey, sought their execution and eventually had them killed. As principal victims of his first coup, it is hardly surprising that the queen and Dorset took sanctuary and henceforth viewed Richard as their enemy. It is less obvious that they did so before 1 May 1483. To favour a speedy coronation did not make them Richard's enemies and, indeed, Mancini tells us that they were not. Their scheme would make Richard chief councillor, but not actually ruler. Earlier evidence does not support a long-standing hostility. Far from objecting to Edward IV's marriage, Richard – then only twelve years old – had shared in the ceremonies that made Elizabeth queen. In 1468-9 he resisted the attacks of Warwick and Clarence on the Wydevilles and in 1469 Queen Elizabeth made him steward of her estates at £100 a year. In 1472-4 she backed him against Clarence over the Warwick Inheritance, in 1477-8 he helped her destroy Clarence, and in 1482 Rivers served under his command and he created Sir Edward Wydeville a banneret. There is no evidence of friction locally. Finally, on 20-25 March 1483, Rivers chose Richard to arbitrate one of his land disputes: a clear mark of trust.

The Great Hall, Prince's Apartments and circular Norman Chapel, Ludlow Castle, where Edward V learned of his father's death.

Friendship not animosity, trust not distrust, also explain the events of the first coup. Rivers had allowed little enough time to bring the young king from Ludlow, where he was on 24 April, to his coronation at Westminster on 4 May, particularly if, as Mancini says, he was meant to arrive three days early. The quickest itinerary lay far to the west of Gloucester's route from York to London. Rivers had no need to meet Richard and could certainly have avoided him had he wished. The fact that all met at Stony Stratford is good evidence in itself that this was their intention and that they were on good terms. So, indeed, Mancini states:

> Both dukes wrote to the young king in Wales, to ascertain from him on what day and by what route he intended to enter the capital, so coming from the country they could alter their course and join him, that in their company his entry to the city might be more magnificent. The king assented to them and did as they requested… [He] halted at a certain village to await there his uncle.

Moreover, Rivers went *back* to meet Richard and Buckingham and spent a convivial evening with them. He was still quite unsuspecting at his arrest next morning and so too were Grey and Vaughan. Unwittingly they had placed themselves in Richard's power as the two dukes had planned. Bereft of their leaders the king's escort succumbed without a blow. Evidently Rivers did not see Richard as his foe and was unaware of any supposed animosity between them. Yet Richard treated him as an enemy. Either Richard had concealed his hostility even from them or else it did not yet exist. They cannot, in either case, have known of his aspirations to be protector.

Mancini opts for concealment. He tells us that Richard was 'sorely displeased' about Edward's marriage but kept it secret. If that was true, he dissimulated. If this was merely what Richard said in 1483, he was dissimulating again, but we have no certain evidence that the duke said any such thing. The crucial evidence here relates to the destruction of Clarence in 1478. Just as Richard, according to Mancini, disapproved secretly of King Edward's marriage, so too following Clarence's death he 'was so overcome with grief for his brother, that he could not dissimulate so well, but that he was overheard to say that he would one day avenge his brother's death'. Hence the Wydevilles feared Richard's vengeance. Secrecy and dissimulation could explain the absence of confirmatory evidence for either. We can demonstrate Mancini's story to be untrue. While the Wydevilles did indeed engineer Clarence's ruin, responsibility rested with the king and parliament. There was nothing improper about their participation nor that of Richard. Not only did Richard attend the crucial planning meetings late in 1477, but he also benefited more than anyone else from the spoils of his brother's destruction. These came not just after his fall, but before it. Those grants that antedate Clarence's death but follow his condemnation were merely in bad taste, but others were made even before Clarence was put on trial and depended for their implementation on his destruction. The grant of Ogmore was as early as 27 November 1477. Here the documentary evidence is conclusive. We must agree with More that Richard 'lacked not in helping forth his brother Clarence to his death; ...[as] if he were heartily minded to his wealth'. There is a third piece of evidence. In a letter for the Irish Earl of Desmond, whose father had suffered judicial murder at English hands, Richard wrote that 'the same thing was and happened since in this realm of England, as well of his brother the Duke of Clarence as other his nigh kinsmen and great friends', and promised him justice against the murderers. The letter proves that in 1483 Richard himself was spreading the story that he had disapproved of Clarence's death. Richard as king distanced himself from the death of his brother which he had promoted as duke, and blamed it on others, presumably those same Wydevilles implicated by Mancini and More, both of whose information derived directly or indirectly from Richard himself. Given the unambiguous message of the documents, Richard could not claim to have opposed Clarence's fall publicly, but instead said that he concealed his real feelings just as he did about the original Wydeville marriage. Remember that Mancini attributes the whole story of a Wydeville-Gloucester feud to Richard himself.

Five points emerge from this. First, there was no hostility, veiled or otherwise, between Richard and the Wydevilles before 1483. It was invented by Richard in April-May 1483. Second, we must therefore reject the heart of the case for the defence, that Richard had to stage his coup on 1 May because the Wydevilles posed a threat to him. There was no such threat. Third, Richard saw advantages in distancing himself from the Wydevilles and court, belittling their co-operation over Clarence. Fourth, he was

The bones in the Clarence vault, Tewkesbury Abbey, which are said to be those of the Duke and Duchess of Clarence.

anxious to saddle the Wydevilles with the blame. 'They had to endure the imputation brought against them by all, of causing the death of the duke of Clarence.' Not only were they unpopular, so Mancini says, but he adds that it was fear of punishment for Clarence's death that prompted their opposition to Richard's protectorate. Obviously the Wydevilles themselves cannot have thought or said that. Fifth and finally, Richard was determined to become protector and was prepared to go to any lengths.

Why did Richard seek to distance himself from the Wydevilles, the court and even from Edward IV's government? Clearly he wished to blame the Wydevilles for all defects of his late brother's regime which, to some extent, he seems to have invented. In terms reminiscent of *Titulus Regius* (and even Crowland) but containing independent elements, Mancini took Edward IV to task in particular for his timorous foreign policy that collapsed before his death, on the unnecessary taxation for wars that did not happen, and on Edward's avaricious hoarding of treasure. He charged Edward with failing in his duty to defend his realm and to 'live of his own' and with abuse of the doctrine of necessity, which entitled him to taxation only for the necessary defence of the kingdom as a whole. Even that, Crowland, Mancini, and the poets show, was not altogether acceptable. The government had been run by the Wydevilles, on whose 'great Rivers', Bishop Russell declared, there could be no reliance or security. They were evil councillors, said Mancini, who had advanced and ennobled themselves at the public expense. This same charge had been levelled at them in 1469, when Edward himself had also been criticized for breaking his pledge to live of his own and for misusing a tax granted for war against France. When therefore his 1475 invasion of France ended in peace, King Edward had remitted an unpaid instalment to the taxpayers, but the Scottish war of the early 1480s caused him to collect it and in 1483 he had secured a new tax for another war against France, which he had not yet declared. Richard thus charged Edward with the sort of misgovernment that had led to depositions in the past and saddled the Wydevilles, unjustly, with the responsibility.

The Wydevilles, so Richard told Edward V, had not cared for the honour and safety of his father, and were therefore unworthy guides for him. Richard himself was loyal, committed to the common weal, concerned about the decay of trade and the inadequate incomes of poor artificers and was best suited as an outstanding soldier to protect the realm against its enemies. He was untarnished by the old regime, for after Clarence's death he had withdrawn from court and concentrated on the good government of the North. So Mancini says. We have already seen how Richard's military reputation had been inflated. But how could Mancini write so favourably of Richard's activity on his 'Gloucester estates' when he did not even know where they were? Where else could he have learnt of this but from Richard himself or Richard's circle? To withdraw from court was a recognized way of courting popularity by those anxious to become 'idols of the multitude', towards whom, so Crowland said, the 'eyes of the common folk, always eager for change, used to turn in days gone by. They regarded the earl of Warwick, the duke of Clarence, and any other great man in the land who withdrew from royal circles as idols of this sort.' Actually Richard had never withdrawn, maintaining and exploiting his court links and attending as frequently as was compatible with his peripheral responsibilities, yet clearly he claimed that he had withdrawn and was believed. Not only had he saddled the Wydevilles with the blame for killing Clarence, but he had also drawn on Clarence's misconceived popularity. 'By these arts [of public relations] Richard secured the favour of the people.' He projected an image of himself designed to be popular rather than true. Richard appealed beyond the political establishment to the commons whose intervention in previous revolutions had been decisive, as he knew and modern historians now know.

So Richard was untarnished by the discredited old regime, the man best suited to rule and moreover the man entitled to do so as the Lord Protector designated by the late Edward IV in his will. That will was never proved and no longer exists. Did it contain any such provision? The wills of Henry V in 1421 and of Edward IV himself in 1475, both made by kings bound for foreign war and leaving under-age heirs, contain no such clauses, and besides Henry VI's council had decreed that kings could not determine government after their death. Richard alone claimed to have been designated protector. He himself may be the source for Mancini in 1483 and for such writers as Bernard André and Polydore Vergil. The fact that he later became temporary protector is immaterial. Perhaps, therefore, the Wydeville-dominated council in London was not only entitled to determine the future form of Edward V's government, as indeed they were, but needed to overturn no provision of Edward IV to achieve it. We have already seen that the decision to do without a protector was made very early, probably on 10-11 April, and Crowland saw this as fulfilling Edward

IV's wishes. Rivers could hardly have failed to see Richard as a rival at Stony Stratford if he was already laying claim to the protectorate. In spite of all this, Richard not only laid claim to the office, which he asserted in his letters, but also succeeded in persuading Mancini and others that he had a right to rule. In reply, we hear only hostile accounts of the Wydevilles, not the justification of the royal council that made the decision.

The Wydevilles had a good case but were hopelessly outmanoeuvred. They appear not to have effectively rebutted Richard's claims of Wydeville or Hastings plots, nor of the precontract story. Here Richard's assertions were absolutely crucial – his claim that they were plotting his destruction and his elevation of this accusation from mere factional fighting to a major public concern. It was this charge that justified his first coup as a pre-emptive strike. It was alleged that the Wydevilles had planned to ambush him with the weapons that he sent in four cartloads to London. Mancini claims these to have been left over from the Scottish war (perhaps at Grafton Regis, the family seat near Stony Stratford?) and More observed that they would be no use in barrels. If such an ambush was planned, it seems unlikely that the perpetrators would themselves have been so easily ambushed. Whether true or false, however, is hardly to the point. Here was another attempt to demonstrate a long-standing feud with Richard and to blacken the Wydevilles that can be traced directly to Richard himself. It was he who publicly paraded weapons in carts to support the allegation. Richard had anticipated any denials: the weapons apparently substantiated his case. In strict law, the actions of the Wydevilles against Richard up to this date were not treason and the council refused to authorize their executions. They had already been damaged by circulation of the charge and in future the council treated them as traitors. Although the council had commissioned Sir Edward Wydeville, it now treated him as an enemy, and by early June Bishop Russell was accusing the Wydevilles of plotting with the French. When Hastings fell, the charge of complicity with him also seems to have stuck, at least at first.

There was no more damning accusation than treason, except perhaps sorcery, and the Wydevilles were tainted with that too – a charge invoked to explain Edward's ill-advised marriage. In his letters to York of 10 and 19 June, Richard asserted not just that the queen was plotting his destruction, but, 'as it is openly known', she had also by 'subtle and damnable ways... forecasted the same': that she had foretold his future by necromancy. This was the charge for which three men had been executed in 1477. In 1469-70 Elizabeth's mother had been accused of sorcery, perhaps in relation to her daughter's marriage. Note the emphasis on the *damnable* nature of Elizabeth's action: it was deserving of hell. The appeal to notoriety also needs to be taken seriously: how else could such an oblique and passing comment have carried weight? It implies the existence of other propaganda now irretrievably lost. Again the source is Richard himself. Should not we perhaps take more seriously the claim of the Tudor chroniclers that Richard also charged her and Hastings with causing his physical deformity by sorcery?

All these points feature in Richard's letter of 10 June that sought military support against the plots of the queen. Written in the same highly coloured and vituperative language as *Titulus Regius*, it demands aid against the queen, her blood, adherents and affinity, which have intended and daily do intend to murder and utterly destroy us and our cousin the Duke of Buckingham and the old royal blood of the realm, and as it is now openly known, by their subtle and damnable ways forecasted the same, and also the final destruction and disinheritance of you and all other men of honour, as well of the north parts as other countries that adhere to us.

In just a few lines, the letter accuses the Wydevilles of murder, treason, rebellion and even sorcery, all offences that were genuinely damnable or deserving of damnation, and appeals to the citizens' respect for the social hierarchy and royalty, their sense of honour, the sanctity of inheritance, their own self-preservation, their regional sentiment and their loyalty to Richard. Even the queen was an upstart when compared to the 'old royal blood of the realm'! Here is the first example of the representation of enemies as threats to inheritance – to property and therefore social status – that Richard later made commonplace. Note also that Richard identifies himself with the northerners, whose rights and interests were intertwined. No doubt such points could be and were amplified by Sir Richard Ratcliffe, 'this bearer', whose additional instructions about musters were all that was noted by the town clerk. Such a letter was tailor-made for its target audience, for only parts could be effective elsewhere – not in London, for example. Though it at first appears comprehensive, there is much else that Richard was saying in the South that was omitted. In his parallel letter to Lord Neville, he appealed merely to the recipient's sense of the common weal. The fact that his letter to York achieved the desired effect was at least partly because no defence was made or could have been possible against such a mixture of prejudice and innuendo.

It was not just the Wydevilles who are denigrated here, of course, but Lord Hastings who is not explicitly mentioned in Ratcliffe's credence. Hastings suffered by sexual association with Edward IV, Dorset and Elizabeth Shore, yet nevertheless was depicted favourably by the principal chroniclers. Crowland aligned himself explicitly with him, identifying him with Archbishop Rotherham and Bishop Morton as 'one of three strongest supports of the new king'. Mancini agrees. All three were 'in age mature, and instructed by long experience of public affairs. [They had] helped more than other councillors to form the king's policy, and besides carried it out'. 'Undoubtedly the protector loved him well', More observed, 'and loath was to have lost him'. Yet Hastings was seized without warning at council on 13 June 1483, charged with treason, and executed. Others were arrested at the same time and a plot against Richard was declared, which was at first accepted by the London mob. Richard's summonses of northern help on 10/11 June, which again allege conspiracy, have been cited as confirmation. However all these sources – the actual letters, the charges and the proclamation cited by the chroniclers – all emanate from a single source, Richard himself. No other confirmatory evidence has ever been found. It is an unlikely story that is most likely to have been Richard's own invention.

Another instance of how Richard blackened the Wydevilles' name concerns the treasure of Edward IV.

> [He] was yet so eager for money, that in pursuing it he acquired a reputation for avarice; ... and so he had gathered great treasures, whose size had not made him more generous or prompt in disbursement than when he was poor, but rather more stringent and tardy, so that now his avarice was publicly proclaimed.

He built up a 'royal treasure, the weight of which was said to be immense'. Here Mancini repeats well informed opinion. Crowland's king was concerned to extract all he could from his subjects, 'to reassemble treasure worthy of his regal estate and from his own resources and by his own effort', and did indeed make himself 'a very wealthy prince'. Immediately after the king's death, a member of his household makes him lament:

> I stored my coffers and also my chests
> With taxes taken of the communalty;
> I took their treasure but of their prayers missed...
> I had enough, but was not content.

Following the first coup, Mancini reports, all this treasure ' was divided between the queen, the marquis and Edward [Wydeville]'. How greedy, selfish, and unpublic-spirited! But there was no treasure. The magnificence of Edward's court was designed to mislead about the real state of his finances and did indeed mislead his historians. Crowland in particular failed to correlate the king's real insolvency (of which he was aware) with his outward display of wealth. Edward's acquisitiveness and timid foreign policy arose not from avarice but from his need to keep up appearances with minimal resources and his inability to finance war. Any balance he had built up had already been spent at his death. When he died, Edward left only £490 in the Exchequer and £710 in his chamber, a total of £1,200: insufficient to pay the costs of £1,496 for his funeral on 18 April, so jewels had to be sold a month later. Moreover, this was widely known, certainly to Crowland, who was one of the royal council who received frequent reports on the parlous financial position from early May, and to the royal executors, who on 12 May refused to administer Edward's will because he had not left enough to meet liabilities and to those present at their renunciation. These included both archbishops, eight other bishops, Richard himself Buckingham, Arundel, Hastings and Stanley 'and many other nobles'. The Wydevilles could not have stolen the treasure: first, because it did not exist; second, because it was part of Edward's estate; and third, because it was not stolen. The £3,670 that Dorset and Sir Edward Wydeville received for foreign defence was authorized by the council. Even before the second coup, Edward's executors, treasury officials, and therefore the councillors knew this truth. Probably Richard already knew too. He knew how much difficulty Edward had in paying for the

Scottish war and how anxious he was to offload and avoid commitments. But the Wydevilles still took the blame. Where did the story publicized by Mancini come from? It came from Richard. A letter nominally from Edward V of 2 May, the day after the first coup and therefore really from Richard, urged Cardinal Bourchier to 'see to the safekeeping of the Tower and the treasure there in'. In short, Richard was responsible for this untrue rumour that slandered the Wydevilles. He skilfully exploited Edward's display of wealth against them.

Most important of all, it appears, were the charges of sexual offences directed against the Wydevilles. Lechery was a deadly sin, the only one that the Church consistently attacked, and sexual offences were the main business of the church courts, which was possible only because the laity were assiduous in reporting offences. We can thus be sure that public opinion was generally hostile to illicit fornication, adultery and prostitution. Edward IV himself was a notorious philanderer and such conduct could not be condoned even in a king. Crowland testifies to his self-indulgence. His fellow whoremongers were Lord Hastings and two Wydevilles: the king's youngest brother-in-law, Sir Edward Wydeville, and his elder stepson, Dorset. All may have shared Mistress Elizabeth Shore. Their sexual misdemeanours were exposed on three occasions at least: to Edward V at Stony Stratford; in *Titulus Regius*; and through the exemplary punishment of Mistress Shore. All three reports derive from Richard himself, who then, as later, found political advantage in publicizing his opponents' illicit sexual activities. Was Richard again behind Mancini's tribute to the his exemplary private life? How much advantage Richard gained from the Wydevilles' peccadilloes, how popular such charges were, we cannot now tell or perhaps fully appreciate.

The label of sexual immorality by itself was politically damaging. Such sinners were unworthy to guide the young king. Moreover Richard attributed to them some responsibility for the late king's peccadilloes, a charge that impressed Lord Chancellor Russell: 'Was not his pestiferous sickness increased by daily remembrance of the dark ways that his subtle friends had led him in?' It was also suggested that their advancement owed something to their share in his exploits. While it was their kinship to the queen rather than such intimacy that gave them their authority after Edward's death, Elizabeth's position was weakened by exposure of her family's sexual misconduct. Many tales were current in 1483 about her marriage to Edward IV. Mancini says that she was too humble and should have been a virgin; that she was refused royal honours by the nobility; that the match displeased the royal family and so annoyed Edward IV's mother that she declared him a bastard; that Elizabeth defended her chastity so well against Edward, even putting a dagger to her throat, that he was obliged to marry her to secure her sexual favours. Already current by 1469, the story may have been encouraged by the Wydevilles themselves. Whether such tales were true is immaterial here. What matters is that they were being circulated, that they were potentially damaging to the Wydevilles if properly exploited, and that they focused attention on the queen's marriage and hence on the legitimacy of her children. There are more specific charges in *Titulus Regius,* which blames the marriage on sorcery and witchcraft

Elizabeth Shore, mistress of Edward IV, Lord Hastings and possibly Marquess Dorset and Sir Edward Wydeville as well. Brass from her parents' tomb at Hinxworth, Hertfordshire.

committed by Elizabeth and her mother the Duchess Jacquetta according to 'the common opinion of the people'. Maybe people did remember Jacquetta's abortive sorcery trial of 1469-70, perhaps on this charge. Richard, as we have seen, accused Elizabeth of necromancy earlier in the month. The marriage had been clandestine and without banns, lacked the assent of the notables and could well have been celebrated in an unconsecrated place. Such irregularities went a long way towards counteracting the virtue and chastity of the dagger story. Elizabeth was no better than her menfolk. In *Titulus Regius* such slurs lead up to the precontract, the invalidity of the marriage, the adultery of both partners and the consequent illegitimacy of their offspring. Incorrigibly immoral, the Wydevilles could be set aside with Elizabeth's bastards.

While *Titulus Regius* makes no direct mention of the supposed bastardy of Edward IV himself, it assumes knowledge of this old story among its readers and exploits it. Richard, it states, was 'born within this land' [at Fotheringhay] and so the three estates 'have, and may have, more certain knowledge of your birth and filiation abovesaid'. His elder brothers Edward and Clarence had been born respectively at Rouen and Dublin. Richard did not need to slander his own mother, as More thought, for the legend could be put to use without doing so. He was not the author of this old story, but it is alluded to in *Titulus Regius* and the chronicles testify to the currency of the story at the time. Allegations of bastardy had become commonplace at such times. We cannot now be sure how this one spread.

And so it is again and again: the sorcery of the Duchess Jacquetta and the Wydeville involvement in the fall of Clarence, for instance. Old stories were recycled, such as the legendary greed of the Wydevilles and their sexual immorality, and new elements were inserted – such as the treasure and the precontract – in familiar contexts that made old tales easier to swallow. Richard used the full gamut of propaganda weapons. He managed public appearances carefully, giving attention to pageantry and ceremony, dressing appropriately and staging his own displays of reverence to Edward V and his brother. It was important to be seen. Like Warwick the Kingmaker, he encouraged people to eat at his table and meet him in person. He did not over-expose himself and employed agents – Cardinal Bourchier, Buckingham, and Ralph Shaa – when appropriate. He used proclamations and open letters, which were carefully phrased, as Mancini appreciated, to achieve the required effect. He was not afraid to intervene directly to scotch a hostile rumour.

He leaked information and started rumours when appropriate. Take the case of the northern army, which Richard summoned secretly by private signet letters on 10-11 June, but which was still at Pontefract on 25 June. Its imminent approach 'within the week' was known in London by 21 June (and perhaps on 18 June, when the York contingent had not yet left) and influenced events. Who leaked the news? To whose advantage was it? Not to Richard's enemies, for Stallworth interprets its purpose favourably. For Richard, then? If the news of the forming of the army was leaked, quelling insurrection and overawing opposition could be achieved without the disorder that accompanies armies and without arousing north-south animosities. This was disinformation, not information. Given that Richard had solemnly led the swearing of fealty to Edward V before his departure southwards and that his letters summoned help against plotters, the troops may well have been unaware that they were accessories to a usurpation of which they may not have approved. Without realizing this, southern dissidents took the northerners' commitment to King Richard on trust. Richard, in short, was a supreme propagandist and manipulator of public opinion with the field all to himself. He determined events not just by his actions, not just by his principal public statements, but by his calculated smears and manipulation of information. He was already, to quote Professor Ross, 'the first English king to use character-assassination as an instrument of policy'. His opponents may have denied the charges, those who knew the truth may have discounted them, though neither is recorded, but they could apparently neither erase the smears nor take the offensive themselves. The mud stuck.

Yet Richard's propaganda was not purely negative. We have already seen that he presented himself in a positive light – as martial, kingly and as loyal as possible – and how he presented himself as acting in the true interests of Edward V, identified himself 'as the only hope for the continuance of the good government of Edward IV' and sought for himself the same loyal service of Edward IV's retainers as they had shown to his brother. Dr Horrox indicates, however, that such ends were incompatible with his attack on the regime of his late brother to which such Yorkists had belonged and therefore that *Titulus Regius* – where the charges were made – must have been written later, in 1484. But Richard did not charge either Edward IV or his servants with the failures of the last regime. Its defects were not those of the king or of his servants as a whole but the responsibility of evil councillors, the Wydevilles, whose bad and indeed corrupt advice was at fault. Here Richard was exploiting a long-standing, well-tried and accepted convention that allowed for attacks on governments without touching the untouchable monarch himself. Whether all the late king's adherents recognized or approved the fine distinction we cannot tell.

The death of Lord Treasurer Essex shortly before Edward died, the dismissal of Lord Chancellor Rotherham and then the execution of Lord Chamberlain Hastings removed those ministers most closely identified with the outgoing regime. The charges alleged against the Wydevilles in their individual rather than public capacities – embezzlement, treason, sorcery and lechery – were too shockingly sinful to be condoned by anybody, even Edward IV's household or administration. Nobody could tolerate sorcery. Even Bishop Russell, who as keeper of the privy seal had been Edward IV's third great minister of state, bitterly denounced the Wydevilles in his parliamentary sermon. Dominic Mancini and Crowland could not condone Edward IV's sexual vices. And Richard's propagandist emphasis on such matters shows that he believed such prurience to be general among the political nation and the public at large. While distancing himself from the Wydevilles and his brother's late regime, Richard convicted the former of bad government while acquitting Edward, and identified them with conduct that all good Christians, including his brother's servants, must find unacceptable. His confiscation of Wydeville property and persecution of their closest associates while relying simultaneously on the rest of the Yorkist establishment illustrates his concern to isolate the queen's family from the other loyal supporters of Edward V. Whether he actually succeeded, as he hoped, or whether Edward IV's servants accepted the validity of his criticisms of the Wydevilles is not clear.

Naturally Richard used his flair for public relations to make his case as convincing as possible. His own arguments had to be presented clearly and substantiated, if necessary with fabricated evidence, but that was perhaps less important than to package himself attractively and to pander to ideas as popular as loyalty, service, military prowess and patriotism. His opponents' arguments were countered not by reasoned debate but by force and were discredited along with their authors. Such arguments could be defeated by making their propagators notorious and such notoriety could be better achieved by slander and innuendo than by legal process. To maximize his case, the very landscape could be altered, so that the political system of Edward IV's last days was reinterpreted and propagated for public consumption. And this propaganda was believed not just by innocent newcomers like Mancini but by old hands like Crowland, who unconsciously assimilated it for our consumption today.

Our history of April-June 1483 is very much Richard's creation, and knowing that, as his contemporaries did not, we cannot accept the contemporary verdict.

The verdict of history

For four centuries the verdict of history was that Richard was intent on usurping the throne throughout these three months. That was what he did, after all. Yet, as we have seen, Richard himself was able to put forward a good case, and one that seems to have enjoyed widespread approval at the time. He has also been revealed as a skilful propagandist, manipulator of opinion and manager of others, who promoted his own case and systematically denigrated that of his opponent. These characteristics apply both before and after his bid for the throne. The fact that he was a propagandist does not prove his guilt, for a propagandist may believe his own propaganda or employ it in a good cause, even when, as here, much of it is untrue. He used methods and arguments first for his protectorate, then to prove his title as king, but this does not mean that usurpation was always his aim. It was merely thrifty. Propaganda is the means to various ends and need not discredit the end itself. But we must be cautious in accepting the propagandist's version of the facts. Our cross-examination has enabled us to identify some elements of Richard's propaganda and to correct his version of events. We may reasonably ask what purpose that propaganda served.

What did Richard achieve in 1483? He became king, of course, but that was the work of the 20-26 June. Before that stage and before revealing that intention, what had he achieved? He had secured power as protector, but only temporarily. He had destroyed both the leading factions of Edward IV's court, the Wydevilles and Lord Hastings, and had cemented his victory in each case by executing the leaders. We know now that he had no prior quarrel with the Wydevilles. That recognition rebuts the kernel of the defence case: that Richard was driven to strike them down in self-defence. Why did he destroy them? 'It seems that Richard was set on becoming protector', says Professor Pollard, 'and would accept no compromise'. But what was the protectorate *in itself*? Was it by itself sufficient incentive or justification enough for what Richard did? To argue that he was prepared to shed the blood of Rivers, Vaughan, and Grey and to inflame the lifelong vengeance of the Wydevilles merely in order to hold the protectorate for six weeks hardly seems credible. It was too high a price to pay. Once protector, what was it he hoped to gain by executing them? Surely he had objectives larger than six weeks rule and stretching further into the future? Similarly Richard had no prior quarrel with Hastings. Hastings was overjoyed at his protectorate. Why did he kill him? There is no independent evidence to suggest that Hastings was plotting against Richard, but there are actions, all commentators agree, that Hastings could not approve. Are we not entitled to suggest that their destruction and deaths were Richard's objectives in picking quarrels with them? And may we not wonder why this was so? What did Richard want that demanded the destruction of both principal factions first?

Initially Richard claimed to be taking power for the good of his nephew. The Wydevilles were an obstacle to this – though not before his first coup – but Hastings was not. Richard wanted to execute Rivers and Grey in early May and did so on 25 June. There is a consistency of intention here that stretches from April to June and a determination to destroy both factions which suggests consistency of motive. Evidently Richard intended to destroy both factions as obstacles to his accession from at least April. But he proceeded to extremes, by executing Rivers and Grey, only when he knew his accession was assured and that he could not be called to

The remains of the brass to Sir Thomas Vaughan, chamberlain to Edward V, at Westminster Abbey. Along with Rivers and Grey, he was executed by the Earl of Northumberland at Pontefract Castle.

account. Before then, he did not have their blood on his hands and did not have to answer for their deaths.

The executions themselves were the work of the Earl of Northumberland and Lord Neville. To execute the brother and uncle of a king risked future retribution and was an act carried out only if immunity was guaranteed. It follows that Northumberland and Neville knew that Richard would become king. It was not a large risk, for that self-same day he deposed his nephew, but that was in London and the executions were in Pontefract. The two lords must have had advance warning of the usurpation. How could they have been told and how could Richard have been sure of their agreement? Surely not by letter, still less by credence. They needed more authority and certainty of immunity than that. Richard must have been certain that they would carry out his wishes. And since they were not together after his march south, he must have told them that usurpation was his object before setting off from the North. They took their oaths of fealty to Edward V intending perjury.

It is striking that it was these two men who were named as commanders of a northern army that included the men of Hull and York and no doubt the rest of the northern peerage and Richard's northern affinity. It was these two whom Richard particularly trusted and they were his confidants. Here is further evidence that Richard planned the usurpation from the start.

It would have been fatal for Richard's true intentions to leak out. They did not and he managed to scotch such rumours as they arose. He was a master dissimulator, who kept his options open and could have recoiled from usurpation at any time. Few, indeed, can have known his intentions at the time: Northumberland and Neville; perhaps Sir Richard Ratcliffe, sent as credence to Lord Neville and to York; William Catesby, if we accept More's story that he sounded out Hastings; Buckingham, of course; and perhaps Lord Howard. His instruments, such as those who arrested the Wydevilles and Hastings, need not have known the whole plan. But obviously not Hastings, nor Chancellor Russell, who penned a sermon for the opening of Edward V's parliament. Each event was carefully prepared to avoid the use of force or the charge of illegality. He preserved the appearance of consensus, accepted rebuffs and sought to persuade rather than coerce. Opinion was manipulated not just overtly but surreptitiously, so that Richard's own slanders and versions of events became generally accepted. He sought to carry with him not just the nobility and the council but also public opinion. It was by consent that he became first protector and then king. His accession was carefully regularized by formal election, enthronement, fealty and coronation to maximize the element of consent. He was not made king by a faction.

Three months of scheming demonstrate that Richard wanted to become king. Ambition and lust for power were the motives imputed to him by Mancini. We can no longer believe that his hatred or fear of the Wydevilles forced him to take power, both because he had invented their enmity and because he had destroyed them. Yet he could still have been driven to take the crown. He might have argued that he was driven to it by the threat to his position posed by the death on 4 May of George Neville, which he may have foreseen. On Neville's death, the right of inheritance to the Neville estates on which Richard had based his power was transferred from his son to Richard Lord Latimer. With the reversion in other hands, Richard could expect his authority as life-tenant to diminish. While Edward V was a minor, Richard could expect no grants in compensation, even if comparable properties became available, nor could he argue the re-partition of the Warwick Inheritance. Indeed, it was a Wydeville – Dorset – who had the custody of the co-heir, Clarence's son Warwick, and intended him as husband for his daughter. Such a re-partition would be against her interests and Richard could expect the united opposition of the Wydevilles to any such proposal. The Wydevilles thus blocked Richard's best route to the future and he needed to destroy them to consolidate his position. Perhaps his acquisition of Warwick's custody by mid-June aimed as much to safeguard his rights to the Warwick Inheritance as to neutralize a potential rival for the crown? But a new partition was impossible with a king and rival co-heir who were both minors. Hence he took the crown himself.

It is an attractive theory but it lacks contemporary support. No chronicler mentions it. The date of 4 May falls inconveniently after the first coup. It is easier to believe that it was an incidental disaster and a supplementary spur, increasing the risks if Richard drew back from the brink, rather than his main motivation in April to June 1483. Richard's usurpation was planned as early as April. He lacked a title acceptable to contemporary conventions and deposed a king for whom there was universal support. He seized the crown not from principle and concern for common weal, but for his own personal advantage. He may well have believed his own propaganda that he was the man best suited to rule, for we must not underestimate his capacity for self-deception. He was indeed the dissimulator, manipulator and propagandist presented by More and Shakespeare. Crowland and other contemporaries, who lived through events and initially took Richard at his own estimation, were right to re-assess these three months as the fulfilment of a preconceived plan. The ***verdict of history*** cannot correspond either to earlier ***contemporary verdicts*** or the ***case for the defence***. It is the ***case for the prosecution*** that must stand.

4 Richard III and Buckingham's Rebellion

One-nation kingship

We cannot now be certain how far Richard succeeded in persuading those who supported him as Lord Protector also to back him as king. It is credible that his accession initially enjoyed widespread support. It is also possible that it depended ultimately on the committed backing of his own faction. Events moved too quickly for us to be sure. But Richard did not rely purely on his popularity or indeed leave anything to chance. We have already seen how from April on he constantly presented himself in the right light, explained his actions publicly and mouthed loyal sentiments, thus identifying himself with his nephew Edward V and cutting the ground from under his opponents. In his capacity as Lord Protector he secured the support of the royal council, the citizens of London and York, and of the subjects in general and retainers in particular of Edward IV and his son Edward V. Richard took over distribution of Edward V's patronage, which he used to advance, reward and strengthen his principal allies – notably Buckingham and Howard – and thus prepare the way for his own accession. The queen and her kin were induced to put themselves hopelessly in the wrong by resisting Richard's first coup and were then discredited by a smear campaign. The Wydeville fleet was suborned. First Rivers and Grey, then Hastings, Morton and Rotherham were removed by force. With their leaders removed, their assets stripped, with Richard in control of both king and government and backed by public opinion, it is hardly surprising that Queen Elizabeth in sanctuary and her son Dorset in flight were unable to orchestrate effective resistance in May and June.

Following his first coup, Richard dismissed Edward V's household, presumably because they were too closely associated with the Wydevilles, but he indulged in no further purges until the autumn and most of Edward IV's servants seem to have passed via Edward V's service to that of Richard without interruption. Given that Richard was simultaneously a member and head adult of the house of York, right-hand man of Edward IV's Yorkist affinity, protector and defender of Edward V and legally head of his government, it is hardly surprising that his authority was accepted and that Richard felt able to employ royal servants as freely as his brother had done. Richard represented continuity. Inevitably there were some vacancies to be filled and naturally Richard introduced his own men, some of them northerners, but there was no wholesale turnover in personnel. Understandably, he also turned to his own men for the performance of delicate and controversial duties demanding unambiguous commitment. As Lord Protector, he had the authority to demand military support from the noblemen and towns of southern England to confront the so-called Wydeville/ Hastings plot in mid-June, but he did not do so. He applied instead to the Earl of Northumberland and Lord Neville, to York and Hull, clearly selecting them specifically because of the ties of obligation that bound them to him as Lord of the North. So, too, it was as a lifelong friend loyal beyond the grave that Richard turned to Viscount Lovell, who took the place in Richard's household that Hastings had held in Edward IV's, becoming Lord Chamberlain, chief butler of England, and a knight of the Garter. Edward Grey of Groby, Lord Lisle, the in-law and enemy of the queen, erstwhile retainer of the Kingmaker and Clarence, ally of Richard over the Warwick Inheritance, waited on Richard after Hastings' fall and was rewarded with his viscountcy and portions of Clarence's lands to which he had claim. Bishops Shirwood of Durham, Langton of St Davids and Salisbury, and Redman of Carlisle, Lord Stanley and his son Lord Strange, Lord FitzHugh, Lord Scrope, and Lord Greystoke were all northerners whom Richard included in his escorts.

At a lower level, it was the Warwick retainer William Catesby who supposedly sounded out Hastings, the northerners Sir Robert Harrington and Sir Charles Pilkington who helped arrest him, Sir James Tyrell who had taken custody of Archbishop Rotherham, Sir Richard Ratcliffe who liaised with his northern supporters, and John Kendall, Richard's secretary as duke, who replaced the unreliable Oliver King to become Richard's secretary as king. A sprinkling of other northerners – Huddleston, Tunstalls, Franke and Nesfield – entered Richard's household in the first months of his reign. Several of these gradually came to the fore. Catesby was head of a prominent family of Warwick retainers and distinguished lawyers and had a successful legal practice before entering royal administration. Richard came to employ him as a councillor, steward of the earldom of March, chancellor of the Exchequer, speaker of the House of Commons, and ultimately gave him land worth £323 a year. He valued Ratcliffe so highly that he gave him sufficient lands to qualify for an earldom; he may have been Richard's right-hand man in County Durham and was certainly commissioned to treat with the Scots at Lochmaben in 1484, but he seems to have been employed principally on council and at court. Tyrell's repeated employment in missions of trust before and after 1483 is consistent with his alleged murder of the princes. He became master of the horse and the henchmen, chamberlain of the Exchequer, and was administratively and militarily responsible for the castle of Guines by Calais, Cardiff and Glamorgan, and the Duchy of Cornwall. Somehow Tyrell escaped the unpopularity of Ratcliffe and Catesby, transferring to the service of Henry VII and becoming his councillor. Such men – and northerners in general – became increasingly prominent as the reign progressed. But Richard could not have become or remained king without the support of noblemen from other parts of England.

The most important of Richard's new allies was Henry Stafford, Duke of Buckingham, who played a key role in each of his *coups d'état* and his usurpation. Buckingham was a younger man than Richard and very much less experienced. He was actually Richard's cousin several times over, for like him he was descended through two lines from Edward III and had been married as a boy to the queen's

Detail of the memorial brass to Sir William Catesby, who was Speaker of the House of Commons under Richard III and was executed after the Battle of Bosworth Field. Ashby St Ledgers church, Northants.

sister Katherine Wydeville. His marriage to such a social inferior, Mancini alleged, was behind his alliance against the Wydevilles in 1483. However that may be, Buckingham was certainly proud of his lineage. Such pride prompted him to adopt the arms of his grandfather Thomas of Woodstock, Edward III's youngest son, and had brought down Edward IV's wrath upon him. Buckingham's estates matched Richard's and had been assembled by successive inheritances like those of Richard Duke of York and Warwick the Kingmaker. Birth, rank, fortune and the declaration of his majority at the early age of sixteen all presaged a brilliant career, but this had not materialized. Admittedly Edward IV had acted as godfather for his eldest son, whom he named Edward, and had appointed the duke as High Steward of England to pronounce the death penalty on Clarence in 1478, but he had done no more and had failed to concede either the national or the local authority that Buckingham evidently considered his due. The Wydevilles had established their sphere of influence in Wales, where Buckingham's great marcher lordship of Brecon lay, and saw no role for him (or Huntingdon) in their plans or even allowed him a place on their Council of Wales. He was also excluded from local office in his home county of Staffordshire. Given the duke's formidable resources and authority, it was unwise to thwart his legitimate aspirations in this way, but such exclusion seemed destined to be his fate indefinitely if his Wydeville in-laws maintained their ascendancy over Edward V and hence over Wales. We cannot know whether it was these grievances that prompted Buckingham to support Richard against his own relatives by marriage and in his bid for the crown, but it is clear that what he wanted most was to dominate Wales himself and to cut a figure on the national stage.

These were legitimate aspirations which Richard could satisfy. Early in Richard's protectorate Buckingham received wholesale and hitherto unparalleled grants of office in Wales that grew into his appointment as chief justice and chamberlain of both north and south Wales, steward of all the royal lordships, constable of fifty-three castles, and military commander of the adjoining shires. He alone had replaced the whole Council of Wales. Buckingham succeeded Richard himself as constable of England – a grandiose honorary office to which he had a hereditary claim – and was the new king's most important supporter and most trusted adviser. And he petitioned to inherit the house of Lancaster's share of the Bohun inheritance, which comprised great estates in eastern England and would make him incomparably the greatest of the Yorkist nobility at the price of seriously dismembering the king's own duchy of Lancaster. Richard conceded even that. However his signed warrant of 27 August 1483, issued at either Nottingham or Pontefract, was never presented by Buckingham to the duchy chancellor for implementation.

John Howard and his son Thomas were both older than Buckingham, from a lower level of society and had earned royal favour by arduous and valuable service. John had thus secured a peerage in Edward IV's first reign and important royal offices, and his son had a place at court. Like Buckingham, however, the Howards found that their legitimate aspirations carried less weight than those of the king's immediate family. The Howards' kinsmen had included the Mowbray dukes of Norfolk and earls of Surrey, the last of whom died in 1476, leaving only his infant daughter Anne between John Howard and a half-share of the Mowbray inheritance. Anne's marriage in 1478 to Edward's four-year-old younger son Richard, henceforth Duke of York and Norfolk, had provided for him at no cost to the king. Anne, however, died in 1481 and Howard should have succeeded. Instead young Richard's title was confirmed by Edward's last parliament and clearly both Edward V and his Wydeville-dominated government would maintain him in possession. The Howards' contacts with Richard III went back at least to 1472 and perhaps to 1469. Thomas helped overpower Lord Hastings in John's presence. John escorted young Richard from sanctuary to the Tower and presided as steward of England over Richard III's coronation. In return John received his half of the Mowbray inheritance, was created Duke of Norfolk, Earl Marshal and Admiral of England, and Thomas became Earl of Surrey.

Richard's sister Elizabeth had married John de la Pole, Duke of Suffolk, the only

The competitors for the Mowbray inheritance.
Right: John Howard, Duke of Norfolk, in a stained-glass portarait once at Tendring Hall, Suffolk.
Below: The skull of Lady Anne Mowbray, child bride of Richard, Duke of York, from her remains excavated at the Minories, Stepney, in 1964. (The hair remains in an extraordinary state of preservation and, when cleaned, was found to be a red-gold 'Titian' colour.)

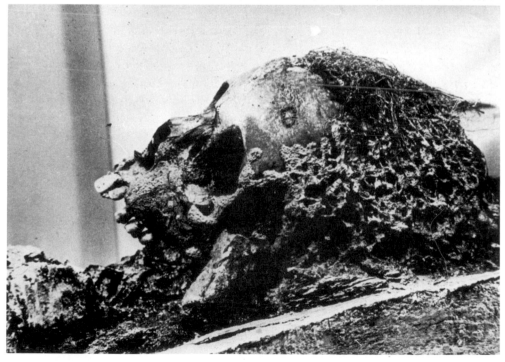

Thomas Howard, created Earl of Surrey by Richard III and later the 2nd Duke of Norfolk, in an engraving of a lost brass formerly at Lambeth.

Effigies of John de la Pole and his wife Elizabeth, Richard III's sister, at Wingfield church, Suffolk.

other English duke, who had found – like Buckingham – that his kinship to Edward IV paid few dividends, perhaps because he was a nonentity. Richard at first promised more, as Suffolk featured prominently in his accession ceremonies, but it was to be Suffolk's son and namesake John Earl of Lincoln – Richard's eldest nephew – who proved more valuable, accompanying him on his progresses and deputizing for him in the North. Another malcontent, whose legitimate interests had been overrun by the Wydevilles, was the Welshman William Herbert of Raglan. His father had ruled Wales in the 1460s on the king's behalf but Herbert himself had been forced to give up his county and earldom of Pembroke in 1479 to the future Edward V in return for a few manors in Somerset and the title of Earl of Huntingdon. This again was the work of Wydeville in-laws and the destruction of the Wydeville rule in Wales was to his advantage. Initially Buckingham took priority but following his fall it was Huntingdon who became the king's chief agent in south Wales and whose loyalty was to be cemented by marriage to Richard's bastard daughter Katherine. Nor were Buckingham, Howard, Suffolk and Huntingdon the only losers under the previous regime. Northumberland, Berkeley, Neville and Abergavenny all wanted wrongs righted and yet others hoped to benefit from the redistribution of royal patronage. There were plenty of people disgruntled with the former regime available for Richard to win over.

Such men provided Richard with the substantial aristocratic support that he needed in the royal council and to control Wales and East Anglia, where he himself was relatively weak and could not concentrate his resources. He retained his personal grip on the North. Those committed to him by loyalty and self-interest constituted a minority of the peerage. Edward V's projected parliament and coronation and Richard's own coronation were occasions when the backwoodsmen turned out in force and their neutrality or hostility could have been decisive. The fact that Richard acceded peacefully was largely due to his military superiority.

The force with which Edward V left Ludlow was dismissed at Stony Stratford and Hastings's supposed conspiracy enabled Richard to restrict the retinues of peers coming to parliament and to the coronation. Richard and Buckingham brought only 500 men to London, but enlarged their retinues by the middle of June. Even so, it was not these retainers who ensured his dominance, but the enthusiasm of the populace, whom he so assiduously wooed to pressurize council and corporation and skilfully restrained. Such popularity, however, was uncertain and needed direction and control. The numerical advantage of his own retainers became overwhelming when account was taken of the northern army summoned on 10-11 June, whose existence and approach was made known by Saturday 21 June. The army was estimated to be up to 10,000 strong and was presumed to be committed to Richard. The advent of the northern army meant that those in London acquiesced – willingly or otherwise – to Richard's actions. Thus far, however, the threat was potential rather than real. The army was actually still at Pontefract on 25 June and may have numbered 4,000 men or less. Once Richard's accession had been effected, the northerners' political support for him was again reinforced by their duty of

A panorama of London, with the Yorkist residence, Baynard's Castle, in the foreground. An Elizabethan engraving by Claus Visscher.

allegiance and the army proceeded to London, arriving on 1 July. Richard ensured that his military superiority was realized by summoning the mayor, aldermen and liverymen to his inspection of the army at Moorfields on 3 July. No wonder that the coronation went off peacefully three days later.

If his succession was to endure, however, Richard had to make himself king of the whole nation like his brother Edward IV. Although his own retainers and those of his allies were powerful, they were inevitably outnumbered by those lacking such personal connections. For future stability and security Richard had to be accepted as king even by those who were neither his natural adherents nor bound to him by mutual self-interest. Acquiescence at his accession was not the same as conviction or commitment, which could not be taken for granted. Richard appreciated this. Far from assuming continuity of his brother's regime and loyalty of Edward's servants, he seems to have worked very hard in his early months to persuade his people – especially the Yorkist establishment – that his kingship was legitimate. Deposition of one monarch and his replacement by another could never be entirely legal, but there were precedents that he followed. *Titulus Regius* set out a title that disqualified all alternative candidates. As in 1399 and 1461, it was an assembly of three estates which resembled parliament that duly elected him as God's lieutenant:

> Our Lord God, King of Kings, by whose infinite goodness and eternal providence all things are principally governed in this world, lighten your soul and grant you grace to do, as well in this matter as in all other, all that may be according to his will and pleasure, and to the common and public weal of this land; so that, after great clouds, troubles, storms and tempests, the Sun of justice and of grace may shine upon us, to the comfort and gladness of all true Englishmen.

Great care was taken to see that Richard's coronation and anointing with holy oil by the Archbishop of Canterbury in Westminster Abbey conformed to normal practice and that it was fully recorded. Those present were not confined to members of Richard's own retinue or faction but were drawn from a broad cross-section of the English nobility and gentry. As Dr Horrox has observed, 'it was a Yorkist occasion, not the celebration of a factional triumph'. Those present acclaimed him as king and the peerage rendered him their oaths of fealty:

> I become true and faithful liegeman unto my sovereign lord King Richard III by the grace of God king of England etc and to his heirs kings of England and to him and them my faith and trouth shall bear during my natural life, and with him and in his cause and quarrel at all times shall take his part and be ready to live and die against all earthly creatures and utterly endeavour me to the resistance and suppression of his enemies, rebels and traitors if I shall know any to the uttermost of my power, and no thing court that in any wise may be hurting to his noble and royal person.

Any with unquiet consciences, like the Calais garrison, because of their earlier oaths to Edward V, were told that their earlier oaths were invalid because they were 'then ignorant of the very sure and true title of our said sovereign lord that now is Richard III has and had since the same time to the crown of England'. *Titulus Regius*, of which a copy was sent to Calais, clarified the position. Whatever private doubts may have been expressed, Richard was king and God's lieutenant, and was entitled to the allegiance of everybody – all, directly or indirectly, had accepted him as king. Such ties reinforced those already due to him as their particular lord. Both *The Rows Roll* and *The Salisbury Roll* proudly depicted him in his coronation robes. No such York Roll survives, but Richard had now succeeded Edward IV as legitimate head of the house of York and leader of the Yorkist affinity.

We have seen how Richard courted approval and popularity in London and Westminster in May and June. Initially this had been in his capacity as his nephew's protector; later, however, it was on his own behalf. Mancini reports that Richard abandoned the mourning-clothes he had worn since his brother's death, and

Richard III's Charter of Incorporation to the City of Gloucester, granted in 1483. It bears a unique variant of his Royal Arms with its white lion and boar supporters and its royal shield set within the rays of the 'sun of York'.

donned purple: he often rode through London with a thousand attendants, appearing in public to seek attention and applause, and entertained large numbers of people to dinner. His popularity was also reinforced by the ceremonial and celebrations leading up to the coronation, in which Londoners and their visitors were made to participate. He made a prolonged progress through the Midlands to the North in the months following his coronation – his motive was to secure his acceptance and win popularity elsewhere. Escorted continually by noblemen and bishops, he proceeded to Windsor, Reading, Oxford, Woodstock, Tewkesbury, Gloucester, Warwick, Coventry, Leicester, Nottingham, Pontefract, York, Gainsborough and Lincoln. At Lincoln his progress was interrupted by Buckingham's rebellion in October-November 1483. Further visits – to Canterbury, for example – came later. There is no reason to doubt the statement of his secretary John Kendall that 'all their progress has been worshipfully received with pageants and other', but we generally have only glimpses of them. At Oxford he attended lengthy speeches and disputations for two days; at Gloucester, whence he had taken his ducal title, and at Pontefract he granted the towns new charters creating councils of mayors and aldermen. So, too, in 1485, when he spent Whitsun (22 May) at Kenilworth Castle in Warwickshire, Corpus Christi (2 June) at nearby Coventry for the play, and then proceeded via Maxstoke to Nottingham, where he stayed until he departed on his fatal campaign. If Richard showed himself and courted popularity, it was primarily in the Midlands and the North.

Centres of the Warwick Inheritance, where Richard could count on loyalty to

Tewkesbury Abbey (left) with (right) a circle of Yorkist suns on the choir roof to commemorate the Yorkist victory at Tewkesbury in 1471.

himself and his queen, featured prominently on his tour. At Tewkesbury Abbey, for example, he made up the £310 still due for the completion of his brother Clarence's tomb. He arrived at Warwick, so Rows records, accompanied by four bishops, the Scottish Duke of Albany and a Spanish embassy, four earls, Lovell his chamberlain, and five barons. The northerners were joined by such local notables as the bishops of Worcester and Coventry, Lords Lisle and Dudley. The presence of Clarence's son Edward, Earl of Warwick, and the arrival from Windsor of Richard's queen, Anne Neville, enabled Richard to pose as heir of the earls of Warwick. His visit may have been the occasion for the preparation of the *Beauchamp Pageant* and the Latin version of *The Rows Roll* and was recorded by Rows both in his English roll and later in his *History of the Kings of Britain*. Richard and Anne were depicted in his sequence of earls and countesses of Warwick as king and queen in their coronation robes. Rows's description of Anne was particularly extravagant:

> The most noble lady and princess, born of the royal blood of divers realms, lineally descended from princes, kings, emperors, and many glorious saints, Dame Anne, by the great provision of God Queen of England and of France and Lady of Ireland, wife first to Prince Edward son and heir of King Henry VI and after his death marvellously conveyed by all the corners and parts of the whole of fortune and eftsone exalted again higher than ever she was to the

145

Queen Anne, King Richard III and their son, Edward, Prince of Wales, drawn from the English version of the Rows Roll.

most high throne & honour over all other ladies of this noble realm anointed and crowned Queen of England wife of the most victorious prince King Richard III.

The next description was of Richard himself:

The most mighty prince Richard by the grace of God King of England and of France and Lord of Ireland by true matrimony without discontinuance or any defiling in the law by heir male lineally descending from King Henry II.

Note Rows' explicit reference to Richard's legitimacy that contrasts implicitly with that of his brother Edward IV, his nephews the Princes, the Tudors and Beauforts, and with the attainder that debarred Clarence's son Warwick. Yet Richard is described much more briefly than Anne, because he is included primarily as her consort, only secondly as descendant of Henry II, grandfather-in-law of Thomas Earl of Warwick (who died in 1262) – a somewhat esoteric observation – and only thirdly as king. It was as king, however, that Richard committed himself to the 'great cost of building' in the castle and granted the townsfolk great privileges. These privileges had allegedly

Warwick Castle in an engraving by S.R.N. Buck.

been granted to them by William the Conqueror but without documentary proof, had been sought unsuccessfully by Clarence and were now granted by Richard at Anne's instance 'of his bounteous grace without fee or fine freely by charter'. Hence his status with Rows 'as special good lord to the town & lordship of Warwick'.

Richard stayed for a week at Warwick, but it was his visit to Yorkshire that was the high point of his tour. He prepared for his arrival by summoning seventy gentry to meet him at Pontefract, which he created a borough and where he endowed the priory, and arranging for an impressive escort to York itself, which was intended to be the culmination of his progress. He stayed there for three weeks from 29 August. York may have been the second city in the kingdom and was certainly the greatest in the North, the one that Richard had most assiduously cultivated as duke, and where he could expect the most enthusiastic reception. His son Prince Edward joined him from Middleham for his formal entry, when Richard, the queen, five bishops, three earls, Lovell, and five other lords were met by the corporation in solemn procession outside the walls and then entered York Minster, where a grand service of welcome featured the Te Deum. Among the ensuing celebrations were two banquets given by the mayor and a performance of the Creed play. The highpoint was on the Nativity of the Blessed Virgin Mary (8 September), when a splendid service in York Minster was followed by the creation of Richard's son as Prince of Wales and a feast in the archbishop's palace, after which king, queen, and prince 'sat crowned for four hours' – a ceremony so grand that Crowland described it as a second coronation. Richard had given the minster 'silver and gilt figures of the twelve Apostles and many other relics'; he had declared his intention of founding a college of a hundred priests at the Minster, overshadowing any of its other ancillary foundations; without being asked he reduced the city's feefarm; and his largesse also embraced other northern churches, towns and individuals.

As Crowland states, Richard was obviously anxious to exhibit his 'superior royal rank' where he was strong and thus to reinforce his power base there. The 'splendid and highly expensive feasts and entertainments' that he arranged were undoubtedly

Micklegate Bar, York, a symbol of the city's medieval strength.

intended 'to attract to himself the affection of many people'. His son's elevation emphasized a secure succession and the fact that Richard's line had come to stay. The Church consecrated his title. The whole visit stressed both the northern character of the dynasty for northern consumption and Richard's popularity and power in the region for southern consumption. All this was quite deliberate. Richard's secretary John Kendall wrote in advance to the York corporation:

> To advise you, as honourably as your worships can imagine to receive him and the queen at their coming [and] dispose you to do both pageants and such speeches as can goodly (this short warning considered) be devised and under such form as Master Lancaster of the

king's council, this messenger, shall somewhat advertise you of my mind in this behalf: as in hanging the streets through which the king's grace will come with cloths of arras, tapistry-work, and other, *for there are coming many southern lords and men of worship with them, which will mark greatly your receiving of their graces ...*

These southerners, whom Richard wanted to impress with his northern popularity, must have consisted principally of the members of his household, unmentioned but present throughout the progress, who had been for the most part members of his brother's household and hailed principally from southern England. No doubt it was also for this reason that Richard had no less than 13,000 of his white boar badges made in advance of his visit. All northerners must have appeared to be Richard's men. Kendall's letter to York corporation continues with firm incentives for the city to support Richard:

Forsomuch as I verily know the king's mind and entire affection that his grace bears towards you and your worshipful city for manifold your kind and loving behaviour to his grace heretofore, which his grace will never forget and intends therefore so to do unto you that all the kings that ever reigned upon you did never so much. Doubt not hereof and make any kind of petition for anything you want granted by his highness.

No doubt the other visits were equally carefully orchestrated to impress those who were not automatically committed to Richard and to persuade them to accept him as king. The people were certainly given many incentives, for his progress was littered with charters and other privileges, such as the disafforestation of parts of Wychwood, gifts of land, church-plate and vestments to religious houses and cathedrals and other marks of royal favour. To make little Scarborough into a new county and to found a chantry college on such a scale were grand gestures indeed. It is striking that Richard's progress was not directed through disaffected areas, as was normally the pattern, but through the places where he was strongest: Gloucester, whence he took his ducal title, the heartland of the Warwick Inheritance and the North. Moreover, most of the recipients of this largesse – such as Tewkesbury and Coverham abbeys and Wilberfosse nunnery – had enjoyed his patronage before. Pre-existing loyalties were rewarded and reinforced. The less committed were to be impressed by the example of Richard's own adherents.

But Richard relied for his acceptance and popularity on more than splendid ceremonies, promises and mutual self-interest. He also set out to right the supposed wrongs of the previous regime. He was determined to avoid the charge of avarice levelled against his brother. At London, Gloucester, Worcester and Canterbury, he 'declined with thanks' the gifts of money that were proffered, 'affirming that he would rather have their love than their treasure'. 'All avarice [was] laid aside,' observed Rows, and indeed he had the forced gifts or benevolences of his brother abolished, denouncing them in his own authentic voice as 'new and unlawful inventions and inordinate covetousness against the law of the realm' and attributing to them the 'utter destruction' of his 'subjects and commons':

> For divers and many worshipful men of this realm, by occasion thereof, were compelled of necessity to break up their households, and to live in great penury and wretchedness, their debts unpaid, and their children unpreferred, and such memorials as they had ordained for the good of their souls were cancelled and annulled, to the great displeasure of God and the destruction of this realm.

'And God Save King Richard!', responded the Pewterers' Company of London in its records.

Richard invited complaints against wrongs committed by the previous regime, receiving numerous petitions from those with grievances against the Wydeville-dominated council of Wales and especially the oppressions of Lord Richard Grey. His disafforestation of parts of Wychwood subjected to forest law by Edward IV fits in with Bishop Russell's denunciation of enclosures and imparking and the concern of John Rows about depopulation and deserted villages. In his concern for trade he insisted that the Prior of Christ Church Canterbury must import his Bordeaux wine in an English ship. *Titulus Regius*'s charges of immorality against Edward and his regime were followed by the public penance imposed on Elizabeth Shore as a common harlot, by further denunciations of the Marquis of Dorset, and by his instructions to his bishops that 'virtue and cleanness of living to be advanced, increased, and multiplied, and vices and all other things repugnant to virtue repressed and annulled'. As a Christian prince, it was appropriate that he should concern himself with the moral health of his subjects.

Richard also projected a positive image of himself from the start as the model of kingship. He frequently spoke of the good of the commonwealth. The essence of mixed monarchy contained in a king's coronation oaths had been hitherto obscured because they were in Latin. Richard, however, chose to swear them in English, which he and his subjects could understand, and kept them in mind as he ruled, referring to them repeatedly in his public utterances and deliberately presenting his actions in these terms. He wanted his people's good 'above all things earthly'.

'You shall keep after your strength and power to the Church of God and the people whole peace and godly concord,' enjoined Cardinal Bourchier. 'I shall keep,' responded Richard. There can be no doubt that Richard feared purgatory and hated heathens. He told a Hungarian visitor that he wished he could go on a crusade. He opposed sexual immorality. He was literate, apparently well-read and interested in learning – sitting through a disputation at Magdalen College, Oxford – and he promoted learned clergy, particularly Cambridge graduates. He was a generous patron of the Church. Besides his foundations at Middleham, Barnard Castle and York Minster, and lesser donations elsewhere, he added major benefactions at Barking and at Windsor. He had already assisted his brother's reconstruction of St

George's Chapel and now he assisted it even more by transferring from Chertsey Abbey the supposedly uncorrupted body of Henry VI, thus making the shrine more accessible to pilgrims and simultaneously adding a potent source of income to the building fund. His foundations were credited to him even by his enemies. No wonder convocation – the Church's parliament – praised him for 'his most noble and blessed disposition'.

'You shall make to be done after your strength and power equal and rightful justice in all your dooms and judgements and discretion with mercy and trouth,' enjoined Cardinal Bourchier. 'I shall do,' Richard replied. Later he recalled 'his solemn profession which he made at his coronation to mercy and justice'. He mentioned 'the administration of justice whereunto we be professed'. He proclaimed 'the love that he has for the administration and execution for the commonwealth of this realm' and his determination 'to see due administration of justice throughout this his realm'. 'For his grace is utterly determined [that] all his true subjects shall live in rest and quiet and peaceably enjoy their lands, livelihood and goods according to the laws of this land which they be naturally born to inherit.' *Titulus Regius* also refers to the law as the inheritance of all subjects. Richard consulted his judges about defects in the law and may have initiated some of the law reforms undertaken by his first parliament. He began on the first day of his reign, when he charged his judges to do justice without fear or favour. His lords were directed to 'see that their countries were well-guided and that no extortions were done to his subjects'. The oaths of office registered in his signet letter book all order justice regardless of rank and without fear or favour. He formalized embryonic arrangements for poor suitors, appointing a clerk to handle petitions for what was to become the court of requests. He did not simply delegate, but exercised his prerogative of mercy with discretion and made his initial itinerary into a judicial as well as a ceremonial progress. He himself reminded his subjects how 'his grace in his own person, as is well known, has addressed himself to divers parts of this his realm for the indifferent administration of justice to every person'. Eyewitnesses agreed. 'In his realm [Richard was] full commendably punishing offenders of his laws, especially extortioners and oppressors of his commons, and cherishing those that were virtuous,' observed Rows from Warwick. 'His lords and judges sat in every place,' Kendall wrote from Nottingham, 'determining the complaints of poor folks with due punishment of offenders against the laws'. 'For many a poor man that has suffered wrong many days has been relieved and helped by him and his commands in his progress,' added Bishop Langton from York.

Defence of the realm was a king's prime duty and failure in this area was a charge made by Richard against his late brother. Whenever possible he presented himself in a patriotic light, contrasting his own determination to repel external threats with the malice not just of foreign potentates but of the treacherous Englishmen who allied themselves with them. Obviously foreign recognition was one of any usurper's top priorities. While at Warwick Spanish ambassadors proposed a marriage alliance between a daughter of Ferdinand and Isabella and Prince Edward. The risk of war with France, initially perhaps increased by Richard's accession, quickly receded with

Louis XI of France, whose death in 1483 left Richard II considerably less at risk of war with France.

the death of Louis XI in August 1483 and the accession of his young son Charles VIII. Richard was negotiating with France while at York, where he received 'a courteous and wise letter' from the Scots who, however, were still besieging Dunbar. The international position improved rapidly and thus justified Rows' comment that Richard enjoyed 'great laud of the people of all the other lands about him'.

Certainly some saw Richard as the model prince that he aspired to be. He was portrayed as such by the visiting Italian humanist Pietro Carmeliano:

> If, in the first place, we consider religion, what prince is there in our time who is more religious? If justice, who do we think is to be preferred to him in the whole world? If we look for prudence in fostering peace and waging war, whom do we judge ever to be his equal? But if we regard wisdom and largeness and modesty of mind, behind whom shall we place our Richard? Indeed, what Christian emperor or prince can be found more liberal and munificent towards the well deserving? None, certainly, none. To whom are theft, rebellion, pollution, adultery,

manslaughter, usury, heresy, and other abominable crimes more hateful than to him? Obviously no one.

If it appears somewhat exaggerated, it was doubtless what Lord Chancellor Russell – to whom it was dedicated – wished to hear and was not inconsistent with his own praise for Richard in his sermons to parliament. Closer attention to Richard's actual conduct lies behind the praise of John Rows and Bishop Langton. 'By the which discreet guiding,' concluded Rows, 'he got great thanks of God and love of all his subjects, rich and poor.' 'He contents the people where he goes best that ever did prince,' remarked Bishop Langton. 'On my trouth I liked never the condition of any prince as well as his; God has sent him to us for the weal of us.' Already by September 1483 Richard seemed to have moved far on the road from factional leadership towards becoming king of the whole nation.

The revolt of the establishment

Richard's claims to be Edward V's loyal subject never enjoyed universal acceptance. The Wydevilles may have been uncertain even before his first coup of 1 May 1483 and certainly doubted him thereafter. Dorset and the queen continued their opposition, albeit in sanctuary or hiding, but few others were prepared to support what was presented as the selfish factional interests of the Wydevilles against the government of the young Edward V. Once Richard ceased to be Edward V's loyal subject and became instead his supplanter, the situation changed: inevitably some supporters of the protectorate opposed Richard as king. But there was no outcry. It was fear, so Mancini said, that explained Richard's unopposed election and coronation, and fear too that drove other Yorkists into sanctuary. The speed of events caught people by surprise and prevented any immediate resistance.

Once Richard's usurpation was complete, however, there must have been many apart from the chroniclers who thought it was all part of a preconceived plan. Mancini and his successors cannot have been alone in reinterpreting Richard's earlier actions and principled utterances as a hypocritical cloak for naked ambition and in recognizing his title to the crown as the mere means to that end. The revelation of the precontract was surprising to all, always disbelieved by some, and was soon to be widely rejected. At the very least it clearly failed to convince all those who strove to reinstate the princes or their sister Princess Elizabeth in and after 1483, and helped to make her queen. No chronicle, Tudor or otherwise, accepted the precontract story.

Even though Richard had promptly removed the princes from public view, Crowland reports a murmuring that summer on their behalf throughout southern England. There was a plot to liberate them from the Tower before the end of July 1483, only a month after Richard's accession and a few weeks after his coronation. A second plot aimed to remove their sisters to safety from sanctuary so that 'the kingdom might some day pass to the rightful heirs'. Neither required Richard's personal attendance, so his progress continued, though he, at least, was aware of dangerous disaffection in the South. He ordered his officers to put on trial and execute the princes' intended rescuers and to blockade Westminster Abbey to prevent the escape of the princesses. These commands are recorded but not those that he probably issued soon afterwards for the murder of the two princes themselves. However that may be, they never appeared alive again and by November – and probably well before – they were assumed to be dead. Such decisive action was ineffective. Opposition escalated into further uprisings (collectively called Buckingham's Rebellion) throughout southern England and the Welsh borders in October and November 1483. Those who rebelled at Bodmin on 3 November and had fled into exile in Brittany at Christmas, convinced that the princes were dead, committed themselves to another candidate in preference to Richard. It was only twenty months later, on 22 August 1485, that Richard was overthrown.

The first conspiracy against Richard was hatched within a month of his accession – this demonstrates the depth of hostility that his usurpation aroused. The extent of such opposition emerges from the roll-call of those involved in the much more serious rebellions in the autumn, who constituted the leading aristocracy and county governors in every shire from Kent to Oxfordshire and Cornwall. It was an insurrection of the whole Yorkist establishment of southern England. Thirty-three were JPs, three were sheriffs and a significant proportion were members of the royal household. The gravity of their decisions cannot be underestimated. Such men were the most unexpected of rebels. They had so much to lose. They risked not only their lives but their extensive properties and the well-being of their families and descendants. They were committing treason, the most serious of crimes, which carried with it dishonour and corruption of blood not only for themselves but for all their descendants, and was, moreover, a sin against God, carrying damnation as an eternal penalty. They were flying in the face of a lifelong duty of allegiance, generally reinforced by service in local government and often at court. If a handful were out of favour, the majority were assured of its continuance or even of future promotion: ten of the rebellious JPs had been appointed by Richard himself.

For men of such standing, for such comfortable and secure establishment figures to risk everything in rebellion, the impulse motivating them was strong indeed. It was decidedly not self-interest. Allegiance to the young Edward V can have been only part of it. For even when they learned that the princes were dead, that Buckingham was dead, that their rebellions had been quashed and they themselves were driven into exile, many of the rebels were not deterred, nor were they content to lay down their arms and make their peace with Richard. Instead they sought – and found – a rival claimant, whom they designated as husband for Edward IV's eldest daughter, Elizabeth of York. This candidate was Henry Tudor, whose claim through his living mother to John of Gaunt's Beaufort bastards was vestigial in the extreme, and his exile since boyhood meant that he was known to nobody. He had little to his credit but his obscurity and untarnished reputation. Such a choice bears the marks of desperation. To back his claim was tantamount to saying that anyone was to be preferred to Richard. It was more important to depose Richard than to choose a candidate to replace him. It is perhaps comprehensible that such a point of view was adopted by a handful of fanatics. But that it should be adopted by enough of these men of substance to make Henry king is astonishing testimony to their hostility to Richard, whose conduct was clearly felt to have put him beyond forgiveness or reconciliation. To these men the usurpation itself was treason, the most shameful and damnable of crimes, and Richard himself was a traitor, who was not entitled to their allegiance. That was still the position of the Yorkist establishment in 1485 when, as Shakespeare shrewdly appreciated, the Bosworth campaign was a successful re-run of Buckingham's Rebellion: erstwhile retainers of Edward IV and devoted subjects of Edward V made the Tudor Henry VII king over the dead body of the Yorkist Richard III. It is clear, therefore, that Richard had disastrously miscalculated. He had not appreciated how vast the gulf was between his role as Lord Protector and that of usurping king. He had wrongly assumed that those who had accepted his authority as protector would continue to do so after his accession. Instead many rejected him and were prepared to resist him by force.

Thus far all is clear. We have long known the names of most of the rebel leaders. Modern scholarship, particularly the work of Rosemary Horrox and Louise Gill, has thrown a flood of light on their backgrounds and earlier careers. Hence we understand much more than earlier historians about the nature, extent, and significance of the uprising. This compensates only to a limited degree for the enormous gaps in the knowledge that we can take for granted about other rebellions and revolutions. We have no contemporary statement by the rebels of their aims, as opposed to Richard's conventional assertion that they sought his death 'and the subversion of this realm and the commonweal of the same'. We have no reliable information how a coherent opposition was put together. No manifestos or placards survive, though we know they existed, and no clear idea of their plan, since the Kentishmen rose prematurely. We are dependent instead on later narratives, of which Crowland is the nearest and most reliable, and on the record of Richard's countermeasures, culminating in the act of attainder against the rebels of January/February 1484.

There seem to be two fixed points, in late July when the rebels first sought to restore the princes and at Christmas when their candidate was Henry Tudor. What happened between was confused and still confuses. Without recourse to any dates but giving an impression of a considerable lapse of time, Crowland reports in turn a great murmuring in the Home Counties on behalf of the princes; a rising throughout the south on their behalf, in which the Duke of Buckingham took the lead; the report of the princes' death, which prompted Buckingham – on the advice of his prisoner Bishop Morton – to invite Henry Tudor to marry Elizabeth and take the crown. Essentially this is also the story of the Tudor historians Polydore Vergil and Sir Thomas More. Vergil's narrative of 1483-5, which is the foundation of all subsequent accounts, is not so much an account of Richard's reign as the prehistory of the Tudors. More depicts Buckingham as a candidate for the crown himself, who

was persuaded by Morton to abandon his own claims in Tudor's favour. Vergil and More locate Crowland's replacement of the Princes as the rebels' figureheads by Henry Tudor *before* the rebellion commenced. Further elaborations appear in the work of later writers seeking to arrange events in more consistent patterns. Thus the chronicler Hall introduces Henry Tudor's mother Lady Margaret Beaufort into the planning stage with Buckingham before the rebellion even broke out and the Elizabethan antiquary John Stow pushes the Tudors' involvement back into the July conspiracy to free the princes, which was certainly too early for them. As such, the standard interpretation is essentially a Tudor version, which explains the rebellion in terms of its result, presents its whole course as Tudor-inspired, and allots a key role to such Tudor stalwarts as Reginald Bray, Hugh Conway and Christopher Urswick.

The name Buckingham's Rebellion is not contemporary, but the invention of subsequent historians who gave priority to the most high-ranking rebel. To some extent it is misleading, since there is general agreement that most of the rebels were members of the Yorkist establishment. 'Modern opinion has tended to play down Buckingham's significance', Horrox observes. The most recent and only full-length account, by Louise Gill, identifies its aim as 'to replace Richard III with Edward IV's eldest daughter [Elizabeth of York], uniting her in marriage with the Lancastrian exile Henry Tudor, thus joining the dynasties of York and Lancaster'. Buckingham's own phase of the rebellion was a complete failure: he was impeded by floods, attacked from the rear by the Vaughans, failed to recruit, took flight, was taken and executed. He is still however credited with much of the planning and orchestration.

Maxstoke Castle, Warwickshire, one of the homes of Henry Stafford, Duke of Buckingham.

Apparently with the king as far as Pontefract on 27 August, the date of his Hereford warrant, Buckingham had left by Richard's 'joyous entry' to York on 29th and probably proceeded westwards at once. Since he never presented his warrant for execution, he may have never visited the capital again. Perhaps he was at his castles at Thornbury in Gloucestershire on 22 September with Lionel Wydeville Bishop of Salisbury and at Brecon on 24 September, when he supposedly invited Tudor to invade. Bishop Wydeville was the Duchess Katherine's brother and any meeting was the obvious occasion to co-ordinate the Wydeville component of the rebellion. Buckingham was one of very few people in Britain who knew Henry Tudor, whose mother Margaret Beaufort had been married in the 1460s to the duke's uncle Henry Stafford. We know quite independently that Margaret was in correspondence with France over her right to the Orleans ransom. It was Buckingham also who was behind the Cornish rebellion which, Gill says, sought ' to "utterly destroy the king" and to set up another in his place, by the command and order of Henry, Duke of Buckingham"' . Buckingham thus backed Henry Tudor for the crown just as the chronicles say. Here the modern and Tudor interpretations coincide.

It could be so, but it seems implausible. These accounts do not explain Buckingham's unexpected change of front. They do not explain why Queen Elizabeth, Dorset and the other Wydevilles, who have a key organizing role, should accept the direction of Bishop Morton and Henry Tudor's mother Margaret

Beaufort at such an early stage. They ignore what appears to be a genuine loss of direction: some rebels remained in arms to little effect for several weeks, longer than most campaigns in the Wars of the Roses, which suggests that the discovery of the princes' deaths and the change of candidate actually occurred in mid-rebellion. And while it is easy to deduce with Drs Arthurson and Horrox and Mr Kingwell that the new unnamed king proclaimed at Bodmin was Henry Tudor, it need not have been. It could, for example, have been Buckingham, for the Cornishmen may not have known of his execution the previous day at Salisbury. If Ralph Arundel joined the rebellion at Buckingham's command and compulsion, there were another three were driven to it by Sir Thomas Arundell of Lanherne. The Cornish inquisition does not state that Buckingham ordered the insurgents to erect another king, as Gill says; that is a misreading of the document.

Most of all, this Tudor interpretation conflicts markedly with Richard's own understanding of events. Richard evidently suspected something. Crowland says that his spies kept him well-informed. He arrested John Welles and seized Bishop Wydevilles' temporalities, but Buckingham's defection was nevertheless a horrible surprise for him. Although we first hear of the Kentish insurrection from London on 10 October, Richard himself at Lincoln next day was clear that the ringleader was Buckingham and it was against him whom he was soon to proceed himself. His proclamations focused on Buckingham and Dorset, not Henry Tudor. It was Buckingham to whom the Cornish uprising was attributed by the prosecution as late as 3 December, and it was he also who took priority in the parliamentary attainder of the rebels in 1484, which allows to Henry Tudor and his mother only walk-on parts. Henry invaded with Breton support and was hence attainted, but the act explains participation by Buckingham's invitation, supposedly despatched on 24 September, and not because he was a candidate to the crown. If Henry Tudor had really been Richard's principal foe, his rival for the crown, he would surely have been given a much higher prominence in the act. Presumably his recognition as their candidate by the defeated rebels at Christmas 1483 was not yet known at the Westminster parliament of January/February 1484.

Crowland, our earliest narrative of the rebellion, states that it was on the advice of Bishop Morton, then Buckingham's prisoner at Brecon, that the duke urged Tudor to invade, marry Princess Elizabeth, and take the throne. The complicity of Morton with Buckingham at Brecon and Buckingham's summons to Tudor are in the attainder of 1484, though attributed to different dates. Neither this act nor any other contemporary source states that Buckingham acted on Morton's advice nor that he invited Tudor to marry Elizabeth of York or take the throne. From where did this information derive? There is no evidence that Crowland was at Brecon or was yet a Tudor partisan: at this stage his chronicle is brief and particularly short on detail. What he later recounts became the Tudor orthodoxy of Polydore Vergil and Sir Thomas More. Had Crowland access to the same information and informants? Was Morton himself the source? Crowland did not write until 1486, after Henry VII's accession. It would not be surprising if hindsight caused him to rationalize events, to read back Henry's candidacy from Christmas to October. Protagonists of the new regime may well have antedated their commitment, presented Buckingham's Rebellion as a Tudor movement from the start, and gave themselves starring roles. Morton himself, most strikingly, was to be rewarded with an archbishopric, the chancellorship, and a cardinal's hat. We owe the standard history of Buckingham's Rebellion to Tudor historians, to Tudor propaganda, which modern historians have taken too easily at face value.

The traditional account of Buckingham's Rebellion, in short, takes a Tudor perspective that made sense in the light of subsequent developments, but which is unlikely to have applied throughout the rebellion and which was subsequently elaborated to create appropriate antecedents for the leaders of the Tudor regime. If the Tudors were indeed implicated in July as Stow says, though the contemporary Frenchman Bishop Basin makes no such assertion, it was on behalf of the Princes. The rumour that the Princes had died and the consequent search for replacement claimants comes later, at the very least after 29 July when the trial of the July conspirators was ordered. The changeover to Henry Tudor, which Crowland does not date, may well have happened after the rebellion had commenced. Probably the Tudors began as mere participants and only back in Brittany did the desperate exiles, like Warwick and Clarence in their restoration of Henry VI in 1470, make Henry Tudor into their figurehead. Indeed there can have been no Tudor adherents other than Henry and his uncle in 1483: they were the creation of Henry's victory and many had been Yorkists earlier in the year. So, too, it was Henry's identification of himself as heir to Henry VI that made Lancastrians once more of those who had reconciled themselves with Edward IV after the destruction of the house of Lancaster in 1471 and who had subsequently joined the Yorkist establishment. They could now hope to recover forfeited property that had been lost in the service of Henry VI.

Richard's victory over the Wydevilles had been temporary. They carried weight throughout southern England arising from their landholdings, ranging from the lordship of the Mote in Maidstone to the east, the ancient queen's lands and Salisbury episcopal estates in central southern England, to Dorset's West Country Bonville barony and Rivers' receivership of the duchy of Cornwall. As queen-dowager, queen-mother and custodian of the Yorkist princesses, Queen Elizabeth was still powerful. Twenty years near the seat of power, two decades of politicking, and a whole series of advantageous marriages had created many other connections. Such ties gave them the influence to hold the rebellion together and create the chain of command that Buckingham could not supply. Wydeville opposition to Richard was to be expected. So, too, therefore was the opposition of their in-laws and clients, such as the Hautes, Pympes and Guildfords in Kent. What was surprising was that so many other southern Yorkists should have joined them. Take Piers Courtenay, Bishop of Exeter, who had come to prominence as secretary of that foe of the Wydevilles, Richard III's own brother Clarence. Take Sir William Stonor of Stonor in Oxfordshire. Beside his friendly contacts with the Marquis of Dorset should be set those he enjoyed with Richard before his accession, his membership of Richard III's household, his prominent role in the coronation and his relations

The effigy of the Yorkist Sir Roger Tocotes in Bromham Church, Wiltshire. Knighted by Edward IV after the battle of Tewkesbury, he was a leader in Buckingham's Rebellion (at Newbury) and was attainted in 1484.

with the Duke of Suffolk and Lord Lovell, both of whom were in the ascendant. Both the king and Lovell presumed on his loyalty against the rebels. 'Cousin Stonor', wrote Lovell confidently:

> I commend me to you as heartily as I can. Forasmuch as it pleases the king's grace to have warned you and all other to attend upon his grace and your company that you will come in my command and my company will be with you. And I am sure that it will please his grace best and cause me to think that you love my honour and I trust shall be to your security.

He went on to state the date and time of the rendezvous of Richard's supporters, which Stonor took into the opposing camp.

Then there is the case of Sir Thomas St Leger. Admittedly he too had contacts with the Wydevilles – who had not? – having betrothed his daughter to Dorset's son, but he was a long-standing royal servant whose fortune had been made by his liaison and subsequent marriage with Richard's late sister Anne, Duchess of Exeter. Surely Richard could be certain of his brother-in-law? But he could not. Surely the pull of the discredited Wydevilles could not have been stronger than Richard's influence? Rather it was allegiance to Edward V and offence at Richard's behaviour which drove such men against their self-interest into rebellion, into alliance, and thus under the direction of the Wydevilles. This was not and could hardly be a general response, given the extreme reluctance of the fifteenth-century aristocracy to break their

Richard's sister Anne, Duchess of Exeter, and her second husband, Thomas St Leger, from a brass plaque in St George's Chapel, Windsor.

allegiance, but it remains remarkable that over such a wide area so many of the leaders of local society with so much to lose did indeed choose this course of action.

However, none of these arguments can explain the desertion of the Duke of Buckingham, for nobody bore greater responsibility for Richard's usurpation. His defection was a grievous blow, as we know from a postscript that Richard wrote to Lord Chancellor Russell in his own hand:

> Here loved be God is all well & [I am] truly determined for to resist the malice of him that had best cause to be true, the Duke of Buckingham, the most untrue creature living, whom with God's grace we shall not be long till we will be in that part and subdue his malice. We assure you [there] was never false traitor better provided for.

Richard's shock was all the greater since Buckingham was 'now of late days standing and being in as great favour, tender trust, and affection with the King our sovereign lord, as ever any subject was with his prince and liege lord, as was notoriously and

161

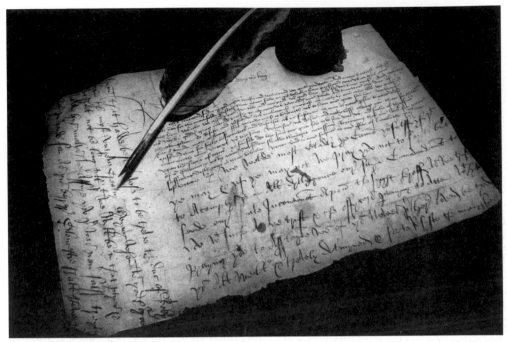

Richard's letter to Lord Chancellor Russell of 12 October 1485. The postscript (bottom and left), in Richard's own hand, calls Buckingham 'the most untrue creature living'.

openly known'. No wonder Richard refused to see the duke after his capture and had him executed forthwith. Another equally personal case was that of St Leger, who was summarily executed despite all his efforts to buy his life. But Richard's alarm was more general than these specific cases suggest, prompting him at one moment to order the seizure of the lands of all the household men in southern England and later to distrust southern officeholders as a breed. It is even possible to argue that such a response was not misplaced if one considers how many such notables were prevented from joining the rebellion by their absence with Richard on progress in the North. Clearly he could not count for his own protection on the peculiarly strong loyalties supposed to exist within a lord's (and, especially, a king's) household.

Richard's language testifies authentically to his belief in the justice of his own title, sense of betrayal, and horror at the heinous treason that had been committed against him. The same message emerges from the prayers added to his personal primer. Hence his summary execution of his former ally and his brother in law. Against other rebels Richard's proclamations adopted his conventional moral tone, identifying himself with the common good, attributing to them 'the utter destruction of our said sovereign lord, the subversion of his realm, and the utter disinheriting of all his true liege people', and denouncing the rebels as offenders against God and man. Once victorious, he could claim God's verdict in his favour. Buckingham was denounced as a 'rotten member of the body politic' and

Right: 'The Angel and Royal', Grantham. In the room above the gateway, Richard III received the Great Seal during his campaign to put down the 1483 rebellion.

Below: Richard III's Great Seal.

parliament attainted 'the great and principal movers, stirrers, and doers of the said offences and heinous treasons'. Gross ingratitude and heinous treason were the charges against Buckingham and St Leger. The Tudors, 'being then beyond the sea in Brittany', were labelled merely as 'great enemies of our sovereign lord'. The participation of the Wydevilles enabled Richard to redeploy the propaganda employed in *Titulus Regius*. Recalling how he had granted a general pardon to his subjects and his judicial progress, he had hoped, so he proclaimed, that 'all oppressors and extortioners of his subjects, horrible adulterers and bawds, provoking the high indignation and displeasure of God, should have been reconciled and reduced to the way of truth and virtue'. But the Marquis of Dorset 'not fearing God, nor the peril of his soul, hath many and sundry maids, widows, and wives damnably and without shame devoured, deflowered and defiled, holding the unshameful and mischievous woman called Shore's wife in adultery'. Now moreover Dorset had rebelled, threatening not merely the death of the king, breach of the peace and damage to the commonwealth, but also the 'unletting of virtue and the damnable maintenance of vices and sin as they have done in time past to the great displeasure of God and evil example of all Christian people'. Such scandalous denunciations sought to prevent any new recruits to the lecher's cause. They were intended to discredit the leadership with their rank and file. Richard's tactic was to separate the leaders, whom he comprehensively denounced as 'traitors, adulterers and bawds', from those ordinary rebels whom they had 'abused and blinded'. Prices were placed on the heads of the ringleaders, while the lesser men were let off. The tactic enjoyed great success. Buckingham was betrayed for the reward. Many Kentish rebels, 'when they knew and understood the said conspired traitors, left and forsook them and as his true subjects since have well and truly behaved them'. By appealing directly to the lesser rebels, Richard separated them from their lords and leaders. It was a technique that he had used before to neutralize Sir Edward Wydeville and he was to use it again later, when he sought to prevent his townsmen or tenants from being retained with other lords or even his own officers. He did not want any intermediaries interrupting his communication with his lesser subjects. In 1483 this technique enabled him to achieve yet another almost bloodless victory.

In retrospect Richard erred in trying to impress southerners with his support in the North rather than directing his progress through those counties where personal loyalty to him was weak. While he moved rapidly and decisively, the insurrections were too widespread for him to suppress them as quickly as would have been necessary had they possessed united and determined leadership. Though different counties rebelled in sequence, from east to west, the campaign took much longer than the fortnight or three weeks of 1460, 1470, 1471, 1485, and 1487. Although uncoordinated, the scale of these rebellions exposed how very limited were the resources available for their suppression. On the other hand, it may have been Richard's own actions that caused the movement to collapse. He invoked the Welsh counterattack that surprised Buckingham and offered the rewards leading to his capture. He may have been behind the publication of the death of the princes that threw the rebels into disarray. Order was successfully restored everywhere. At first sight his victory appeared to be decisive. His enemies were dead, defeated, dispossessed and scattered. When Henry Tudor pledged himself to marry Elizabeth of York in Rennes Cathedral at Christmas 1483 and his fellow exiles swore fealty to him as king, he was in precarious exile and it required a considerable feat of imagination to regard him as a threat. Richard appeared unassailable.

So thought the parliament of January 1484, which – perhaps from fear – confirmed *Titulus Regius* and attainted his enemies. So presumably thought the mayor, aldermen, and burgesses of London to whom the king's title was once again explained. So thought almost all the lords and the gentlemen of the king's household, who now swore allegiance to Prince Edward as his father's heir. So also thought the Earl of Huntingdon, who agreed to marry Richard's bastard daughter Katherine and received in return the Welsh lordships forfeited by Buckingham. And so in particular thought Queen Elizabeth, now resigned to the death of the princes, but not to the permanent seclusion of herself and her daughters in Westminster Abbey nor to the exile of Dorset. Abandoning any hope that Henry Tudor might overthrow Richard and marry her eldest daughter, she preferred the more certain incentives available from the king. He offered safe conduct to her daughters if they came out of sanctuary. He promised to treat them as his kinswomen, to grant them pensions and to marry them to gentlemen with appropriate dowers. A husband was indeed found for the second daughter Cecily. Subject to the oversight of a royal squire, he would also pension Queen Elizabeth:

And moreover I promise to them if any surmise or evil report be made
to me of them or any of them by any person or persons, that then I shall
not give thereunto faith or credence nor therefore put them to any kind
of punishment before that they or any of them so accused may have their
chance to defend themselves and answer.

Signed by the king and witnessed by the City corporation on 1 March 1484, it was
guarantee enough for Elizabeth and her daughters to emerge from sanctuary. Dorset
was recalled from exile. As in 1461, the Wydevilles considered their cause to be
irretrievably lost.

Once the Tudors were extradited, the object of Richard's diligent diplomacy in
1484, the last rival to Richard's throne would be eliminated, the last figurehead for
conspiracy would be removed, and the opposition once again disarmed. It might then
have been possible to offer clemency to the Yorkists in exile and Richard could have
re-established himself as king of the whole nation.

Such motives lie behind the relative moderation of Richard's countermeasures
against the rebels when compared with the alarm of his earlier pronouncements. Of
course such grave offences as treason and rebellion had to be discouraged. Hence
the handful of executions of notorious ringleaders and the attainders of a hundred
others. Regret and reconciliation, rather than rigour and revenge, were the
dominant theme. Ringleaders must be punished as a deterrent to others, the
preamble states, but in his 'great benignity and pity' the king had granted 'to divers
persons culpable in the offences his grace and pardon'. In time many could have
earned forgiveness, bought pardons, recovered their estates and even returned to
public office. Thus Lady Margaret Beaufort was deprived of her estates only for
these to be granted for life to her husband Lord Stanley: he would have been
understandably aggrieved as a loyal subject to lose heavily for his wife's fault.
Similarly Richard was lenient in his treatment of those who were allowed to pay
fines, who offered sureties for their good behaviour or even recovered portions of
their property. Grants of forfeited lands were widely recognized to be insecure and
were commonly revoked when the original owners had expiated their offences.
This was the pattern after earlier attainders, almost all of which were eventually
reversed. Whatever Richard's intentions were, however, there was not time to allow
this process to work. Less than two years were to pass before he lost his throne.
Meanwhile the continuous haemorrhage of new defections forced him to place less
emphasis on mercy than on deterrence. Whereas earlier executions had been
commuted to mere beheading, William Collingbourne and others were hanged,
drawn and disembowelled as prescribed by law.

The anti-Ricardian conspiracy did not end with Buckingham's Rebellion. Henry
Tudor was a new figurehead for the opposition. If many of the rebels fled abroad,
there were others, who although they had ostensibly made their peace, remained
disaffected. Moreover, further treason trials, arrests and sureties, forfeitures, fines
and dismissals from office reveal Richard's discovery of many further plots and

The effigy of Margaret Beaufort by Pietro Torrigiano, Westminster Abbey.

plotters, who in 1483 had escaped involvement or at least discovery. Among them were yet more of Richard's local officers and household. Why had they not rebelled in 1483? What now drew them into treason with all the risks that it entailed? Perhaps they were late converts to the villainy of Richard's usurpation. If so, who converted them and how? Perhaps they were appalled by the character of the regime. Perhaps instead they were shocked by Richard's further crimes. If so, how did they learn of them? Indeed, how was opinion formed in Ricardian England? The number of unsavoury exposures and Richard's evident alarm indicate that he was the victim of a sustained campaign of vilification. The propaganda initiative passed to his enemies. Hence the stream of defections and perhaps also the declining morale among even his adherents and the unwillingness at least of some of them to fight for him at Bosworth Field.

Involuntary tyranny

Richard presented Buckingham's Rebellion as a continuation of the misdemeanours of the Wydevilles. It was sufficient for him simply to recycle old propaganda. The lechery of the Wydevilles was legendary, Buckingham's treason was patent and collectively they had abused and deceived the people. Henry Tudor was different. At first Richard ignored him; then in 1484 he presented him not as a dynastic rival,

An early drawing of Henry Tudor, in the 'Recueil d'Arras'.

but as a traitor in collusion with England's enemies. Such traitors had promised to cede English possessions to foreign enemies: certainly an allusion to the surrender of Hammes by Calais to the French and perhaps also a reminder of Henry VI's transfer of Berwick to the Scots. They threatened English property rights. Only in June 1485 did Richard publicly acknowledge the dynastic threat, attacking Henry's title as a bastard on both sides: through Owen Tudor's liaison with Henry V's widow and through the Beaufort bastards of John of Gaunt. He ignored Henry's proposed marriage to that other bastard, Elizabeth of York, declining to publicize what was potentially Henry's trump card. Apparently Richard could find nothing to exhume from Henry's uneventful and blameless career. Once the invasion had taken place, Richard confined himself to conventional charges. Henry sought his 'utter destruction, the extreme subversion of this our realm, and the disinheriting of the same'. Richard pledged himself to resist, summoned his retainers on pain of forfeiture and threatened his opponents with attainder. He warned, correctly, that Henry would do likewise.

Against the Wydevilles, Richard could take the offensive, attack their record and offer new hope. Against Tudor, there was no scope for character assassination and precious little for a positive programme. Buckingham's Rebellion had discredited Richard's claim to be the automatic and legitimate heir of his brother's regime. He was on the ideological defensive, and was never to recover the ideological initiative: eventually he found his position indefensible. So too with practical politics. He could not attack the Tudors, execute them or drive them abroad, for they were safely beyond his reach. His attempt to extradite them, though almost successful, disastrously misfired, for it drove them into France, whose rulers were prepared to allow military backing for an invasion. Richard had to await this repeatedly delayed threat of invasion, defend the coastline and control recalcitrant localities, all at a financial cost he could not afford. He found himself obliged to resort to discredited financial expedients and could not honour all the promises he had made on his progress. Where he had promised peace and stability, he brought civil war and continuous plots. Instead of victory abroad, he was obliged to sue for peace and even to abandon his garrison at Dunbar, to his shame especially in the North. Where he had offered justice, his reputation was scarred by rough-and-ready responses to emergencies. These weaknesses forced him to rely increasingly on his own personal retinue, to the eternal destruction of his claim to govern for all, and exposed him moreover to charges of tyranny. His inability to rule as he wished and to achieve his objectives cast doubt on his intent, which later chroniclers emphatically echoed.

In retrospect it was Richard's misfortune that his usurpation and the defeat of Buckingham were so bloodless and left so many of his foes alive, recalcitrant and beyond his reach in France. Had they been killed, their absence would have had to be accepted. Had they capitulated, they would have been obliged to accept him. As it was, his own chosen substitutes were bound to have to combat and overcome nostalgic memories for these exiled foes among their colleagues, kinsmen, neighbours, officers and tenants. Richard had to redistribute forfeited lands and offices among those he trusted. Because Buckingham's Rebellion had been the uprising of the southern establishment, the forfeited lands, offices and authority had inevitably to be given to outsiders, who had no natural place in the community of each shire.

Worse still, since Richard had alienated the leaders of every southern shire, he had perforce to turn to northerners, even though hostility between North and South was even stronger then than now. It dated back to at least 1461, when the depredations of Queen Margaret's northerners had caused London to close its gates to her with decisive political effects. We have seen the irrational fear of the aged Countess of Oxford for the 'north country'; in 1486 one writer speaks of 'the North, whence all evil spreads'; and Crowland's hostility is notorious. It is clear that Richard had appreciated the need to tread carefully and had hitherto made sparing use of his most committed supporters. While happy to present himself as a northern king in the North, he was more cautious in the South and employed northern pressure as indirectly as possible. Thus news of his northern army was substituted for its actual presence at his usurpation and on its arrival it was bivouacked outside London rather than billeted within, so that southerners were exposed to his popularity in the North without their animosity being stirred by too close proximity. Even so the City of London, Cambridge University and Crowland were alarmed by the 'frightening and unheard of numbers' and Londoners ridiculed the northerners' unfashionable equipment.

Buckingham's Rebellion forced Richard to replace unreliable southerners in his household with northerners, giving the court a distinctively northern character. It compelled him to import northerners into the southern counties, not always to high office but often in relatively humble roles. And he was obliged to grant large estates to particular northerners in particular localities to give them local standing and sometimes even to transfer whole areas to northern rule. Thus he brought Sir Marmaduke Constable of Flamborough Head in Yorkshire to rule the town and district of Tonbridge in Kent and ordered local people to obey him. Such men were obvious intruders, lacking the natural authority of those they had replaced, speaking unfamiliar dialects, wearing different clothes and with outlandish manners. They had a distinct identity, different from those around them, and appeared to be the principal beneficiaries of an alien regime. Such men actually were not numerous – they were certainly not a majority of the ruling elite in any shire – but they stood out: in 1484 two-thirds of the sheriffs south of the Thames and Severn were intruders. It was not sufficient that Richard was anxious that they ruled well.

The attainder of the rebels in parliament also shocked Crowland. 'We nowhere hear of the like even under the triumvirate of Octavian, Anthony and Lepidus' appears alongside the marginal heading 'Unheard of proscriptions of lords and magnates'. Is it more than chance that he refers here to Marcus Emilius Lepidus, the model of a good custodian appointed by the Roman Senate, whom Bishop Russell had intended comparing to Lord Protector Gloucester in his opening speech to Edward V's parliament, never delivered there, but perhaps well known? Attainders on such a scale and on such occasions were inevitable, as in 1461 and again before Crowland wrote in 1485, but never had they been concentrated on the South. To Crowland, of course, the rebels had been *right*: they represented the Yorkist establishment, the mainstream loyalists for whom *Richard* was the aberration. Worse still, Crowland continued, the rebels' lands were distributed among the king's northerners, 'whom he had planted in every part of his dominions to the shame of all the southern people, who murmured ceaselessly and longed each day for the return of their old lords in place of the tyranny of the present ones'.

Concrete evidence, of course, is almost entirely lacking. There was to be no outburst of popular enthusiasm on Henry's arrival in 1485 like that which swept earlier regimes away in 1460 and 1470. Some credence however is lent to his claim to popular hostility by a carol *The Briar and the Periwinkle* written in the broadest Kentish dialect that comes from Ashford in mid-Kent. The carol laments the wrongful exclusion of the [rose-]briar, the principal local lord Sir John Fogge, treasurer of Edward IV's household and long a Wydeville partisan, by 'great treason', and his replacement by a periwinkle, most probably the recipient of his lands, the Yorkshireman William Malliverer. Malliverer's badge was probably not a periwinkle, which was traditionally the flower used to crown a traitor. Though the hated periwinkle had laid the briar's 'leaves low', yet 'all his roots were strong', the

Kentish rustics sang. With the help of God, 'the King of Bliss', they looked forward to when

> The Periwinkle shall have right evil ending,
> And all his roots be raised.

Naturally Crowland was unconcerned that these sufferings had many precedents in those of Lancastrians under Edward IV. It was also irrelevant to him that Richard had no choice, because the local rulers had rejected him. It was not the quality of the northerners' rule that Crowland objected to, but the fact that they were there at all. Richard's response to the rebellion generated further discontent and, in Crowland's eyes at least, made him a tyrant. Only a few years later Henry VII was to exploit this fear by proclaiming that northern rebels wanted to destroy the south parts of the realm.

Doubtless the northerners appreciated their wholesale promotion, but it was damaging to Richard and probably restricted his policy options. Since he could not dispense with their services, he may have felt unable to offer the full restoration to the disaffected that he may have wished. Spreading those whom he trusted thinly across southern England deprived him of the immediate services of the relatively few retainers who were both able and reliable. It is striking that his key man in South Wales, Sir James Tyrell, was inescapably committed in another essential role at the time of Henry Tudor's invasion in 1485. Perhaps the control by Richard's agents of the localities was indeed less effective than that of natural lords and they had to be more continually present. Richard's rule was no authoritarian absolutism. To import northerners was not a mark of strength but a tyranny of weakness. Moreover Richard responded to hostility in southern England not by personally enforcing his rule, but by absenting himself. Horrox has shown that he was seldom in the South in 1484-5, spending instead long periods in Yorkshire and the Midlands, especially Nottingham.

Importing northerners also cost Richard income, for he was obliged to grant them the lands that had been forfeited, both as rewards for their services and to buttress their local authority. Richard was generous, as More admits, but also, as More also says, 'above his power liberal, ... for which he was fain to pill[age] and spoil in other places and get him steadfast hatred'. The threat of invasion from abroad along the lengthy coastline of England and Wales forced on Richard defensive preparations that had to be maintained for the long months that Tudor's expedition was delayed. The cost exceeded Richard's means and impelled him to levy forced loans. These were technically different from benevolences because he intended to repay them, but this fact carried weight only with those who considered repayment to be in his power. For those who did not, the distinction was purely semantic, a matter of words. Richard seemed to be reviving practices that he had only just repudiated and indeed abolished by act of parliament. Just as Richard had attacked the Wydevilles for misusing Edward IV's treasure, so Crowland blamed him for wasting it. He charged Richard with extravagance. He denounced him for

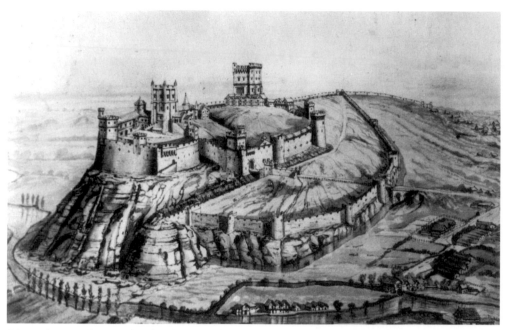

Nottingham castle, one of Richard III's many Midland and northern strongholds, as it appeared in the fifteenth century.

reviving benevolences, which he called malevolences, and for extortion from the clergy. The charges are taken up by others and crop up in several chronicles. The king who had refused taxes and gifts and had condemned his brother's levying of unnecessary taxes was tarred with the same brush. Both *The Twelve Triumphs of Henry VII* in 1486 and Rows in 1490 describe Richard as a miser: the same charge as that already made against Edward IV and to be made against Henry VII. Such financial expedients undermined Richard's claim to good government with those whose approval he needed to win – it is striking that the London chroniclers were so critical – and it identified him with that mark of tyranny that he had himself denounced, the levy of unnecessary taxes.

The Wydevilles never doubted that Richard was a usurper. Nor did Mancini, whose history was entitled *The Usurpation of Richard III*. Nor did the rebels of 1483 or Crowland. Usurpers, to contemporary eyes, were tyrants. So, too, were any kings who ruled not for the benefit of the people, but for themselves. The death of his only son made Richard appear the sole beneficiary of his regime and thus placed him firmly in this category. On Crowland's evidence many in the South, including those who were perhaps neutral or uncommitted, regarded the northern occupation as tyranny and their continued resistance forced Richard into financial expedients that he had himself previously regarded as tyrannical. The injustice of such charges, the quality of Richard's rule and his good intentions are all irrelevant. What matters was that Richard was presented in this way. It was a commonplace by 1485, when Tudor's letters describe Richard as 'that homicide and unnatural *tyrant* that now bears dominion over you' and 'that odious *tyrant* Richard late Duke of Gloucester'. There is no argument, no justification, no evidence. Richard's tyranny is presumed, can be taken for granted, and needs no discussion. The time for discussion was past. Richard's tyranny justified his own deposition and Henry's accession. Richard's tyranny was widely accepted in his own lifetime and not merely because of what he was and what he did. In an era before modern communications, such facts cannot have been generally known and anyway facts do not speak for themselves. They have to be presented. It was the achievement of Richard's enemies that Richard's tyranny and Richard's monstrosity became common currency in 1484-5.

5 Richard III's defeat and defamation

A monster in his own lifetime

'England's black legend' of Richard III – usurper, tyrant, and monster – dates back to the histories of John Rows, Thomas More and William Shakespeare. All were Tudor writers subject to the Tudor dynasty. All, therefore, so Ricardians claim, were peddling Tudor propaganda, defaming Richard III to justify Henry VII. But Richard's character was already blackened before Bosworth. It was partly because he was vilified that he lost Bosworth and, indeed, had to fight it. He was already dubbed 'that homicide and unnatural tyrant'. This was not necessarily because Richard was a monster and the charges were deserved. The evidence is at best ambiguous and sometimes non-existent. It was because he was presented as such. Tudor propaganda preceded Bosworth. Wydeville propaganda preceded Tudor propaganda. To justify Henry Tudor, Richard had to be discredited. We do not know how the propaganda was disseminated. We do not know where it was formulated or how far it was directed by Henry Tudor: how far he was the organizer as well as the beneficiary. We cannot attribute roles to Pembroke and Oxford, to Margaret Beaufort and John Morton, to Bray, Urswick, Collingbourne or the others whose names we know. Most probably it originated in London rather than abroad. We possess only Collingbourne's rhyme:

> The Cat, the Rat, and Lovell the Dog
> Rule all England under a Hog.

The allusions are to Richard's trusted lieutenants, Catesby, Ratcliffe and Lovell. Though the rhyme is too brief to carry much analysis, it attributes great authority to them (maybe too much for men of such lowly rank?), ridicules them and perhaps hints at the bestiality of their rule. Richard's emblem of a white boar ultimately gives rise to many hoggish references.

Apart from this, however, we wholly lack those proclamations, manifestos and placards like those at Bodmin that once existed and which Richard denounced. He leaves us in no doubt about their number and the gravity with which he viewed them:

> And where it is so that divers seditious and evil disposed persons both
> in our city of London and elsewhere within our realm enforce
> themselves daily to sow seed of noise and slander against our person
> and against many of the lords and estates of our land to abuse the

Georges Vertue's engraving of the royal portrait of Richard III. Above, 'The Cat the Rat, and Lovell the Dog / Rule all England under a Hog.' Below, the Tudor Welsh dragon sinks its teeth into Richard's boar.

multitude of our subjects and avert their minds from us... some by
setting up of bills, some by messages and sending forth of false and
abominable language and lies, some by bold and presumptuous open
speech and communication one with another...

Therefore, he ordered the York corporation to arrest the culprits,

> as oft as they find any person speaking of us or any other lord or estate
> of this our land otherwise than is according to honour, truth, and the
> peace and righteousness of this our realm, or telling of tales and tidings,
> whereby the people might be stirred to commotions and unlawful
> assemblies, or any strife and debate arise between lord and lord, or of us
> and any of the lords and estates of this our land ...

How we would like to know which lords were provoked into conflict and which
were wrongfully exposed to Richard's anger by this kind of propaganda! It leaves us
in no doubt of its effectiveness, nor indeed does his statement elsewhere in the same
document that

> innocent people which would live in rest and peace and truly under our
> obeisance, as they ought to do, are greatly abused and oft put in danger
> of their lives, lands and goods, as oft as they follow the steps and devices
> of the said seditious and mischievous persons.

So seductive was this material that Richard ordered that any that were confiscated
should not be read but posted to him unread! The king's capacity for crowd
management had been taken over by the opposition. We can guess at some of the
reasoned arguments. We know something of the ridicule, the non-sequiturs, the
smears and the innuendoes that were deployed against him. Some, indeed, are
preserved in later, post-Bosworth, works. Propaganda does not have to be true – much
of it was not – but it has to be effective, and it was.

The Wydevilles began with what proved to be a false start. The counterpart of
Richard's crimes were the virtues of his victims, who were presented as completely
innocent. When John Rows reports the unjust executions of Rivers and Grey, he
records also Earl Rivers' verse meditations on the vagaries of fortune and describes
'how the innocent humbly and peaceably submitted to a cruel fate from their enemies
butchers'. Rivers, moreover,

> was found to be wearing, at the time of his death, the hair shirt which he
> had long been in the habit of wearing against his bare flesh, [which]
> consecrated hair shirt of Earl Anthony was long after hung before the
> image of the Blessed Mary the Virgin at the Carmelite Friars at
> Doncaster.

Note the emotive words 'butchers', 'innocent', and 'consecrated', which we will encounter again. Rivers' death is depicted as a martyrdom, like the start of one of those cults that developed around such defeated politicians as Thomas Becket at Canterbury, Edward II at Gloucester, Archbishop Scrope at York and Henry VI at Chertsey and Windsor. When did it begin? Are there not hints even in Mancini's idealized portrait of this realistic politician? 'Lord Rivers', he wrote, 'was always considered a kind, serious and just man, and one tried by every vicissitude of life'. So too that abnormal teenager, Edward V, whom Mancini eulogizes. Likewise Lord Hastings, whose posthumous encomium contrasts with a ruthless reality. Such idealizing of Rivers was current by July 1483. Faced by death, he left an exemplary will. Did he also compose exemplary verses, tailor his demeanour and dress to a future cult, and plan the publicity that brought it to Rows' ears? The fact that there was no cult and no canonization merely illustrates the lack of continuity between Wydeville and Tudor propaganda. There were better opportunities for ideological warfare than the rehabilitation of the Wydevilles! When one ceased, the other began.

Richard's weakest point was always his title as king and it was not merely rebels who questioned it. Multiple copies were produced of *Titulus Regius*, which recorded Richard's election by the three estates, and were shown to doubtful officials to convince them of his right. Buckingham's rebels were not persuaded and even after their defeat 'divers persons, so it said', impugned the validity of the election because the estates were not then assembled in parliament and were anyway insufficiently learned to judge the justice of Richard's case. Crowland certainly thought them so, for such matrimonial suits as precontracts were subject to the canon law of the Church. Without questioning the validity of his original case and since parliament's authority was generally accepted as supreme, therefore, Richard asked parliament in 1484 to confirm his title, which it duly did. The rumours were not stilled, however, and in April 1484 Richard had summoned the City livery companies to Westminster 'at the which time the king's title and right was showed'. It did not suffice. Even before Bosworth, on the strength of the homage and fealty rendered to him at Vannes, Henry Tudor posed not as a claimant but as the rightful king set on 'the recovery of the crown of our realm of England to us of right appertaining'. Richard was at best king de facto. No earlier pretender had claimed to be king before overcoming his rival. Not only did this claim further discredit Richard, it may also have helped Tudor sympathizers to justify to themselves their support for Henry, and indicated that resistance to them would carry the penalties of treason. Indeed, when Henry was victorious, in spite of parliamentary opposition, he dated his reign from before Bosworth and thus attainted as traitors those who fought for the de facto king, though his chosen date was not Christmas 1483, but the eve of Bosworth itself.

Richard's position would be strengthened by the removal of those who had better claims. By July 1483 the Princes in the Tower had already disappeared. What had happened to them? Mancini had his suspicions in July and by autumn they were generally assumed to be dead. Most likely Richard killed them, just as other

'*The Burial of the Princes*', an engraving of the painting by James Northcote.

usurpers eliminated their predecessors and concealed their fate to avoid condemnation. The fact that Richard failed to produce the princes to exculpate himself does not of course prove him guilty, for he may well have thought support for Henry Tudor was less dangerous than support for Edward V, if Edward was shown to be alive. None of our informants knew for sure the answer to this well-kept secret. But Richard's guilt was taken for granted in January 1484 by the chancellor of France, in 1485 by Henry VII's parliament, in 1486 by Crowland the Englishman, by the Italians Giovanni Gigli and Pietro Carmeliano in London, by the Welshman Dafydd Llwyd, and the Spaniard Diego Valera and thereafter by many others. So what? What lasting harm did Richard II's death do to Henry IV or Henry VI's to Edward IV? Their deaths were allowed for in politics, just as politicians dropped the princes from their plans after November 1483. No doubt Richard merely intended the disappearance of the princes to be permanent and for them to be quietly forgotten. But Richard's enemies found more political dynamite in the murder of these princes than in those of earlier kings: because they were *innocent*, as Valera pointed out; because they were *infants*, as Rochefort and Valera noted; and because Richard was their *protector* and they were in his care. The essence of the charge was there from the start, even before their fate was certain, when Mancini records the tears that were shed on their behalf. Tears meant the same in the fifteenth century as now. It was not a long step to compare the princes to the Holy Innocents and thus Richard to King Herod, the archetypal wicked king of the mystery plays. Llwyd actually writes of the 'sin of Herod' and Rows compares Richard's rule to that of Herod. This view was commonplace in Henry VII's London, but it occurs in Wales in 1486 and was probably held earlier. Richard's attainder late in 1485 refers to his 'shedding of *infants'* blood' and Henry's pre-accession letter calls him a '*homicide*'. That was why Henry VII failed systematically to dishonour him, if he did not. There was no need. Richard had taken the blame for the deaths of the princes and had paid the price. Whether he was actually guilty was a side issue.

If Richard was weak as an individual, his position would be much stronger if he headed a dynasty that would outlast his own life. Unfortunately he had no brothers living and only one legitimate son. He made the most of him. Prince Edward was created Prince of Wales in September 1483 at York, lieutenant of Ireland, and then, in February 1484, he was recognized by the lords and members of his household, who swore oaths of fealty to him. But in April 1484 he died. His parents were understandably distraught. Crowland was probably not alone in identifying the hand of God. Richard could not manage without an heir. At first, Rows says, he recognized Clarence's son Edward, who also commanded the loyalty due to the Kingmaker. To set aside Clarence's attainder, however, was to give Warwick's title precedence over his own. For a second time Richard placed him in custody. His next choice, Lincoln, son of his sister Elizabeth, was a Yorkist prince old enough to be politically effective with a title decidedly inferior to Richard's own. Since it was certainly weaker than those of Edward IV's daughters, Lincoln's nomination, now apparently confirmed by a family pedigree roll, brought Richard no new accession

An effigy at Sheriff Hutton Church, Yorkshire, said to be that of Edward, Prince of Wales, Richard II's only son.

of power. What Richard really needed was a son, but Queen Anne apparently could not oblige. To have another son, Richard needed another wife, preferably one who would strengthen his own title. Hence the proposal to replace Queen Anne by his own niece, Elizabeth of York, eldest daughter of Edward IV and eldest sister of the Princes in the Tower, supposedly even before his queen's death. Not only could Richard have assured the succession, but he could also have deprived Henry Tudor of the support of such erstwhile Yorkists who placed dynastic legitimacy before revenge against Richard. Indeed tales about the proposed marriage supposedly frightened Henry Tudor into contingency marriage plans to one of the Herberts of Raglan.

Crowland reports that at Christmas 1484 Richard stopped sleeping with his queen and dressed her and Princess Elizabeth in similar clothes:

> The people spoke against this and the magnates and the prelates were greatly astonished: and it was said by many that the king was applying his mind in every way to contracting a marriage with Elizabeth either after the death of the queen or by means of a divorce for which he believed he had sufficient grounds. He saw no other way of confirming his crown and of dispelling the hopes of his rival.

On 16 March 1485 Anne died. But Richard's marriage to Elizabeth did not follow. Instead, northerners objected to the discarding of Queen Anne, churchmen to the

179

Three of Edward IV's daughters, including (left) Elizabeth, future wife of Henry VII. The Royal Window, Canterbury Cathedral.

marriage of an uncle and a niece, and the king had to repudiate any intention to marry her. Not only could he not marry Elizabeth, who remained available for Tudor, but his denial was not believed: not by Crowland, nor on his testimony either by Catesby and Ratcliffe, whom Crowland says knew better, nor by the Londoners, who considered his statement 'more by the will of these councillors than his own'. Worse still, he was rumoured to have poisoned Anne. The story was current in London and York almost as soon as Anne was dead, it came to the ears of Crowland and Commynes, and became a fact for John Rows and *The Great Chronicle of London*.

What truth is there in the stories? They were already current by 29 March 1485, when Richard publicly denied them at the London Guildhall. Some confirmation for the marriage scheme after Anne's death exists in a supposed letter in favour from Elizabeth herself. But our main source is Crowland, who believed all the tales. It is he who, with hindsight, attributes an incestuous motive to Elizabeth's Yuletide attire, and who discounts Richard's denials. We cannot know his grounds nor how widespread the tales were. Whether the stories are true, however, matters less than the fact that they were believed to be true, that the marriage project was extended (scarcely credibly) into the murder of the queen, and that they served to blacken Richard.

Much the same is true of Henry VI, whose body Richard had moved from Chertsey Abbey to St George's Chapel, Windsor in August 1484. We cannot tell precisely why. Was it merely an act of piety towards an uncanonized saint? Was it to divert the offerings of the faithful to Windsor's building fund? Was it at the wishes of Queen Anne, whose first husband had been Henry's son? Was it thus to appropriate Henry's prestige to Richard himself? Or was it to deny such prestige to Tudor, who may already have been claiming to be Henry's designated heir? Whatever his reason, it was presumably to dispel such benefits and indeed to counterbalance them that Richard was alleged to have murdered Henry, an accusation which became historical orthodoxy until the 1950s. Only then was it demonstrated that Richard probably did not kill Henry and certainly did not bear the responsibility. That, however, is not the point. In his own lifetime he was stained with another heinous regicide and the martyrdom of a saint. Rows alludes to the story about 1490, but it was already mentioned by Gigli, Carmeliano and Llwyd in 1486. When Crowland denounced Henry's murderer as a *tyrant*, he appears to be referring to Richard, except that the previous sentence, penned in 1486, implies that the culprit was still living. 'He is the accursed one who, ready for any crime, likewise ran me through by thrusting his sword into my entrails,' Carmeliano makes the sainted king say. Richard did it with his own hands, both Rows and More aver. The story was *current* in 1486, when it was repeated by four independent sources, and therefore it was probably circulating earlier. Was it to *dispel* such rumours that Richard translated Henry's body in the first place?

Admittedly Richard's title was weak and open to attack. The assaults discussed here go beyond reasoned justification and additionally smeared him with regicide, homicide, infanticide, martyrdom, incest and adultery, against which no defence was possible. Richard was receiving the treatment he had dealt out to others. What is most striking is how thoroughly he was discredited. Even traitors against him received a sympathetic reception from the crowd around the scaffold. Richard dared not let even the aldermen of York read the rebel placards that they were taking down. His subjects, even those at York and members of his council, were prepared to believe him guilty of infanticide, the murder of his wife and marriage with his niece. His denials were not enough and his word was not trusted. Three times he appeared reluctantly at the Guildhall to promulgate his title anew, to publish his agreement with Queen Elizabeth, and to deny the murder of his wife. Public statements and appearances had worked before. Yet now, Crowland says, he was not believed. If even Catesby and Ratcliffe were unconvinced by him, how could anyone else be? Must he not have been the monster that he was portrayed as being?

The monster magnified

Such propaganda probably encouraged support for Tudor and discouraged loyalty to Richard. Some changed sides with their retainers, the Earl of Northumberland refused to take his division into conflict and others certainly stayed away altogether. It seems that Richard failed to deploy all those bound to him by allegiance and personal loyalty that a king could reasonably expect. But propaganda alone was not enough. The crown had to be won by force. Though perhaps less committed, Richard's army was probably still the larger at Bosworth, but was relatively small when compared to those of the victors of Towton (1461) or Barnet (1471). However effective Tudor's propaganda was in denying Richard support, it failed to attract either substantial numbers of Tudor, Lancastrian, Yorkist or Wydeville partisans from within Wales and the Midlands or the mass popular turnout that had proved so overwhelming in 1450, 1460, or 1470 and perhaps even for Richard's own revolution in 1483. Bosworth was hard fought, the result hung in the balance, there were substantial losses on both sides including Henry Tudor's standard-bearer, and ultimately it was foreign mercenaries and the treason of the Stanleys that decided the day. Had Richard won, little would be known of his monstrous reputation. That he lost was fatal to his historical standing. Winners write history, not losers. Nobody wrote on Richard's behalf. Besides justifying their own victory, Richard's enemies reinforced his notoriety.

Initially they had no choice. Bosworth appears decisive only in retrospect. Supporters of Richard fought on, rallying behind successive Yorkist princes, and enlisted international support. There were risings in 1486, an invasion and hard-fought battle in 1487, and conspiracies continued for another twenty years. It is not clear why. Not all Yorkists accepted the dynastic claims of Henry VII, and nostalgia for Richard's good government in Yorkshire, for his resident lordship in Richmondshire and his beneficial legislation, persisted well into Henry VIII's reign.

Above: Henry VII and his standard-bearer arrive at Atherstone, from a mural in the 'Three Tuns', Atherstone, Warwickshire.

Right: The tomb and effigy of Sir Robert Harcourt, KG, at Stanton Harcourt, Oxfordshire. A standard-bearer to Henry VII at Bosworth Field, the remains of the flag still hang above his tomb.

King Henry VII was a king elected by proportional representation. He was the first choice of very few, but he had won the first transferable vote of Tudors, Lancastrians, Yorkists, Welshmen and Frenchmen, each with their own axe to grind, who knew nothing substantial against him and hated Richard. Such coalitions of convenience commonly lasted only so long as the object of their hatred before they disintegrated. The second reign of Henry VI in 1470-1 is a good example. If Henry VII was to survive, he had to become more than a mere figurehead, he had to justify his kingship positively – to win acceptance as king in right as well as in fact – and he also had to destroy any lingering nostalgia for his predecessor and the cause he had represented. The two were inextricably intertwined.

Conquest and election were not enough. Henry VII needed also to reign by hereditary right. His early propaganda sought to strengthen his hereditary title. Apparently even before his accession he presented himself as the heir of Lancaster, wrongfully deposed by the house of York, and in particular as heir of his uncle, the saintly Henry VI, who was later said to have designated him as his heir and to have

Henry Payne's 'The Plucking of the Red and White Rose in the Old Temple Gardens'. In the marriage of Henry Tudor to Elizabeth York and its issue in Prince Arthur, the roses of York and Lancaster were finally joined.

prophesied his accession. Lancastrian credentials took precedence over his marriage to Elizabeth of York, which he had promised in 1483, but which he was careful to postpone until after his coronation. What would have happened to him otherwise if she had died childless? This marriage, which made him heir to the Yorkists, united the claims of both houses and ended the Wars of the Roses, was literally made in heaven. 'The father of the gods nodded approval of the solemn ceremonies from his lofty heavenly seat; wonderful to say, he made their two bodies one flesh, and sanctified and united their minds; the high heaven gave a sign.' So wrote Giovanni Gigli; his compatriot Carmeliano presented it as devised by St Henry VI himself. The union bore as fruit Prince Arthur, the reincarnation of King Arthur, whose return portended a golden age. Henry's succession was the fulfilment of the prophecy of Cadwallader. Drama and pageantry, genealogies, verses and history enshrined this Tudor symbolism.

Perkin Warbeck, one of Henry VII's rivals for the English throne, from the 'Recueil d'Arras'.

There is emphasis in each instance on supernatural and often divine authority. Henry was king by divine right. He had claimed already to be king before Bosworth and attainted those who had fought against him. His victory at Bosworth was God's verdict on his cause, an exercise of divine judgement in his favour. He was God's providential instrument to destroy tyranny. Henry was sent to free his people from the evils which had hitherto afflicted them beyond measure'. His role as saviour of the people demanded an exemplary early career, which was duly provided for him by court poets like Bernard André. Henry evidently believed it himself, ordering in his will that a kneeling effigy of him receiving his crown from God should be placed on top of St Edward's shrine in Westminster Abbey. Henry's triumph brought peace and ended internecine strife. Lambert Simnel and Perkin Warbeck were presented as tiresome little pretenders, not the formidable dynastic rivals of reality, and he secured for them as small a place in English history as Richard III had reserved for Buckingham's rebels. From the start Henry, like Richard, portrayed himself as a Christian prince committed to Christian renewal and a good ruler committed to justice. Even today he remains in popular consciousness the king of the Star Chamber, the scourge of bastard feudalism and the over-mighty subject.

All this image-making started surprisingly early. One of Henry's letters from France promised an end to enslavement not just for the English but also for the Welsh and it was apparently before his accession that the Welsh poet Lewis Glyn Cothi yearned for the Tudors to cast the Yorkists from the throne. Writing early in

Detail showing Richard's charge against Henry Tudor, from Abraham Cooper's 'The Battle of Bosworth Field', 1825.

1486, Crowland observed already that 'out of this warfare came peace for the whole kingdom' and compared 'the new prince' to 'an angel sent from heaven through whom God designed to visit his people'. Even before Prince Arthur's birth, Giovanni Gigli tells of Henry VII's inheritance from Henry VI, alludes to the Arthurian legend, and stresses the new king's marriage. Pietro Carmeliano, later in 1486, expands on the Lancastrian heritage and marriage, and lauds Arthur's return as a source of peace and concord. John Rows about 1490 accepts Henry's divine right to rule, sees in him the fulfilment of prophecy, and in Arthur the hope of the future. A host of others follow.

Successive writers amplify the material, but it is clear that it originated with the king's own propagandists. Though doubtless well advised, it was Henry VII himself who associated himself with Henry VI, postponed his marriage till after his coronation and selected the name for his son. His reasons were explained and disseminated, picked up and transmitted by foreigners such as Gigli and Carmeliano. Like Mancini, they could only know what they were told. More surprisingly, the image was accepted also by well-informed Englishmen like Crowland and Rows, neither of whom had been uncritical of Richard. To denounce the aged Rows as an unprincipled timeserver for his anti-Ricardian alterations to his *Roll* and hostile line in his *History* is unfair. In 1483-4, when he had celebrated the succession of Anne Neville (and thus Richard) in his rolls of the Earls of Warwick, he had made little of, not forgotten, Richard's maltreatment of the Countess Anne, which he resurrected in his *History*. The deaths of Queen Anne and Prince Edward freed him to interpret Richard's character in the light of his own experience. Undoubtedly Rows had assimilated Tudor propaganda by 1490. Crowland indeed was influenced as early as 1486.

All this positive propaganda demanded the denigration of Richard III. This too began very early. We have already seen how much was made of his murder of the Princes and of Henry VI by Crowland, Llwyd, Gigli, Carmeliano and Rows. These crimes had become commonplace. As early as April 1486 Crowland accepted the Tudor myth that Bosworth was God's judgement for Richard's sins. He provides hard evidence for this in the terrible dreams of demons that Richard experienced the night before, in the fact that he did not eat breakfast and had no chaplains to celebrate mass, and also in Richard's ghastly appearance on the day of battle. But were these facts or were they invented after the event? Crowland did not fabricate them. They were invented or at least perpetuated by those interested in Bosworth as a providential event with ominous portents. Likewise the fate of Richard's body, buried like a dog in a ditch, has become part of the Ricardian myth, already current early in 1486:

> And King Richard's body having been discovered amongst the dead ... many other insults were offered and after the body had been carried to Leicester with insufficient humanity, a noose being placed around the neck... (Crowland)

> He ordered the dead king to be placed in a little hermitage near the place of the battle and had him covered from the waist downwards with a black rag of poor quality, ordering him to be exposed there three days to the universal gaze... (Valera)

> And another took his body and put it before him on his horse and carried it, hair hanging, as one would bear a sheep. And so he who had miserably killed numerous people ended his days iniquitously and filthily in the dust and mire, and he who had despoiled churches was displayed to the people naked and without any clothing, and without royal solemnity was buried at the entrance to a village church... (Molinet)

Once he was victorious, Henry had deliberately defiled and dishonoured the corpse, thus publicizing Richard's shame that denied him honourable burial. So, too, almost alone, Henry ordered the execution of Catesby, the unacceptable face of Ricardian rule, at the same time as he claimed, scarcely justifiably, to be merciful and forgiving to those who had been misled into supporting Richard. Henry's later unpublicized

Henry VII with the naked corpse of Richard III after the Battle of Bosworth Field, from the mural at the 'Three Tuns', Atherstone, Warwickshire.

honourable interment of Richard and his restoration of the Catesbys did not lessen the propaganda impact of his actions at the time.

It is clear that the new Tudor government immediately presented a favourable image: Henry himself projected a complex hereditary and mythological title, and denigrated his predecessor. As usual, we lack the propaganda offerings of government, and must reconstruct them from the writings of private individuals: Crowland, Valera, Rows, Llwyd, Gigli and Carmeliano. They wrote in different localities and none were direct employees of government. But how independent were they in fact? Much of their information emanated from the government and they were concerned to please their Tudor patrons. None could escape rumour, common opinion and official propaganda. But the fact that all agree so early that Richard had killed the Princes in the Tower suggests this was also the government line. Modern Ricardians argue that Henry VII did not accuse Richard of this murder and find parliament's reference to 'the shedding of innocent blood' ambiguous. It was not ambiguous at the time but stated a commonplace, that was probably supported not merely by prejudice but by speeches in parliament that were not committed to paper and certainly do not survive.

Only later, it seems, was Sir James Tyrell presented as the actual murderer on the evidence of a confession that may or may not have existed and which may or may not be true. Tyrell was executed in 1502 not for this crime, but for new treasons. There is no surviving copy of his confession, but its validity was accepted by *The Great Chronicle of London*, the *Histories* of Vergil and More and all subsequent writers. The Tudor

An emotive portrayal of the murder of the 'Princes in the Tower' by James Northcote.

regime had already executed other potential rivals, Clarence's son Warwick and Perkin Warbeck, to reinforce Prince Arthur's title on the eve of his Spanish marriage. It was consistent therefore to spread rumours or even copies to strengthen the ruling dynasty. Whatever such a confession might have contained, Sir Thomas More presented a circumstantial account in which Tyrell implemented King Richard's explicit commands. Already the princes were termed 'babes', an early indication perhaps of the cross-fertilization between the Princes in the Tower and the tale of the Babes in Wood that had occurred by the 1590s. Both innocent pairs suffered from a wicked uncle.

Richard's treatment of his nephews was merely an extreme form of the contempt for normal human obligations that he had already showed to his brother, mother, and in-laws and was yet to reveal to his wife. Richard 'violated the ties of kin and friendship', observed Mancini: admittedly an Italian, with perhaps a heightened sense of family. Had Richard's disrespect for such conventional ties been realized, he could never have succeeded as he did. He managed it because he dissembled, as all the major narratives from Mancini and Crowland to Rows and More agree. 'He received his lord King Edward V blandly, with embraces and kisses, and within about three months or a little more he killed him together with his brother'. Does this not sound like the renegade apostle, Judas Iscariot, who betrayed Christ? 'He letted not to kiss whom he thought to kill', More remarked more explicitly. Richard was Antichrist, Rows concluded.

Where does truth end and fiction begin? What elaborations of the various stories add genuine information and which are pure invention? Certainly the stories grew in the telling, sometimes perhaps with official prompting, sometimes prompted by others. Thus it was Rows in 1490 who first mentions Richard's two years in the womb and his birth with teeth and hair, but it was More who makes the point of it all clear: 'that nature changed its course in his beginning, which in the course of his life many things unnaturally committed'. Was this already implied before Henry's victory by his description of Richard as 'unnatural'? So too *The Great Chronicle of London* records both the prayer that Henry supposedly uttered on landing at Milford Haven and his coronation at Bosworth by Sir William Stanley. This particular account obviously dates from before 1495, when Sir William was executed; and the crowning was subsequently attributed to his brother Thomas Lord Stanley, presumably by the Stanleys, whose role was also stressed in the *Ballad of Bosworth Field* and the ballad *Lady Bessy* of about 1500. Rows added Lord Stanley to those arrested (and indeed wounded) at Hastings' death and it was later even suggested that he had differed with Richard during the Scottish campaign of 1482. The role of the Stanleys also became more important as the story of Buckingham's Rebellion was rewritten in a more overtly Tudor way. Lord Stanley's wife Lady Margaret Beaufort, the future Cardinal Morton, Reginald Bray, Hugh Conway and Christopher Urswick were assigned more prominent parts as the story was embroidered – doubtless because of their testimony – by Polydore Vergil, Sir Thomas More, and Edward Hall under Henry VIII and even later by John Stow under Elizabeth I, all of whom added extra participants. One tradition said that

The crowning of Henry Tudor on Bosworth Field.

Henry VII owed his throne to Hugh Conway! From 1495 the French historian Robert Gaguin and his successors attributed Henry's victory at Bosworth to King Charles VIII. Places in the campaign were found for the Welsh poet Dafydd Llwyd and, in a later *Life*, for Sir Rhys ap Thomas.

Nor was this rewriting of history confined to the Bosworth campaign. In 1495, for example, the Earl of Oxford declared that Richard's disinheritance of his mother was notorious, but feared that it would nevertheless be forgotten and his recovery of her estates therefore impugned. It is true that no chronicle recorded the incident, but Oxford arranged for the preparation of an official record, which survives to this day. Even notoriety did not last; it had to be recorded if it were to be remembered. So firmly were the Wydevilles intermarried into English nobility and indeed into royalty that their descendants could not allow their reputation to be so tarnished. Soon after his disparaging references to Edward IV's marriage, Polydore Vergil wrote of the noble ancestress of the Earl of Essex, obviously at his instance and without realizing that she was one of Queen Elizabeth Wydeville's sisters. To disparage the marriage, particularly in the way Richard had done, was to question the legitimacy of Henry VII's queen and her sisters. No wonder Henry sought to destroy all copies of *Titulus Regius*. A more positive image was presented in a sixteenth-century painting depicting the wedding as a perfectly normal public ceremony in church conducted by a bishop! If Lord Rivers did indeed die well, who transmitted the information to John Rows, and who ensured for Hastings such a good write-up? Some of these later additions have become historical orthodoxy, some have not. Some need weeding out, yet others are still being assimilated, but which, if any, are true?

Only Richard, it seems, is consistently treated worse the later the writer writes. While the authors in 1486 have nothing to say about Richard's birth and appearance, Rows describes both about 1490 and the hunchback story was current in York in 1491. Subsequently it becomes a commonplace and even Richard's portraits were amended to suggest deformity. A monstrous body was the natural casing for a monstrous mind. Just as the heroic and divine elements of Henry VII's image demanded an exemplary rewriting of his early history by his court poets, so the image of Richard the Monster was magnified by his unnatural birth, his deformity and his dishonourable death.

The Great Chronicle of London marks the stage that the Ricardian myth had reached in London by about 1512. Entries are arranged under mayoral years and do not add up to a coherent narrative or biography. What makes it anti-Ricardian is the interpretation of individual events, as much as the events themselves. Richard was dissimulating during April to June 1483, secured the younger prince before killing Hastings, and his public utterances were disbelieved and indeed received with hostility. Queen Anne may have been poisoned and Tyrell may have killed the Princes, so that most gentlemen 'grudged so sore against the king for the death of the Innocents that they as gladly would be French': a nice touch, which one wishes was contemporary. Richard attempted to buy support, extorted loans from clergy and city that were not repaid, and when he urged his men to rule the localities well and prevent extortions, 'he taught others to exercise just and good which he would not do himself'. Dr Shaa, who preached his title, died in miserable remorse, while those traitors whom he executed died exemplary deaths. Richard is implicated in Henry VI's death, but not yet in those of his son or Clarence. Indeed, hostile though the chronicle is, it does not bring together all elements of the later myth – notably Richard's appearance – and gives no sense as yet of an inherently wicked character beyond redemption even before 1483:

> And thus ended this man with dishonour as he that sought it, for had he continued still protector and suffered the children to have prospered according to his allegiance and fidelity, he should have been honourably lauded over all, where as now his fame is dirtied and dishonoured … but God that is merciful forgive him his misdeeds…

The *Great Chronicle* is not a comprehensive collection of anti-Ricardian propaganda, nor does it project a coherent, consistent or convincing portrait of the monster. That was the achievement of Polydore Vergil, Sir Thomas More, Edward Hall and William Shakespeare.

The monster myth

As heir to both Lancaster and York, Henry VIII did not have his father's need to give priority to his Lancastrian title and thus his historians were free to devise a more

732   Richard the third.   *An.Dom.1483.*

(marginal note) I made match to coosen the people.

(marginal note) Iuuenal. sat. 3.

the king (for so was he from that time called) and the people departed, talking diuerslie of the matter, euerie man as his fantasie gaue him. But much they talked and maruelled of the maner of this dealing, that the matter was on both parts made so strange, as though neither had euer communed with other thereof before, when that themselues wist there was no man so dull that heard them, but he perceiued well inough that all the matter was made betwéene them. Howbeit some excused that againe, and said all must be done in good order though: and men must sometime for the maners sake, not be aknowen what they know (though it be hard to outreach the circumspect, wise, & vigilant minded man; as the poet saith:

——non facile est tibi

Decipere vlyssem.]

For at the consecration of a bishop, euerie man knoweth well by the pateng for his buls, that he purpo-

seth to be one, & though he paie for, nothing else. And yet must he be twise asked whether he will be bishop or no, and he must twise saie naie, and the third time take it, as compelled therebnto by his owne will. And in a stage plaie, all the people know right well, that one plaieng the Soldan, is percase a sowter: yet if one should can so little good, to shew out of season what aquaintance he hath with him, and call him by his owne name while he standeth in his maiestie, one of his tormentors might hap to breake his head (and worthie) for marring of the plaie. And so they said, that these matters be kings games, as it were stage plaies, and for the more part plaied vpon scaffolds, in which poore men be but the lokers on. And they that wise be will meddle no further. For they that sometime step vp, and plaie with them, when they can not plaie their parts, they disorder the plaie, and do themselues no good.

Thus farre Edward the fift, who was neuer king crowned, but shamefullie
by his vncle slaine, as in the processe following appeereth.

Richard the third, third sonne
to Richard duke of Yorke, and vncle
to Edward the fift.

(marginal note) Anno Reg.1. 1483.

The next daie the protector with a great traine went to Westminster hall, & there when he had placed himselfe in the court of the kings bench, declared to the audience, that he would take vpon him the crowne in that place there, where the king himselfe sitteth and ministreth the law, bicause he considered that it was the chiefest dutie of a king to minister the lawes. Then with as pleasant an oration as he could, he went about to win vnto him the nobles, the merchants, the artificers, and in conclusion all kind of men, but especiallie the lawiers of this realme. And finallie, to the intent that no man should hate him for feare, and that his deceitfull clemencie might get him the good will of the people, when he had declared the discommodities of discord, & the commodities of concord & vnitie, he made an open proclamation, that he did put out of his mind all enmities, and that he there did openlie pardon all offenses committed against him.

And to the intent that he might shew a proofe ther-

is in a manner deiected to a seruile flatterie [which refuseth no dutifulnesse, tend the same is neuer so hie a degrée of indignitie ; which one noteth, saieng :

——rides? maiore cachinno

Concutieur; flet, si lachrymas aspexit amici;

Frigescis? piget; si dixeris Æstuo sudat.]

When he had begun his reigne in the moneth of June, after this mockish election, then was he crowned king in the verie same moneth. And that solemnitie was furnished, for the most part, with the selfe same prouision that was appointed for the coronation of his nephue. But here to shew the maner of his coronation, as the same is inserted in this pamphlet of sir Thomas More, by maister Edward Hall and Richard Grafton (although not found in the same pamphlet) thus we find it by them reported.

First, to be sure of all enimies (as he thought) he sent for fiue thousand men of the north against his coronation, which came vp euill apparelled, and woorse harnessed, in rustie harnesse, neither defensible, nor scoured to the sale, which mustered in Finsburie field to the great disdaine of the lokers on. [By which beginning it appeered to the world that he had his state

(marginal notes) (*) This that is here betwéene this marke & this marke (*) was not written by maister More in this historie writ-ten by him in English, but is translated out of this historie which he wrote in Latine.

(marginal note) From this marke(*) to this (*) is not found in sir Thomas More, but in maister Hall and Grafton.

A page from Edward Hall's 'Chronicle', detailing how Edward V was 'shamefullie by his uncle slaine'.

coherent providential pattern to fifteenth-century history. Others already existed: a lament on Edward IV implied that avarice threatened his salvation and Crowland thought the ensuing upheavals could also be his punishment. Such early suggestions were superseded. By April 1486 Crowland was already influenced, if unconvinced, by Henry Tudor's role as God's chosen instrument. Subsequent historians could present Richard II's deposition by the Lancastrian Henry IV as a sin, that was punished by the dethroning of the latter's grandson Henry VI in 1461; God's instrument then, the rightful Yorkist King Edward IV, was nevertheless punished in the person of his son Edward V for his usurpation; and Richard III, both a usurper and a tyrant, was the victim of divine providence in the person of Henry VII in 1485. The pattern appears in Vergil's *English History*, was clarified and streamlined by Hall, and provided the overarching framework for Shakespeare's eight fifteenth-century history plays.

If Richard features in the Tudor Myth in a uniquely unfavourable light, it was the presentation of his whole life and reign that has done most to besmirch his reputation. He was the victim of two outstanding historians. While Polydore Vergil was Henry VII's official historian, he was also a conscientious scholar of independent mind, critical of established orthodoxies, praiseworthy in his respect for evidence and with endless time for research and revision of his text. Sir Thomas More was a successful lawyer, a brilliant classicist of international reputation, and not yet the royal minister or Catholic fanatic. Both assimilated a vast range of information, some from existing histories (Vergil almost certainly from Crowland, Rows and the London chronicles), much from questioning eyewitnesses and others in the know, some perhaps from documentary sources. The depth and range of More's knowledge is especially impressive. He thought so deeply about what he wrote that one constantly finds new layers and perceptions within the studied ambiguities. Each produced comprehensive and well-documented accounts that deservedly superseded those already in circulation.

Having said that, neither account was comprehensive. Begun in both Latin and English and unfinished, Sir Thomas More's *History* confines itself to 1483. After filling in the background and outlining Richard's career through flashbacks to his earlier life, it comprises an extremely detailed and elaborate analysis of the usurpation and breaks off in the preliminaries to Buckingham's Rebellion. Had More written at such length for the whole reign, the result would have been enormous, which may have been why he broke off. Polydore Vergil's account is much briefer on the areas which both cover. Thereafter he concentrates principally on the build up to Henry Tudor's accession, which his informants could tell him about, rather than the last two years of Richard's life. We have already seen how indispensable his account has proved for the rebellions of 1483. Doubtless Vergil thought the rise of Henry VII to be more important than the decline of Richard III. It has meant that the opposition story is as well known as Richard's own. But it also meant that the usurpation story was much more familiar to Tudor audiences than the rest of the reign. Understandably therefore, when Shakespeare came to write his *History*, he omitted altogether the events between Buckingham's Rebellion and the Bosworth campaign, which he skilfully amalgamated.

Facts by themselves are of little importance; it is how they are presented that counts. Just as hostile to Richard as earlier writers, Vergil and More were far more coherent, consistent and convincing. Both rejected Richard's denigration of his brother's regime, demonstrating that despite Edward IV's faults 'this realm was in quiet and prosperous estate'. Wydeville greed and Wydeville-Hastings rivalries were not the cause of the crises, which were initiated by Richard from his 'execrable desire for sovereignty' in defiance of the common good. Richard was the prime mover of the whole sequence of events. Hearing of Edward IV's death, at once 'he began to be kindled with an ardent desire of sovereignty', plotted with 'spiteful practice and sleight' to achieve his end, and progressively destroyed all obstructing his path and his subsequent reign. Both stress the wickedness and sinfulness of his actions. Moreover behind all this, they found the roots of Richard's character. 'But forasmuch as this duke's demeanour ministers in effect all the whole matter whereof this book shall entreat', so both delineate an evil man whose wickedness had earlier antecedents, who had slain both Henry VI and his brother Clarence. He was beyond reform and redemption. 'Richard', writes Vergil, 'was not able to change his savage nature, and did not long persevere in goodness, but immediately returned to evil and did everything thenceforward, as is evident in the case of his wife's death, under a cloak of hypocrisy.' Damning though his character sketch is, More makes it genuinely monstrous by setting it in the context of Richard's unnatural birth and deformity. An evil and unnatural character, to early sixteenth-century thinking, should surely be encased in an ugly or deformed body and surely also anticipated by an unnatural birth. Richard's birth should have foreshadowed and his appearance betrayed both his personal monstrosity and his horrific career.

Here, of course, is the origin of Shakespeare's portrait, which derives from both writers through the media of the chronicles of Edward Hall and Raphael Holinshed. More's intense study of Richard's character and the usurpation story recurs at the heart of Shakespeare's play and is completed after Buckingham's Rebellion, where More breaks off, from Vergil. Of course Shakespeare's portrait included other material and other characters, some of it his own invention, but essentially his portrait is a dramatic adaptation of More and Vergil. In drama statements cannot be qualified, digressions are eschewed, events are presented chronologically and everything must be presented in direct speech. More's lengthy character study becomes Richard's opening soliloquy and Richard's ambitious malice is the mainspring of events. Shakespeare borrowed much from More's *History* when preparing his own, but there was also much that he omitted: while some of More's best lines and scenes recur in the new setting, many do not, and the result is far more than 'the play of the book'. Though theatre audiences never doubt Richard's wickedness, Shakespeare successfully conveys the plausibility that enabled Richard the dissembler to carry the political nation with him to their doom and ultimately his own. The story is essentially the same, but the action is more concentrated and the narrative proceeds at breakneck speed through Richard's triumph to his tragedy.

Shakespeare still drew, so it has been argued, on independent popular traditions and much more than the dramatizer of earlier Tudor writings. That the legends grew need

'Transparent villainy' – John Hutton's etched-glass portrayal of Shakespeare's Richard III at the Shakespeare Centre, Stratford upon Avon.

This Victorian playing-card typifies the evil image of Richard III.

not mean that they are untrue, merely undemonstrably contemporary. If all those who later claimed to have supported the Tudors in 1483 or 1485 had indeed done so, we would know of only a fraction of those participated. There is a real distinction between sources and histories, but it is notoriously difficult to draw. It is not acceptable to label Vergil and More as historians, as mere interpreters, rather than historians. Nor can we safely ascribe resemblances between the narratives of Mancini and More to discussions with the same informants thirty years apart. They were commonplaces of the whole Yorkist establishment. What Tudor historians valued from the usurpation story, as shared by Mancini, was the critique of Richard III. What they did not want, because irrelevant, was material favourable to the Wydevilles or Hastings. What they added approved the end of the story and their own experience. As time passed, they supplemented it with authentic material not yet written down, with elaborations and exaggerations, and above all with interpretations that with hindsight saw better where everything fitted. More, Vergil, and perhaps even Shakespeare had new source material to add. Shakespeare, however, was the last.

For almost four hundred years Shakespeare's play has been the most popular and utterly damning presentation of Richard, both on paper and on the stage. Through the centuries a host of historians, professional and commercial alike, recycled and repeated what More and Shakespeare had codified. They supplied the interpretation for James Gairdner's *History*, for much of the twentieth century the standard life, who poured newly discovered records into the same old interpretative bottles, and for those of A.L. Rowse in 1966 and Desmond Seward in 1983. This tradition was repeatedly renewed as further Shakespearean productions plumbed ever more chilling or monstrous depths of villainy in a part that every great actor must play. Richard's monstrosity received its ultimate visual expression, so far, as the black-clad four-legged hump-backed thing depicted by Anthony Sher in 1984/5. Richard has never been more chillingly portrayed than as a tin-pot modern dictator. The Tudor stereotype remains in everyone's subconscious. Each issue of the Richard III Society *Bulletin* contains still more unexpected attacks.

Also for almost four hundred years the Tudor historians supplied the material for the defence. There was fact and paradox in More, Vergil, and Crowland, as first Sir George Buck in 1619 and subsequently Walpole in 1768 found, for defences of Richard to be constructed. At first thought eccentric, their time has come. There were no longer any witnesses for the prosecution to clarify ambiguities that were unambiguous to contemporaries or to supply the evidence anachronistically required to meet modern standards of proof. From Gairdner on, the widespread and systematic research into and publication of records provided material for comparison and criticism of traditional orthodoxies and traditional sources. Few of these could withstand the scholarly application of the comparitor microscope, still less the sweeping dismissal of anything Tudor or recategorization from History to Literature. The real Richard was never as interesting or as popular as he is today.

6 The man behind the myth

We have charted Richard's descend from a man into a monster. We have seen him in the light of the political conventions of his day and the Christian providential framework connecting sin and punishment that he and everyone else accepted. We have observed how Richard's unnatural birth and dishonoured death were potent elements in his notoriety. None of these ideas are current today and yet we find it difficult to replace the compelling portrait that Shakespeare wove around them. His Richard III is intensely believable, dynamically alive and utterly fascinating. If he was writing drama not history, Shakespeare was surprisingly faithful to his sources and his interpretation was not original. He had no choice what to write, not because Tudor censorship prevented him taking an independent line, but because there was no other line to take. He could have found no sources favourable to Richard on which to draw but only the tradition transmitted by Vergil and More. They, indeed, could have gathered the new information and interviewed the different eyewitnesses necessary for a more favourable portrait. Instead they imposed a consistent anti-Ricardian bias on miscellaneous material of diverse antiquity, origins and reliability, some Wydeville, Tudor, and Stanley, some even Ricardian. In the process they overlooked much propaganda and postdated rewriting of history. We can hardly blame them when even Richard's contemporaries could not recognize the truth. The fact that More's *History* so closely resembles Mancini's has been used to argue for More's reliability. But, as we have seen, Mancini's account cannot be taken at its face value. It too incorporates propaganda and the material that he so rigorously analysed was not everything he thought. The resemblance of More's history to Mancini's account thus demonstrates only the continuity of a suspect tradition. Professor Carr once wrote that a historian can only record what he thinks he knows. If that was true even of Mancini, what hope had Shakespeare, More or Vergil? And what hope have we?

We know that Richard was not the monster he was portrayed as being, but for many generations his tyranny and monstrosity were indisputable. His notoriety helped buttress the Tudor regime, in discrediting rebels, preserving order, and generally encouraging the disaffected to rest content for fear of worse. The inaccuracy of the tradition was quite irrelevant. Richard had done the same himself. The propaganda he had devised in 1483, which his enemies thereafter disseminated, had influenced and determined events. What happened sometimes mattered less than what was thought to have happened. When we as historians strip away errors and later accretions in our quest for objective truth, we often reject what we need for understanding. Undoubtedly Richard was innocent of certain charges laid against him, but he took the blame and paid the price. The fiction mattered more than the fact.

If Richard's notoriety was magnified by the Tudor tradition and the hostile propagandists of his own day, it owed much also to the brevity of his reign and his disastrous end. We must not lose sight of the speed of events. However worthy were Richard's intentions, he had no time: only twenty-six months to repair the legacy of Edward IV, to devise and implement his own policies, and to carry through any reforms. There was no time to relieve innocent bystanders inevitably hurt by attainder, to accustom and reconcile the South to the presence of northerners, and to secure the submission and restoration of former rebels. If Edward IV or Henry VII had had so little time, their records would have been no better, especially if they had suffered, like Richard, from a Crowland to denounce such early failings. Richard's intentions are destined forever to be might-have-beens and we cannot fairly condemn him for failing to fulfil them. His honeymoon period, if any, lasted only three months, the interminable wait for the Bosworth campaign less than two years, and the whole reign was dominated by security considerations and shaped by his reaction to events. Richard was unfortunate. Yet we cannot leave it like that. Richard had so little time because his regime collapsed. It collapsed because of the alienation of the Yorkist establishment. That was no accident or misfortune but was a direct consequence of his own usurpation, which was also the cause of the hostile propaganda and histories mentioned above.

Yet it had all begun so differently. For much of his adult life Richard had the best press possible because he had the best of public relations officers: himself. Nobody could sell Richard better than Richard could sell himself, in different guises and to different audiences: to potentially hostile northern noblemen, to the city of York, to the royal council and to Londoners, to northerners and southerners, to the Church, the nobility, townsmen and even rebels. Always he tailored his message and his language to his audience. To the Earl of Desmond, he lamented, falsely, the murder of his brother also by Edward IV's government. To Nicholas von Poppelau, he declared his enthusiasm for the crusade. Truly or falsely? We cannot now tell. Von Poppelau believed him, though nothing came of it. Did Desmond believe him? In modern parlance, Richard had great interpersonal skills. He was the master of the public statement and press conference, the open letter and manifesto, the inspired leak and innuendo, the personal appeal and the restatement of accepted values. We can see the self-confidence that prompted his appeals direct to the people. We must presume what we cannot demonstrate: his eloquence, charm, persuasiveness and charisma. He understood contemporary psychology, as we cannot, knew what attracted and repelled, and manipulated his audience accordingly. Thus he denounced his enemies as traitors, sorcerers, lechers, misers and evil councillors. He appealed to their allegiance, loyalty, honour, patriotism, regionalism, respect for hierarchy and royalty, sense of justice (especially to the poor) and of service, the sanctity of inheritance, the concept of the commonweal, the doctrine of necessity and the need for substantial counsel. Of course he had ulterior motives, but he must nevertheless have shared such values to some extent at least, for nobody can escape the values of his age. Of course he did not always live up to them: who ever can? Perhaps he was hypocritical. Bishop Langton notes that behind the puritanical facade 'sensual pleasure increasingly holds sway', but added that 'I do not consider that this detracts from what I have said' in Richard's favour. Yet it was against these standards which he propagated that his subjects found him wanting and rejected him.

Therein lies Richard's fatal error. There can be no doubt that he appreciated the strength of some of these sentiments. His care always to present himself as loyal in May and June 1483 shows that he appreciated what a difference it made: that otherwise he could not command loyalty or obedience even as Protector. He overstepped this convention when he usurped the throne. At that moment, in contemporary theory and for many Englishmen in practice, he outweighed all his estimable qualities and meritorious achievements, changed himself from a loyal subject into a usurper and traitor, committed treason, betrayed his allegiance, lost his honour, corrupted his own blood and that of his descendants and incurred damnation. Treason was the most heinous of crimes and sins. Nothing that he suffered in future could match his own offence: he could not be 'more sinned against than sinning'. Presumably he hoped that those who disapproved would nevertheless accept the *fait accompli*. They did not. The disasters of his reign and subsequent vilification all stemmed from that. People saw through him once he had usurped the crown. Perhaps, indeed, they saw too far, attributing everything to evil motives, and taking straightforward honesty to be hypocrisy as well.

Was his error in character with the rest of his career? Ricardians remind us of his estimable behaviour as duke. Can it be regarded as a tragic miscalculation? Or is it consistent with what else we know of the man? It does not seem that Richard changed greatly when he ceased to be a subject and became a sovereign. The intellectual depth and political ability was always there. So too were the gentler qualities of piety and generosity. The charm, persuasiveness and self-advertisement are constant features. The aggression, ambition, opportunism, foresight, dissimulation, and ruthlessness of the acquisitive duke are present also in the usurpation story. There is a striking similarity in his exploitation of legitimate heirs who happened to be in his power, notably those two wards, George Neville and Edward V. He appealed to principle when it suited him and rejected it when it did not. Before and after 1483 he appealed to law and inheritance when advantageous and disregarded them when it suited him. For much of the time, public interest and self-interest coincided, but when they did not he resisted the constraints that his brother sought to place on him. Ultimately his own interests came first: above his family and above also his obligations as a subject, a knight, a guardian and as a king towards his people. He was always the prime mover in his own career. In this context, his usurpation seems in character. Faced by the opportunity, it was natural for him to seek the throne. He was not the man to be mere caretaker, as Henry VI's uncle Bedford was for many years. Like so many other noblemen who were war heroes abroad and law-breakers at home, Richard's energies would have been better channelled, as he himself had planned, into aggression in Scotland rather than into domestic politics. Instead he pursued his ambitions in England, where the scope for self-aggrandisement was hedged around with deeply ingrained convention. Ricardians are right to remind us of his many sterling qualities, which need to be accounted for, but in the last resort Richard must be judged by what he did.

The traits listed above are almost a caricature of the great nobleman: Warwick the Kingmaker, Earl Rivers or Lord Hastings. It is not surprising that Richard conformed to the conduct of his class but it will not satisfy those who want him lily white. Moreover these qualities were not unworthy of a king. In the rough world of medieval politics, the most effective kings were not the most engaging of men: Edward I and Henry V spring to mind. Perhaps Richard was the best man for the job, as he himself supposed. But the medieval political system did not operate like that. It was not a meritocracy, in which the best man could rise through his talents to the top, but was instead a hereditary monarchy. When Richard took the crown, he breached a whole series of conventions: hereditary legitimacy, the obligation of allegiance, and the need in a mixed monarchy to accede and rule with consent. The fact that he subsequently secured approval from the assembled estates and parliament failed to repair the damage. Just as he had engineered his accession, so his own actions determined his fall. The denunciations of him as King Herod and Antichrist, as a tyrant and a monster, demonstrate the outrage felt by the political establishment. They could conceive of nothing worse. They swept him away and would indeed have done so in 1483 had they found a leader. Richard's fate illustrates once again how incapable were late medieval English kings of resisting the will of their subjects. It demonstrates the power of principles to determine political events. And it was their version of Richard that prevailed.

Chronology

1452	2 October	Richard is born at Fotheringhay Castle, Northamptonshire, the youngest son of Richard Duke of York (d.1460) and Cecily Neville (d.1494)
1459	12 October	The Rout at Ludford. The rebellious Duke of York flees into exile and is subsequently attainted by Parliament. The Duchess Cecily and her three younger children Margaret (b.1446), George (b.1449), and Richard are arrested by Henry VI and placed in the custody of Cecily's sister the Duchess of Buckingham.
1460	26 June	Successful invasion of England by Richard's eldest brother Edward and the Yorkist earls, who take over the government.
	10 September	The Duchess and her children take up residence at Fastolf's Place in Southwark.
	31 October	The Act of Accord, which makes Richard's father York Lord Protector during Henry VI's life and his heir after his death.
	31 December	Richard Duke of York is killed in battle at Wakefield.
1461	After 17 February	George and Richard are sent to Burgundy for safe-keeping.
	4 March	Richard's brother Edward IV declares himself to be king
	18 April	George and Richard arrive at Bruges, where they are fêted by the Duke of Burgundy, before proceeding home as royal princes, brothers of the new king.

1461	2 June	The formal public reception of George and Richard in London by the City corporation and livery companies.
	26 June	George and Richard are knighted.
	28 June	Richard attends the coronation of Edward IV.
	1 November	Richard is created Duke of Gloucester and his brother George becomes Duke of Clarence.
1461–3		Margaret, George and Richard live quietly at Greenwich palace.
1464–5		Richard is already in the household of Richard Neville, Earl of Warwick, the Kingmaker.
1465	September	Richard attends the splendid enthronement feast of Archbishop Neville at Cawood near York.
1468	25 June	Richard is at Margate with the king to bid farewell to his sister Margaret when she departs to marry Charles the Bold, Duke of Burgundy.
	? October	Richard is declared of age, aged 16.
1469	16 January	Richard's first judicial commission, at Salisbury, where two Lancastrian nobles, Henry Courtenay and Sir Thomas Hungerford, are condemned and executed for treason.
	13 May	Richard attends a Garter Chapter at Windsor that offers the Order to Charles the Bold.
	14 May	Richard's agreement with Margaret Lady Hungerford.
	June	Richard accompanies Edward IV on pilgrimage in East Anglia. He is at Walsingham on 21st, Castle Rising on 24th, King's Lynn on 25th, and thence at Fotheringhay.
	24 July	Edward IV's Welsh army is destroyed at Edgecote by northern supporters of Warwick and

		Clarence. The king is imprisoned and Warwick briefly takes over the government.
	13 October	Richard escorts the king, who has been released, to London. He attends the subsequent Great Council at Westminster at which the warring parties are reconciled.
	November	Richard is despatched from Westminster to restore order in Wales.
1470	26 March	Richard is at Hornby Castle (Lancs.) during his 'variance' with the Stanleys.
	18 June	Richard presides over the Great Sessions at Carmarthen.
	July	Richard helps suppress Lord FitzHugh's rebellion in the North.
	26 August	Richard is appointed warden of the West March.
	September	Warwick successfully invades and restores Henry VI as king (the Readeption). Edward IV flees abroad on 29 September.
	November	Richard, apparently travelling later, arrives at Veer in the Low Countries.
1471	11 March	Richard embarks with Edward IV from Flushing; on 24th they land at Ravenspur in Yorkshire.
	11 April	Edward IV and his army, including Richard, enter London
	14 April	Edward defeats Warwick decisively at Barnet; Richard is slightly wounded.
	4 May	Edward defeats Queen Margaret at Tewkesbury. Richard participates and, as constable of England, summarily tries the captured leaders, who are executed.

1471	21 May	The death in the Tower of Henry VI; Richard may have been present.
	3 July	Creation of the future Edward V as Prince of Wales. Richard swears allegiance to him.
	14 July	Edward IV grants Richard Middleham and Warwick's other forfeited Neville lands in the North.
1472	17 February	Edward, Clarence and Richard meet at Sheen Palace to discuss the division of Warwick's estates, Richard having decided to marry the earl's younger daughter Anne and George, husband of her sister Isabel, wishing to keep the whole. By 18 March the king had imposed a settlement.
	Around Christmas	Richard arrests Elizabeth Countess of Oxford at Stratford (Essex.), takes her into custody at Stepney and compels her to surrender her inheritance; the deeds are dated 9 January 1473.
1473	13 May	The royal council at Nottingham imposes order on Richard, whose self-advancement in the North has been encroaching on the offices and retinue of the Earl of Northumberland.
	3 June	It is reported that, since Clarence is resisting the division of the Warwick Inheritance, Richard has taken action to break the deadlock by removing the countess of Warwick from sanctuary at Beaulieu into his own custody.
	6 November	The two dukes are still at odds and private war threatens.
1474	20 July	The two dukes agree the details of a partition of their estates. This is confirmed by two acts of parliament in 1474-5.
	28 July	Northumberland accepts the lordship of Richard, who promises not to interfere in his affairs.

1475	4 July	Richard is among Edward's army that invades France. Peace is agreed at Picquigny (29 August), to which Richard objects, and the army returns via Calais (4 September) home to England.
1476	21-30 July	Richard is chief mourner at the reinterment of his father at Fotheringhay College.
1478	14 January	Richard attends the marriage celebrations of Edward IV's younger son Richard Duke of York to Anne Mowbray.
	January-February	Richard attends parliament, at which his brother Clarence is tried and condemned to death.
	4 July	Richard issues the statutes for his new college at Middleham.
1480	12 May	Richard is appointed King's Lieutenant of the North against the Scots.
1481	22 August	Richard dubs knights and bannerets at Hutton Field by Berwick.
1482	May	Richard raids Dumfries in Galloway.
	12 June	Richard is re-appointed the King's Lieutenant in the North.
	24 August	Richard's army captures Berwick.
1483	January	Parliament congratulates Richard on his victory and grants him the hereditary palatinate of Cumberland and wardenship of the West March.
	9 April	Edward IV dies; his son succeeds as Edward V next day.
	1 May	Richard's first *coup d'état*. Richard and Buckingham seize control of Edward V at Stony Stratford, arresting or dismissing his entourage, while declaring their loyalty to him.

1483	By 8 May	Richard has been recognized as Lord Protector.
	13 June	Richard's second *coup d'état*. Richard seizes and executes Lord Hastings.
	16 June	Richard secures possession of Edward IV's younger son, Richard, who joins Edward V in the Tower.
	25 June	Election of Richard as king by an assembly of notables.
		Execution at Pontefract of Earl Rivers, Lord Richard Grey, and Sir Thomas Vaughan.
	26 June	Richard accedes as Richard III.
	6 July	Richard III's coronation.
	27 August	Richard licenses Buckingham to enter the Hereford inheritance.
	8 September	Creation of Richard's son Edward as Prince of Wales at York Minster.
	11 October	Richard already knows of the outbreak of Buckingham's rebellion and takes vigorous action against it.
	2 November	Execution of the Duke of Buckingham at Salisbury.
	3 November	Cornish rebels recognize another king at Bodmin.
	25 December	Henry Tudor is recognized as king by English exiles at Vannes Cathedral in Brittany.
1484	January	Richard III's parliament, which recognizes his title and attaints his enemies
	29 February	Contract for the marriage of Richard's illegitimate daughter Katherine to William Earl of Huntingdon.

	1 March	Agreement between Richard and Queen Elizabeth, who leaves sanctuary with her daughters.
	April	Death of Richard's only son Edward Prince of Wales.
	12 September	Scottish conference at Nottingham, that results in a truce excluding Dunbar.
1485	16 March	Death of Queen Anne.
	31 March	Richard III publicly denies any intention to marry his niece Elizabeth of York.
	7 August	Henry Tudor lands near milford Haven.
	22 August	Defeat and death of Richard III at Bosworth. Accession of Henry VII.

Bibliography

General

There are many histories and historical novels of Richard III, but most are very biased and of little original value.

Surveys
The best survey of his reign is C.D. Ross, *Richard III* (rev.edn., Yale U.P., London 1999). A.J. Pollard's *Richard III and the Princes in the Tower* (Sutton Publishing, Stroud, 1991) is a well-illustrated and critical overview. There is much extra detail principally on patronage, in R.E. Horrox, *Richard III: A Study of Service* (Cambridge U.P., 1989). P.M. Kendall, *Richard III* (Allen & Unwin, London, 1955), strongly pro-Ricardian, is a pioneering study that is still worth reading. A mass of fascinating material is collected in P. Tudor-Craig, *Richard III* (2nd edn., Boydell, Woodbridge, 1977)

Shorter pieces
Many modern contributions take the form of articles, some in *The Ricardian* (journal of the Richard III Society). Some valuable collections are in J. Petre (ed.), *Richard III: Crown and People* (Richard III & Yorkist History Trust, 1985); P.W. Hammond (ed.), *Richard III: Loyalty, Lordship and Law* (Richard III & Yorkist History Trust, 1986); R.A. Griffiths & J.W. Sherborne (eds.), *Kings and Nobles 1377-1529: A Tribute to Charles Ross* (Alan Sutton, Gloucester, 1986); M.A.Hicks, *Richard III and his Rivals : Magnates and their Motives during the Wars of the Roses* (Hambledon Press, London, 1991). An important recent collection is J. Gillingham (ed.), *Richard III: A Medieval Kingship* (History Today Books, London, 1992)

Specific studies
Three recent books have focused on particular aspects of Richard's life, his books and his religion. A.F. Sutton and L. Visser-Fuchs have studied *Richard III's Books* (Sutton Publishing, Stroud, 1997) and *The Hours of Richard III* (Richard III & Yorkist History Trust, London, 1990). For the context see J. Hughes, *The Religious Life of Richard III: Piety and Prayer in the North of England* (Sutton Publishing, Stroud, 1997), which contains relatively little on Richard himself. Much still remains to be said about Richard's piety.

Sources

The popularity of Richard III and the subventions of the Richard III & Yorkist History Trust have permitted modern editions of the basic sources. The most valuable narratives are now: D. Mancini, *Usurpation of Richard III* ed. C.A.J. Armstrong (2nd edn Alan Sutton, 1984); *The Crowland Chronicle Continuations 1459-86*, ed. N. Pronay and J. Cox (Richard III & Yorkist History Trust, London, 1986); T. More, *History of King Richard III*, ed. R. Sylvester (Yale U.P. 1963; paper-back version 1976); *The Great Chronicle of London*, ed. A.H. Thomas and J.D. Thornley (1938; microprint edn., Alan Sutton, Gloucester, 1983). There are several collections of documents in translation. The standard collection is A.R. Myers (ed.), *English Historical Documents 1327-1485* (Eyre and Spottiswoode, London, 1969). P.W. Hammond and A.F. Sutton (eds.), *Richard III: The Road to the Throne* (Constable, London, 1985) is the most comprehensive collection, but is marred by a poor commentary. K. Dockray, *Richard III: A Sourcebook* (Sutton Publishing, Stroud, 1997) is a succinct and up-to-date collection of extracts regrettably removed from their original contexts.

Both A. Hanham, *Richard III and his earlier historians* (Oxford U.P., 1975) and H.A. Kelly, *Divine Providence in the England of Shakespeare's Histories* (Harvard U.P., 1970), though regrettably out of print, usefully analyse the literary sources and contain some edited material, e.g. relevant extracts from John Rows' *History of the Kings of England* in Hanham and poems by Pietro Carmeliano in Kelly. These are no substitutes for the original documents for the serious student, who should also consult *British Library Harleian Manuscript 433*, ed. P.W. Hammond and R.E Horrox (4 vols. London 1979-83); R.E. Horrox (ed.), 'Financial Memoranda of the Reign of Edward V', *Camden Miscellany* XXIX (Camden Society, 4th series, 34, 1987); *The Coronation of Richard III*, ed. A.F. Sutton and P.W. Hammond (Gloucester, 1983). Hammond, Sutton and L. Visser-Fuchs are systematically publishing the less familiar ceremonial and occasional pieces exploited here, such as those on the funerals of the house of York, and a translation of Nicholas von Poppelau's travel description in *The Ricardian* 127, 143-6 (1994-9).

The fullest bibliography in R.E. Horrox, *Richard III: A Study of Service* (Cambridge U.P., 1989) is usefully updated in the foreword to the revised edition of C.D.Ross, *Richard III* (Yale U.P., 1999).

1 The England of Richard III

This chapter owes enormous debts to the English school of constitutional and institutional history.

Political theory

On political theory, the standard work is S.B. Chrimes, *English Constitutional Ideas in the Fifteenth Century* (Cambridge University Press, 1936), which reprints Russell's sermons of 1483. Some guidance from the Tudor period is provided by

E.M.W. Tillyard, *The Elizabethan World Picture* (London, 1943); W.R.D. Jones, *The Tudor Commonwealth 1529-1559* (1970). I have also consulted specific works by Fortescue in *The Governance of England*, ed. C. Plummer (Oxford U.P., 1885) and *De Laudibus Legis Anglie*, ed. S.B. Chrimes (Cambridge U.P., 1942); *Four English Political Tracts*, ed. J.-P. Genet (Camden 4th series, XVIII, 1977); E. Dudley, *The Tree of the Commonwealth*, ed. D.M. Brodie (Cambridge, 1948); and especially *Three Chronicles of the Reign of Edward IV*, ed. K. Dockray (Alan Sutton, Gloucester, 1988). I also found useful A.J. Pollard, 'The Tyranny of Richard III', *Journal of Medieval History* III (1977); A. Allan, 'Yorkist Propaganda: Pedigree, Prophecy and "British History" in the Reign of Edward IV', in *Patronage, Pedigree and Power in Later Medieval England*, ed. C.D. Ross (Alan Sutton, Gloucester, 1979); 'Royal Propaganda and the Proclamations of Edward IV', *Bulletin of the Institute of Historical Research* LIX (1986); C.D Ross, 'Rumour, Propaganda and Public Opinion in the Wars of the Roses', in *Patronage, The Crown and the Provinces in Later Medieval England*, ed. R.A Griffiths (Alan Sutton, Gloucester, 1980); and G.L. Harriss (ed.), *Henry V: The Practice of Kingship* (Clarendon Press, Oxford, 1985). R.E.Horrox (ed), *Fifteenth Century Attitudes* (Cambridge U.P., 1994) is wide-ranging and original.

Government

A.L. Brown, *Governance of England 1272-1461* (Edward Arnold, London, 1989) codifies much scattered material. On the immediate background, see C.D. Ross, *Edward IV* (rev. edn, Yale U.P., 1997). For the household and court, see *The Household of Edward IV*, ed. A.R. Myers (Manchester U.P., 1959), and *The English Court: From the Wars of the Roses to the Civil War*, ed. D. Starkey (London, 1987). On politics generally, see M.A. Hicks, *Bastard Feudalism* (Longman, Harlow, 1995); 'Bastard Feudalism, the Overmighty Subject, and Idols of the Multitude during the Wars of the Roses', *History* 85 (2000); K.B. McFarlane, *England in the Fifteenth Century* (Hambledon Press, London, 1981).

2 Richard III as Duke of Gloucester

The surveys by Kendall, Ross, Horrox and Pollard devote much space to Richard III as Duke of Gloucester, which is the focus of many of the essays also. Hicks, Pollard and Grant in particular have repeatedly revisited the same topics. Richard's physical appearance is authoritatively treated in Petre, *Richard III: Crown and People*. For his upbringing, infancy and relations with his brother Clarence see M.A. Hicks, *False, Fleeting, Perjur'd Clarence: George, Duke of Clarence, 1449-1478* (rev.edn., Headstart History, Bangor, 1992). The fullest overview of his career as duke remains M.A. Hicks, *Richard III as Duke of Gloucester: A Study in Character* (Borthwick Paper 70,1986) reprinted in Hicks, *Richard III and his Rivals*. For his wife's 'Warwick Inheritance' and relations with Northumberland, see M.A. Hicks, *Richard III and his Rivals* and *The Rows Roll*, ed. W.H. Courthope (2nd edn.

Alan Sutton, Gloucester, 1980); for his Middleham connection and operations in County Durham see especially A.J. Pollard (ed), *The North of England in the Age of Richard III* (Suttons, Stroud, 1997); and for relations with York and the Stanleys see the essays by D.M. Palliser and M.K. Jones in R.E. Horrox (ed.), *Richard III and the North* (Hull U.P., 1985). Particular use has been made of M.K.Jones, 'Richard Duke of Gloucester and the Scropes of Masham', *The Ricardian* 134 (1996). Richard's responsibility for the borders is analysed by D. Dunlop, 'The "redresses and reparacons of attemptates": Alexander Legh's instructions from Edward IV, March-April 1475', *Historical Research* LXIII (1990). For Middleham College, see especially J. Raine (ed), 'The Statutes ordained by Richard Duke of Gloucester for the Church of Middleham', *Archaeological Journal* XIV (1857); *Documents relating to the Foundation and Antiquities of the Collegiate Church of Middleham*, ed. W. Atthill (Camden Society XXXVIII, 1847).

3 Richard III's usurpation of the throne

This chapter relies on the standard published authorities, both the chronicles – especially Mancini and Crowland – and the relatively few surviving documents. These are mainly collected in P.W. Hammond and A.F. Sutton, *Richard III: The Road to the Throne* (Constable, London, 1985); a few others are in Historic Manuscripts Commission *12th Report Appendix III* (MSS of Southampton and King's Lynn); *The Cely Letters 1472-88*, ed. A. Hanham (Early English Text Society, CCLIII, 1975).The full text of *Titulus Regius* is in *Rolls of Parliament* (6 vols. Record Commission 1767-77), vol. V. The narrative of events relies heavily on those in A.F. Sutton and P.W. Hammond, *The Coronation of Richard III* (Alan Sutton, Gloucester, 1983) and on C.T. Wood, *Joan of Arc and Richard III* (Oxford University Press, 1988). For Mancini, see also A.J. Pollard, 'Dominic Mancini's Narrative of the Events of 1483', *Nottingham Medieval Studies* XXXVIII (1993), with which this author fundamentally disagrees.

On the Wydevilles, see E.W. Ives, 'Andrew Dymmock and the Papers of Antony Earl Rivers, 1482-3', *Bulletin of the Institute of Historical Research* XLI (1968); M.A. Hicks, 'The Changing Role of the Wydevilles in Yorkist Politics to 1483', in *Richard III and his Rivals*; D.E. Lowe, 'The Council of the Prince of Wales and the Decline of the Herbert Family during the Second Reign of Edward IV (1471-83)', *Bulletin of the Board of Celtic Studies* XXVII (1976-8); D.E. Lowe, 'Patronage and Politics: Edward IV, the Wydevilles, and the Council of the Prince of Wales, 1471-83', ibid. XXIX (1980-2); C.E. Moreton, 'A Local Dispute and the Politics of 1483: Roger Townshend, Earl Rivers and the Duke of Gloucester', *The Ricardian* 107 (1989). Other new material is to be found in B.P. Wolffe, 'When and Why did Hastings Lose His Head?', *English Historical Review* LXXXIX (1974); R.F. Green, 'Historical Notes of a London Citizen 1483-88', *English Historical Review* XCVI (1981).

4 Richard III and Buckingham's Rebellion

Richard's progress and reforming intentions are treated in A.F. Sutton, 'The Administration of Justice whereunto we be professed', in Petre, *Richard III: Crown and People* (1985); A.F. Sutton, ' "A Curious Searcher for our Weal Public": Richard III, Piety, Chivalry, and the Concept of the Good Prince', in P.W .Hammond (ed.),*Richard III: Loyalty, Lordship and Law* (1986). Favourable comments come from *The Rows Roll*, ed. W.H. Courthope (2nd edn. Alan Sutton, Gloucester, 1980); *Christ Church Letters*, ed. J.B. Sheppard (Camden Society, new series XIX, 1877) for Langton; and H.A. Kelly, *Divine Providence in the England of Shakespeare's History* Plays (Harvard, 1970) for Carmeliano. 'The Briar and the Periwinkle', in Kent Archive Office MS U182Z1, is published in R.L. Greene (ed.), *The Early English Carols* (2nd edn., Oxford, 1977), no.424.1, pp.257, 471-3. Richard's proclamations and letters are in *Foedera etc*, ed. T. Rymer (20 vols. 1704-35*); British Library Manuscript 433*, ed. R.E. Horrox and P.W. Hammond (Gloucester,1979-83); *York Civic Records*, ed. A. Raine, I (Yorkshire Archaeological Society XCVIII, 1939) now republished as *The York House Books*, ed. L.C. Attreed (2 vols., Richard III & Yorkist History Trust, 1991).

The basic source for Buckingham's Rebellion is *Three Books of Polydore Vergil's English History*, ed. H. Ellis (Camden Society VI 1844). The best modern account of the rebellion is now in R.E. Horrox, *Richard III: A Study of Service* (1989) and of the Tudor dimension in R.A. Griffiths and R.S. Thomas, *The Making of the Tudor Dynasty* (Alan Sutton, Gloucester, 1985). There is some additional material in L. Gill, *Richard III and Buckingham's Rebellion* (Sutton Publishing, Stroud, 1999); I. Arthurson and N. Kingwell, 'The Proclamation of Henry Tudor as King of England, 3 November 1483', *Historical Research* LXIII (1990); J.A.F. Thomson, 'Bishop Lionel Wydeville and Richard III', *Bulletin of the Institute of Historical Research* LXIX (1986); M.A. Hicks, 'Unweaving the Web: The Plot of July 1483 against Richard III and its wider significance', *The Ricardian* 114 (1991). For his tyranny, see A.J. Pollard, 'The Tyranny of Richard III', *Journal of Medieval History* III (1977).

5 Richard III's defeat and defamation

The materials for this chapter are drawn from a range of scattered sources that have largely been cited above. Particular debts are owed to H.A. Kelly, *Divine Providence in the England of Shakespeare's History Plays* (1970) and A. Hanham, *Richard III and his earlier historians* (1975). See in addition, L Attreed, 'From Pearl Maiden to Tower Princes', *Journal of Medieval History* (1983); G. Buck, *History of King Richard III*, ed. A.N. Kincaid (Alan Sutton, Gloucester, 1979); R.A. Griffiths and R.S. Thomas, *The Making of the Tudor Dynasty* (1985).Full citations of *The Great Chronicle* and Thomas More appear above. For Shakespeare, see W. Shakespeare, *History of King Richard III*, ed. A. Hammond, (The Arden Shakespeare, 1981).

Index